# AUDIO TECHNOLOGY SYSTEMS:

## Principles, Applications, and Troubleshooting

# AUDIO TECHNOLOGY SYSTEMS:

## Principles, Applications, and Troubleshooting

*Derek Cameron*

*RESTON PUBLISHING COMPANY, INC.*
*A Prentice-Hall Company*
Reston, Virginia

**Library of Congress Cataloging in Publication Data**
Cameron, Derek
  Audio technology.
  1.  Sound—Recording and reproducing.  I.  Title.
TK7881.4.M53      621.389′3      77-10969
ISBN  0-87909-050-2

© 1978 by Reston Publishing Company, Inc.
*A Prentice-Hall Company*
Reston, Virginia 22090

10   9   8   7   6   5   4   3   2   1

PRINTED IN THE UNITED STATES OF AMERICA

# Contents

# Preface

Audio technology is one of the most rapidly growing areas of electronics. The high-fidelity field, in particular, has evolved greatly within recent years. To provide optimum perspective in a coverage of the prevailing state of the art, this text employs a descriptive/design/troubleshooting format. This unique approach facilitates the learning process and establishes a broad base for comprehension. In turn, this is an essential text-handbook for the classroom and home-study student, audiophile, junior engineer, experimenter, and audio troubleshooter. Mathematics has been held to a minimum in the text, and quantitative relations are presented in graphical form. However, the reader is assumed to be familiar with basic algebra, plane trigonometry, and electrical circuit calculations.

The first chapter provides an introduction to audio technology; it discusses high-fidelity component systems, audio amplifier design basics, distortion analysis, and basic audio troubleshooting principles. Decibel measurements are also explained, and common pitfalls are noted. In the second chapter, audio preamplifiers are considered. Basic amplifier parameters are noted. Component and device tolerance effects are explained. Various types of negative feedback are analyzed. Worst-case design factors are tabulated. Additional troubleshooting techniques are detailed, including quick checks and in-circuit test methods. The third chapter covers audio power amplifiers. Class A, AB, B, D, and G modes of operation are explained. Design principles of complementary-symmetry amplifiers are developed. Pulse-width-modulation amplifiers are outlined. Various methods of troubleshooting audio power amplifiers are explained.

In the fourth chapter, FM tuners and stereo decoders are discussed. Fundamentals of RF circuit operation are outlined, with essential design parameters. Troubleshooting techniques for FM tuners and stereo decoders are included, with notes on audio channel cross-checks. Electrophonic music systems are described in the fifth chapter. The basic function generator is explained, with basic programming methods. Unconventional scales such as the open and the pentatonic scales are noted. Subharmonic generation is analyzed. The sixth chapter covers quadraphonic sound systems. Both discrete and synthesized four-channel sound sources are discussed. Audioscope monitor operation is included. Biphonic sound fundamentals are outlined.

Electronic organs are discussed in the seventh chapter. Basic organization and functions are stressed. Voicing arrangements and formant filters are detailed. Each function is illustrated with circuit diagrams. In the eighth chapter, problems of audio system interference are considered. Audio rectification is analyzed, and basic interference filter arrangements are shown. Trap action of a properly designed shielded cable is explained. The text concludes with a comprehensive glossary and eight appendices. Profuse illustration is employed throughout the text to clarify the technical points that are discussed. Numerous charts have been included for summarization of relations and data.

The format and the treatment are the outcome of many years of teaching experience, both on the part of the author and of his associates. In a significant sense, this book represents a team effort, and the author gratefully acknowledges the constructive criticisms and suggestions of his co-workers. In addition, the author is indebted to numerous electronic manufacturers, as noted throughout the text, for illustrative material and various technical data.

It is appropriate that this text be dedicated as a teaching tool to the instructors and students of our junior colleges, technical institutes, and vocational schools.

DEREK CAMERON

# AUDIO TECHNOLOGY SYSTEMS:

## Principles, Applications, and Troubleshooting

# 1

# Introduction to Audio Technology

## 1-1 GENERAL CONSIDERATIONS

Audio technology is primarily concerned with electrical and electronic processing of vocal and musical information in the frequency range from 20 Hz to 20 kHz. In its broader aspect, audio technology is also concerned with the generation of waveforms corresponding to sounds, tonal patterns, and timbres with novel characteristics. Audio technology extends further into fields of scientific exploration, such as psychophysics, wherein the relations between physical and mental events are investigated. In turn, audio technology includes diverse disciplines; it is primarily a science, secondarily an art form that transcends the useful arts, and ultimately a psychological tool with philosophical facets.

Devices, circuits, systems, and audio instruments enter into consideration in the theory and practice of audio technology. A block diagram of a typical high-fidelity system is shown in Fig. 1-1. This system employs various kinds of devices, such as diodes, transistors, integrated circuits, crystals, and thermistors. It utilizes components such as resistors, capacitors, and inductors. It also uses various forms of hardware, including heat sinks, switches, needles, magnets, transformer cores, and so on. Circuits include amplifiers, oscillators, mixers, detectors, equalizers, filters, control networks, and power supplies. Both active and passive types of filter circuitry are utilized.

Most industry authorities agree that high-fidelity reproduction involves a frequency response that is uniform within ±1 dB from 20 Hz to at least 20 kHz, with a harmonic distortion less than 1 percent at any frequency within this range. Component systems, such as that illustrated in Fig. 1-2, are very popular, and are often preferred by critical audio enthusiasts. For example, a chosen set of speakers may be utilized with a preferred type of amplifier, plus a selected type of record player (turntable), a chosen design of AM-FM tuner, a selected reel-to-reel tape deck and/or an eight-track deck, or a preferred type of cassette deck. There is a marked trend to the inclusion of stereo fre-

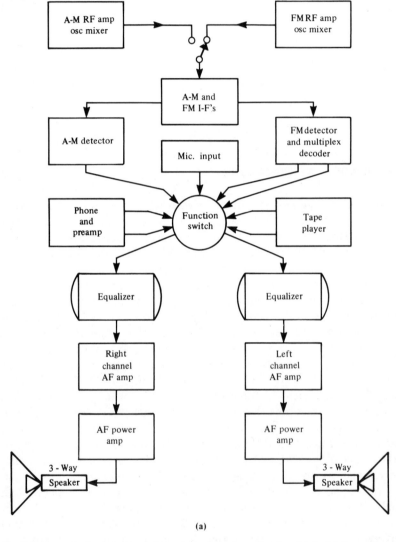

(a)

**Figure 1-1**   Block diagram of FM/AM Stereo multiplex high-fidelity system: (a) arrangement;

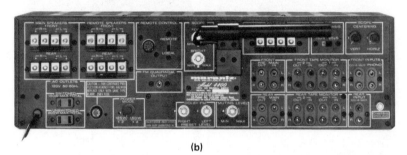

(b)

**Figure 1-1** *Continued* **(b)** appearance of a hi-fi system. (*Courtesy of Marantz.*)

quency equalizers (Fig. 1-3) in component systems. Frequency equalizers are more elaborate than conventional tone controls, in that they permit the operator to increase or decrease the frequency response through five sectors of the audio-frequency range.

High-fidelity stereo-quadraphonic systems are also designed in unitized form and housed in elegant furniture cabinets. A unitized system is called a *console,* and it contains at least two speakers. Another type of stereo-quad design, called the *compact,* has separate speakers with a record turntable and a stereo amplifier on the same base. The chief unit in a compact may include an FM or FM/AM tuner with a multiplex decoder, plus a turntable. Another design of compact features a record changer mounted on top of the main unit, protected by a clear plastic cover. Hi-fi enthusiasts also refer to a compact as a *modular system.* Note that a hi-fi speaker enclosure is usually designed with several speaker units of various sizes, as shown in Fig. 1-2(b). The largest speaker in a group is termed a *woofer,* and it operates to reproduce low bass tones. Most of the audio power is contained in the bass tones.

**Figure 1-2** Appearance of a component system: **(a)** individual components. (*Courtesy of Radio Shack, a Tandy Corp. Company*)

**Figure 1-2** *Continued* **(b)** interior view of typical speaker enclosure. (*Courtesy of Heath Co.*)

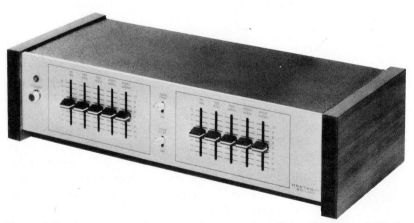

**Figure 1-3**   Appearance of a stereo frequency equalizer. (*Courtesy of Heath Co.*)

The smallest speaker in a group is called a *tweeter;* it reproduces the high treble tones. Also, a speaker enclosure includes an intermediate size of speaker, often called a *squawker* or *midrange speaker,* that reproduces the middle tonal range between low bass and high treble tones. Some designs of enclosures contain a pair of midrange speakers, one of which is larger than the other. As a general rule, the size of a speaker is proportional to the amount of audio power that it can radiate. Speakers in an enclosure operate in association with crossover networks that direct suitable ranges of audio frequencies to each speaker. The speakers with their associated electrical networks in an enclosure are called a *speaker system.* A component system may include an audio power meter, as illustrated in Fig. 1-4, to monitor the power levels for each enclosure.

**Figure 1-4**    An audio power meter, used with a speaker system. (*Courtesy of Heath* Co.)

Stereo headphone jacks are often provided in stereo amplifiers and compact units. A pair of stereo headphones is illustrated in Fig. 1-5. Some hi-fi connoisseurs prefer headphones because of their acoustical characteristics. Other hi-fi enthusiasts utilize them for privacy. Various amplifier input facilities are provided. As an illustration, an appropriate input jack is customarily provided for an FM/AM tuner, for a reel-to-reel tape deck, and for a cassette player. A hi-fi amplifier is also designed with various features, such as tone controls, loudness-type volume control, terminals for additional speakers, stereo balance control, and various input facilities (see Fig. 1-6). Hi-fi connoisseurs who make their own tape recordings require an amplifier that provides an appropriate stereo signal for a particular tape recorder.

**Figure 1-5**   A pair of stereo headphones. (Courtesy of Radio Shack, a Tandy Corp. Company.)

A receiver for a hi-fi system is basically a tuner; it must be supplemented by an amplifier to operate a speaker system. Some component systems are designed with a separate tuner and a separate stereo amplifier. All stereo tuners include a multiplex decoder section to reconstitute the two stereo signals from the incoming encoded FM signal. Note that a tape recorder provides both recording and playback facilities, whereas a tape player lacks recording facilities. A tape deck lacks a built-in amplifier, and is operated with an external amplifier and speaker system. Tape decks may or may not include recording facilities. Tape recorders are designed as monophonic, stereophonic, or quadraphonic units. Audiophiles tend to prefer reel-to-reel machines over cartridge or cassette-type machines. Eight-track cartridge tape players, however, are popular because of their compactness and simplicity of operation. Most eight-track cartridge tape machines are designed as player decks. In other words, a player deck lacks recording facilities. All eight-track tape players provide stereo reproduction, and many qualify as high-fidelity units.

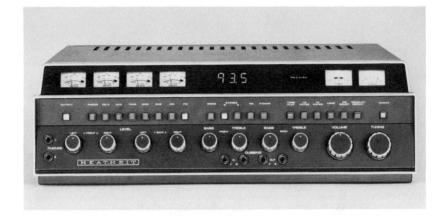

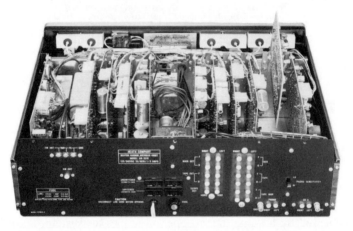

**Figure 1-6**    Controls and input/output facilities for a hi-fi system. (*Courtesy of Heath* Co.)


## 1-2    AUDIO AMPLIFIER DESIGN BASICS

An audio amplifier is designed as a part of a system, as exemplified in Fig. 1-7. An audio-amplifier channel in a high-fidelity system may have a maximum usable gain (MUG) of 5000 times, or more. System distortion is customarily less than 1 percent total harmonic distortion (THD). Amplitude and phase characteristics for a typical hi-fi amplifier system are shown in Fig. 1-8(a). Percentage of distortion is generally stated for maximum rated power output at 1 kHz. In addition, power bandwidth is defined as the frequency range between an upper limit and a lower limit, at a power level 3 dB below maximum rated power output,

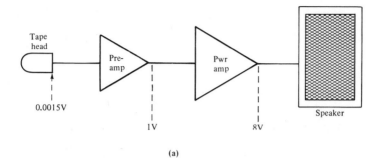

(a)

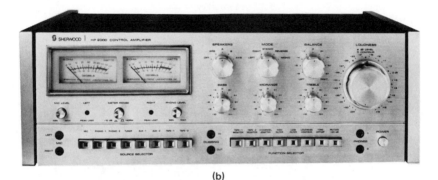

(b)

**Figure 1-7**  Audio voltage levels in an amplifier system: **(a)** block diagram; **(b)** appearance of a control amplifier. (*Courtesy of Sherwood.*)

where the harmonic distortion starts to exceed the value that occurs at the midband frequency with maximum rated power output. The definition of power bandwidth is illustrated in Fig. 1-8(b).

Also, the music-power rating of an amplifier is defined as the peak power that can be delivered to the speakers for a very short period of time, with no more harmonic distortion than at the maximum rated sine-wave output. This period of time is generally considered to be 1 millisecond, (ms), at a repetition rate of 100 pulses per second. In other words, a music-power rating for an amplifier denotes its ability to process sudden peak musical waveforms without objectionable distortion. Music-power output is limited chiefly by the capability of the power-supply filter capacitors to sustain the peak current demand of the amplifier. Note that the peak-power value of a 10-watt sine wave is 20 watts. On the other hand, a musical tone that has 20 watts of peak power may have less than 5 watts of average (rms) power. For this reason, hi-fi amplifiers are often rated for both rms power and music power output.

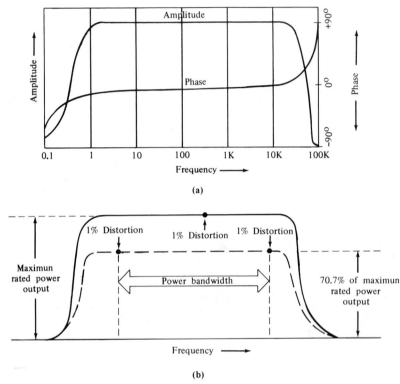

**Figure 1-8** Basic amplifier parameters: (a) typical frequency and phase characteristics; (b) power bandwidth.

Most hi-fi amplifiers can be classified into preamplifier and power-amplifier types. However, a driver amplifier occupies an intermediate position between the input and the output amplifiers. Typical input/output parameters for a preamplifier are noted in Fig. 1-9. Observe that four inputs are provided, to accommodate a low-impedance microphone, a tape player, a phono player, and an FM tuner. Each input port is rated for a different signal level. Thus, the rated input signal level for the low-impedance microphone port is 350 $\mu$V, whereas the rated input signal level for the FM tuner port is 250 $\mu$V, or a ratio of 700 to 1. Also, the frequency response for each port is different. Examples of equalization curves are shown in Fig. 1-10. The maximum available gain (MAG) in terms of voltage for this preamplifier is 69 dB, and an output of 1 V rms is normally delivered to a 10,000-ohm load, regardless of the input port that is in use. Note that RIAA denotes the Record Industry Association of America.

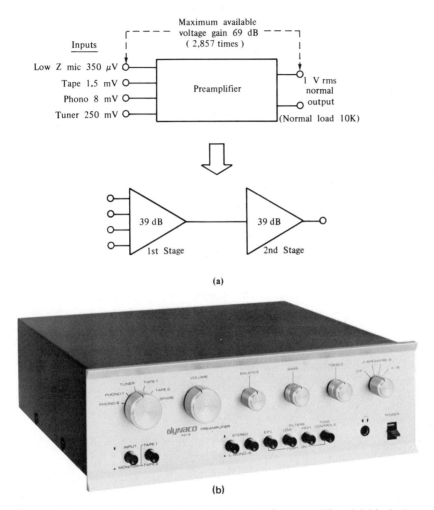

**Figure 1-9**  Typical voltage-gain values for a hi-fi preamplifier: **(a)** block diagram; **(b)** appearance of a high-performance preamplifier (*Courtesy of Dynaco.*)

Next, consider the typical voltage-gain and power-output values
for the power amplifier exemplified in Fig. 1-11. A signal-voltage gain
of 18 dB is provided, and an input of 1 V rms will produce approximately 8 V rms output across an 8- or 16-ohm load. Since the input
impedance of the power amplifier is 10,000 ohms, its power gain is
greater than its voltage gain; the power gain is approximately 38 dB.
A preamplifier is provided with tone controls, and often with additional
frequency-response controls. The characteristics of typical tone and

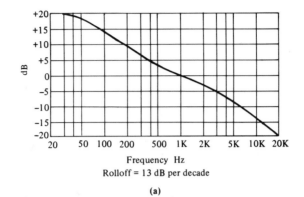

Frequency Hz
Rolloff = 13 dB per decade

(a)

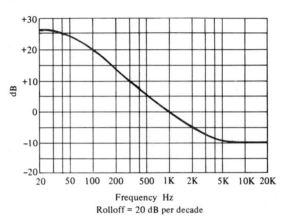

Frequency Hz
Rolloff = 20 dB per decade

(b)

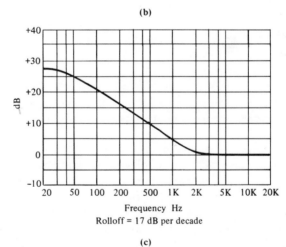

Frequency Hz
Rolloff = 17 dB per decade

(c)

**Figure 1-10** Examples of standardized input frequency characteristics: **(a)** RIAA equalization curve for playback of records; **(b)** NAB standard playback curve for 7.5 in./s tape; **(c)** MRIA playback curve for 3.75 in./s tape.

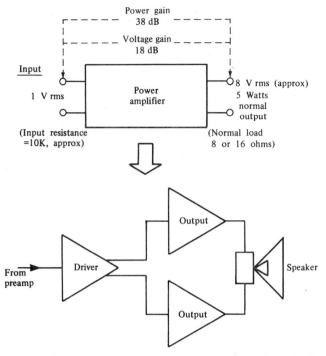

**Figure 1-11**  Typical voltage-gain and power-output values for a hi-fi audio power amplifier.

frequency-response controls are shown in Fig. 1-12. A loudness control is a compensated volume control. It is a combined volume and tone control that boosts the bass frequencies at low volume levels to compensate for the inability of the ear to respond to these bass frequencies. Some loudness controls provide similar compensation at the treble frequencies.

A presence control is basically a potentiometer used in a three-way speaker system for controlling the volume of the middle-range speaker. A three-way speaker system employs a woofer, a midrange speaker, and a tweeter. A rumble filter operates to minimize or eliminate the low-frequency vibration that is mechanically transmitted to a reproducing turntable and superimposed on the audio signal. Rumble can also be caused by a marginal tape transport. A scratch filter is a low-pass filter that minimizes the needle-scratch output from a phonograph pickup by suppressing the higher audio frequencies. If an equalizer is included in an audio channel, the operator can boost or cut frequencies in the 60-, 240-, 1000-, 3500-, or 10,000-Hz regions, as

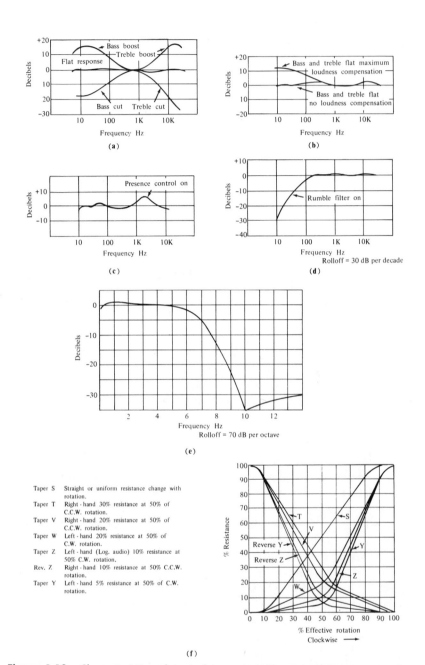

**Figure 1-12** Characteristics of typical tone and frequency-response controls: **(a)** action of bass and treble boost and cut controls; **(b)** effect of loudness compensation; **(c)** midband boost produced by presence control; **(d)** rumble filter characteristic; **(e)** scratch filter characteristic; **(f)** standard tapers for potentiometer controls.

**14**

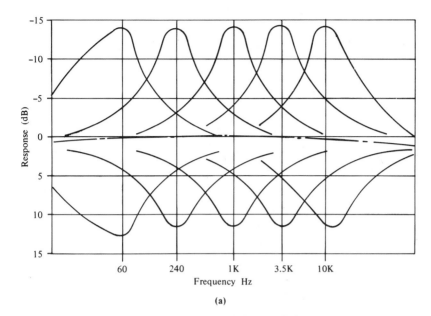

(a)

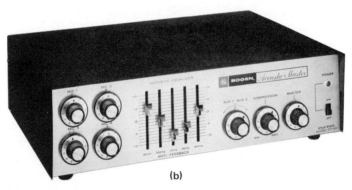

(b)

**Figure 1-13**   Representative equalizer frequency responses: **(a)** response curves; **(b)** appearance of equalizer unit. (*Courtesy of Bogen.*)

depicted in Fig. 1-13. A typical equalizer provides a boost or cut range up to 12 dB.

## 1-3   DISTORTION IN AUDIO SYSTEMS

Distortion is defined as a change in shape of an audio waveform. Thus, noise, interference, or hum are not considered forms of distortion. With reference to Fig. 1-14, the chief forms of distortion are frequency,

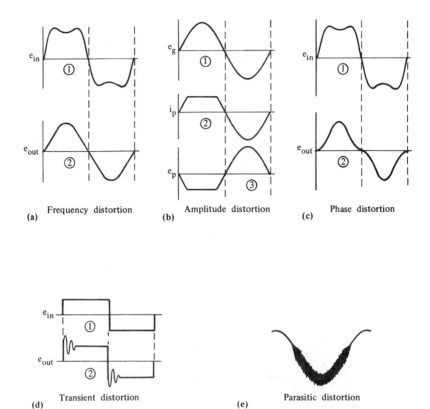

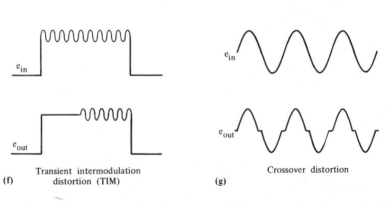

**Figure 1-14**   Basic types of distortion: **(a)** frequency distortion; **(b)** amplitude distortion; **(c)** phase distortion; **(d)** transient distortion; **(e)** parasitic distortion; **(f)** transient intermodulation distortion (TIM); **(g)** crossover distortion.

amplitude, and phase distortion. For example, if a fundamental frequency and its third harmonic are applied at the input of a narrowband amplifier, the third-harmonic component may be attenuated or eliminated, with only the fundamental frequency remaining in the output waveform. In this example, the amplifier is said to impose frequency distortion on the input waveform. Frequency distortion is characterized by an output waveform with fewer frequencies than are present in the input waveform. In turn, a change in shape of the waveform occurs, and the output waveform is "smoother" than the complex input waveform.

Amplitude distortion also produces a change in the shape of a waveform. It is characterized by an output waveform that has more frequencies than are present in the input waveform. For example, if a sine wave is applied to an amplifier that is overdriven, one or both peaks of the sine wave may be compressed or clipped. This change in waveshape is accompanied by the generation of new frequencies that are harmonically related to the frequency of the input sine waveform. Amplitude distortion and frequency distortion are independent processes. In other words, amplitude distortion is not necessarily accompanied by frequency distortion; frequency distortion is not necessarily accompanied by amplitude distortion. Of course, if a narrow-band amplifier is overdriven, it will impose both amplitude distortion and frequency distortion on the input waveform.

Phase distortion is also an independent form of distortion. It is characterized by a change in the phase angle between the fundamental and one or more harmonic components of a complex waveform. For example, if a fundamental frequency and its third harmonic are applied at the input of an amplifier, and the output waveform exhibits the third harmonic in a shifted phase with respect to the fundamental, the input complex waveform has undergone phase distortion. In practice, phase distortion may be accompanied by frequency and/or amplitude distortion. From the viewpoint of the audiophile, phase distortion is much less serious than is amplitude distortion or frequency distortion. The reason for this evaluation is that moderate amounts of phase distortion are imperceptible to the listener. However, phase distortion can become discernible in some situations; for example, if an amplifier processes a square wave that undergoes extensive phase distortion, the output waveform has a noticeably different timbre compared with that of the undistorted square wave.

Transient distortion is not an independent form of distortion, in the strict technical sense of the term. In other words, transient distortion is a function of frequency and phase distortion. However, this function is complex, and it is much more convenient for the audio technologist to consider transient distortion as if it were an independent process.

Transient distortion is generally evaluated from the standpoint of square-wave reproduction. It is characterized in terms of rise time, fall time, overshoot, preshoot, ringing, tilt, and curvature. A distorted square wave is customarily treated as a simple or derived exponential waveform. Although exponential waveforms can be expressed as various series of sine waveforms, the equations are prohibitively involved. However, from an intuitive standpoint, the audio technologist occasionally finds it informative to consider that a square wave, for example, is built up from an infinite series of sine waves.

Parasitic distortion is something of a misnomer, in that it denotes the introduction of a spurious high-frequency sine-wave component into an audio waveform. It is a self-generated form of interference that does not constitute distortion in a strict technical sense. Parasitic oscillation usually occurs over the peak portion of an audio signal waveform. It is distinguished from transient ringing in that parasitic oscillation is produced by a negative-resistance condition, instead of shock excitation. Parasitic distortion is undesirable, not only because it impairs the quality of the reproduced sound, but also because it imposes additional power dissipation on the output transistors, and can cause overheating or burnout.

Amplitude distortion does not always occur over the peaks of the audio signal waveform. For example, crossover distortion (Fig. 1-15) occurs near the zero level of the waveform. It is encountered in class B output stages that are operated at zero bias. In turn, the transfer characterististics of the output transistors exhibit nonlinearity in the vicinity of zero collector current. This nonlinearity results in distortion of the output waveform, as shown in Fig. 1-15(c). Crossover distortion can be minimized or eliminated by applying a small forward bias on the output transistors. Note that excessive forward bias must not be applied, or an overcompensated type of crossover distortion, called *stretching distortion,* will occur. It is also a form of amplitude distortion. A significant distinction between clipping distortion and crossover distortion is that the former increases as the audio output power is increased, whereas the latter increases as the audio output power is decreased.

When amplitude nonlinearity causes peak compression or clipping in an amplifier, as exemplified in Fig. 1-16, harmonic frequencies are generated. Amplitude nonlinearity can be measured either with a single-tone test signal or with a two-tone test signal. If a single sine-wave frequency is used to measure amplitude nonlinearity, a harmonic-distortion meter is employed. The HD meter indicates the combined amplitudes of the harmonic voltages as a percentage of the fundamental voltage in the output signal. If a two-tone test signal is used, consisting

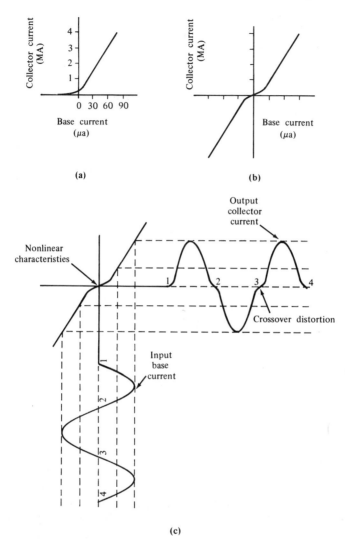

**Figure 1-15** Development of crossover distortion in a class B stage: **(a)** transfer characteristic for a single transistor; **(b)** transfer characteristic for both transistors; **(c)** development of crossover distortion.

of two sine waves with different frequencies, an intermodulation-distortion meter is utilized. The **IM** meter indicates the percentage of amplitude modulation that is impressed on the higher-frequency test signal by the amplifier nonlinearity (see Fig. 1-17).

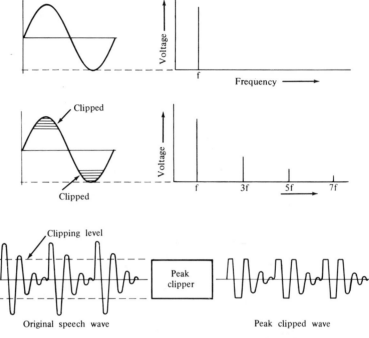

**Figure 1-16** Frequency spectra for a sine wave and a clipped sine wave.

Harmonic-distortion meters and intermodulation-distortion meters both contain audio-frequency filters for signal processing. Thus, an HD meter employs a sharply tuned filter that eliminates the fundamental frequency from the signal under test. In turn, the harmonics (if any) are passed on to an AC voltmeter with a scale calibrated in HD percentage units. In the same manner, an IM meter employs high-pass and low-pass filters with a detector to develop the modulation envelope of the distorted IM test signal. In turn, this envelope waveform is applied to an AC voltmeter with a scale calibrated in IM percentage units. A harmonic-distortion test is ordinarily made at a frequency of 1 kHz; however, the test may be made at any audio frequency. An amplifier will develop different percentages of harmonic distortion at different test frequencies. An intermodulation-distortion test is typically made with a 60-Hz and a 6-kHz two-tone signal. As exemplified in Fig. 1-18, harmonic-distortion and intermodulation-distortion values have the same general trend, although they are seldom identical. With the exception of crossover distortion, both HD and IM percentages will increase as the power output from an amplifier is increased.

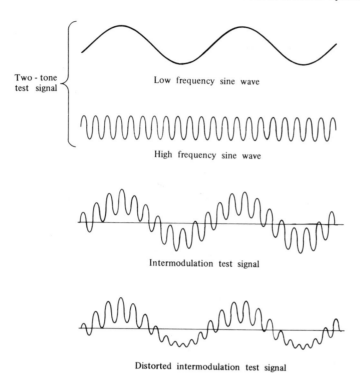

Two - tone test signal

Low frequency sine wave

High frequency sine wave

Intermodulation test signal

Distorted intermodulation test signal

**Figure 1-17**  Composition of an IM test signal, and example of distortion.

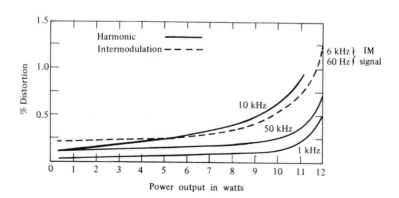

**Figure 1-18**  Comparison of IM and HD percentages for a typical amplifier. (*Redrawn with permission of General Electric Co.*)

Transient intermodulation distortion (TIM) is caused by the employment of a large amount of negative feedback in a configuration that produces objectionable envelope delay.


## 1-4  BASIC AUDIO TROUBLESHOOTING PRINCIPLES

Audio troubleshooting requires suitable tools, instruments, and service data. Most present-day audio equipment employs printed circuitry, often with modular construction. Solid-state design is almost universal, with devices such as integrated circuits, transistors, and semiconductor diodes to process the audio signal. Construction is very compact, necessitating small tools and pencil-type soldering guns. Instrument test leads should be terminated in needle-point prods, both to puncture insulation on printed-circuit conductors, and to minimize the possibility of short-circuiting adjacent terminals or conductors. Because solid-state devices can be instantly ruined by momentary overloads, appropriate care must be taken in test procedures. Service data for the equipment under test are essential, unless the technician has had long experience with the particular unit.

Circuit boards may be damaged if subjected to substantial stress or strain in removal of faulty devices or components. Careless soldering procedure can permit excess solder to short-circuit adjacent conductors or terminals. Conversely, cold-solder joints can lead to puzzling circuit malfunctions. Suitable heat sinks should be utilized during soldering operations, to prevent thermal damage to semiconductor devices. Remember that leakage in a soldering iron can cause the tip to be as high as 117 V above ground potential. Similarly, metal cases of test instruments may be above ground potential. It is good practice to keep all instrument cases permanently connected to a good ground, such as a cold water pipe. Most audio troubleshooting jobs do not require elaborate tools. For example, an assortment of various kinds of pliers, a set of small and medium-sized screwdrivers and Phillip's-head screwdrivers, a diagonal cutter, and a set of hex wrenches are often sufficient. Some jobs also require a set of Allen-head wrenches.

A high-impedance voltmeter, such as that illustrated in Fig. 1-19, is the most basic troubleshooting instrument. Although a digital meter is not mandatory, its high accuracy and ease of reading recommend it to the professional audio technician. An analog-type transistor voltmeter (TVM) will serve the same basic purpose. Even a 20,000 ohms-per-volt volt-ohm-milliammeter (VOM) is often adequate. However, it is advisable to avoid low-sensitivity meters, such as 1000 ohms-per-volt VOM's, in audio troubleshooting procedures, because of the

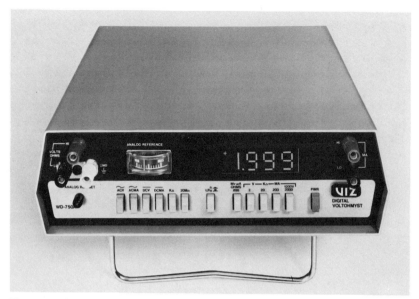

**Figure 1-19**   Appearance of a digital volt-ohm-milliammeter. (*Courtesy of VIZ.*)

comparatively heavy loading that they impose on the higher-impedance circuits. Excessive circuit loading causes subnormal scale indication and can mislead the technician. Most audio service data specify the minimum sensitivity that should be provided by a DC voltmeter to test the equipment circuitry.

Most audio technicians consider that an oscilloscope is second in importance only to a basic transistor voltmeter. A dual-trace oscilloscope with a calibrated vertical amplifier and a triggered/calibrated time base is illustrated in Fig. 1-20. An oscilloscope serves as an audio signal tracer, as a stage-gain or section-gain indicator, as a preliminary distortion indicator, as a noise and/or hum analyzer, as a transient analyzer, and as a phase-measuring instrument. A calibrated vertical amplifier permits the technician to quickly measure the peak-to-peak voltage of a displayed waveform. Although an economy-type oscilloscope is adequate for signal tracing, and can also be used for approximate gain measurements, it has some limitations in high-fidelity tests. For example, unless an oscilloscope has highly linear vertical and horizontal amplifiers, it cannot be used to approximate the percentage of distortion in a high-fidelity circuit. In general, the test equipment used in high-fidelity troubleshooting procedures should have better characteristics than the equipment under test.

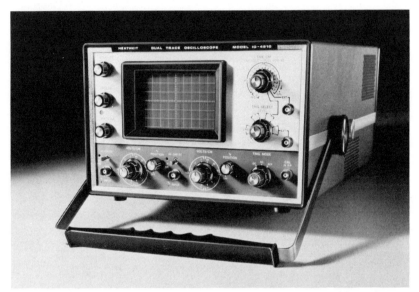

**Figure 1-20** Appearance of a dual-trace oscilloscope with a calibrated vertical amplifier and time base. (*Courtesy of Heath Co.*)

Audio generators of sine-wave and square-wave signals are also basic audio test instruments. Sine-wave and square-wave functions may be combined in a single instrument, as illustrated in Fig. 1-21. A sine-wave generator should have a very low percentage distortion, so that deficiencies of the test equipment will not be falsely attributed to the hi-fi unit under test. A sine-wave generator should provide a wide frequency range, such as from 20 Hz to 100 kHz, so that hi-fi amplifiers with extended high-frequency response can be completely checked. A wide-range attenuator is desirable, so that suitably low-level signals can be applied to preamplifiers without the use of supplementary attenuator arrangements. A maximum output of 6 or 8 V is helpful for testing passive audio components. The chief requirement for the square-wave signal is a sufficiently fast rise time; a rating of 100 nanoseconds or less is adequate.

Troubleshooting of FM stereo systems requires the availability of a stereo signal generator. It is helpful to the technician to have stereo analyzer facilities combined with the generator, as illustrated in Fig. 1-22. This instrument provides dB meters for measuring separation, and a wattmeter function for measuring audio power output. In addition to a complete series of stereo test signals, the instrument also supplies an FM RF/IF sweep-alignment signal with crystal-controlled markers, and

**Figure 1-21**   A combination audio sine-wave and square-wave generator. (Courtesy of B & K Precision, Div. of Dynascan Corp.)

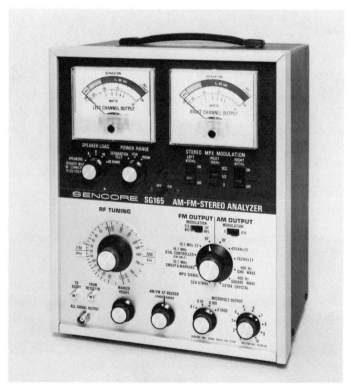

**Figure 1-22**   An elaborate AM-FM stereo analyzer. (Courtesy of Sencore, Inc.)

an AM RF/IF test signal. A 400-Hz square-wave function is also provided, for checking the transient response of audio amplifiers. A wide
range of attenuation is available, so that the output signal can be reduced to the noise level for checking system sensitivity.

Percentage of harmonic distortion is measured with a harmonic
distortion analyzer, such as that pictured in Fig. 1-23. A distortion
measurement can be made at any frequency from 5 Hz to 100 kHz, at
values down to 0.03 percent. The instrument also functions as an AC
rms voltmeter, with a first full-scale range of 1 mV, and an upper limit
of 300 V. An automatic null circuit is included, so that measurements
can be made quickly and accurately. Its input impedance is 1 megohm
(mΩ) with a shunt capacitance of 70 pF, so that loading of audio
circuitry is minimized. Note in passing that hum and noise (if present)
will be indicated on the scale of a harmonic-distortion meter, although
these spurious components are not considered as distortion products in
a strict technical sense.

**Figure 1-23**    A harmonic distortion analyzer. (*Courtesy of Heath Co.*)

Audio technicians often supplement a harmonic-distortion
analyzer with an intermodulation-distortion analyzer, as illustrated in
Fig. 1-24. This type of instrument can measure IM percentages down to
0.01 percent. Measurements are made in accordance with standards of
the Society of Motion Picture and Television Engineers (SMPTE),
with a choice of other test conditions. It contains built-in 60-Hz and
7-kHz oscillators. The instrument input circuitry has a 3-dB bandwidth
from 5 Hz to 1 MHz. It contains a built-in AC voltmeter with an input
impedance of 1 megohm and full-scale ranges from 10 mV to 300 V.
A percentage scale is provided for indication of IM distortion values. A
decibel scale is also provided.

**Figure 1-24**   An intermodulation distortion analyzer. (*Courtesy of Heath Co.*)

**Basic Electrical Testing Procedures**   DC voltage and resistance measurements are basic in hi-fi troubleshooting procedures. Normal voltage and resistance values are specified in audio service data. Circuit malfunctions are often accompanied by changes in DC voltage and/or resistance values. For example, defective transistors can often be tracked down by in-circuit voltage measurements. Typical *NPN* and *PNP* bipolar germanium transistor circuits, with specified operating voltages, are shown in Fig. 1-25. Germanium transistors are usually operated with a base-emitter bias voltage of 0.2 V. Note that silicon bipolar transistors, on the other hand, are usually operated with a base-emitter bias of 0.6 V. Bias polarity is such that class A operation is obtained; forward bias current flows at all times.

If a transistor develops collector-junction leakage, excessive collector-emitter current flows. The stage gain decreases, and the transistor may generate excessive noise. With reference to Fig. 1-25, excessive collector-emitter current flow produces an abnormal voltage drop across $R1$. In turn, the emitter voltage becomes higher than normal. An abnormal voltage drop also occurs across $R2$, with the result that the collector-emitter voltage of the transistor becomes lower than normal. In an extreme condition, with the collector junction short-circuited, practically all of the supply voltage drops across $R1$ and $R2$, and the collector-emitter voltage of the transistor is virtually zero.

An opposite type of fault may occur, in which the collector junction of the transistor burns out and becomes open-circuited. In such a case, the collector-emitter voltage of the transistor becomes abnormally high. Of course, a change in transistor terminal voltages can be caused by defects in associated circuit components, instead of transistor faults. For this reason, the technician must often analyze and interpret

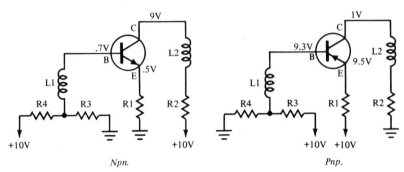

**Figure 1-25**  Typical operating voltages in germanium bipolar transistor circuitry. All voltages measured with respect to ground.

the DC voltage distribution that he finds in an improperly operating circuit. With reference to Fig. 1-26, consider the possible causes for loss of base and emitter bias voltages. (Base and emitter terminals are at zero-volt potential with respect to ground.) Inasmuch as the base bias voltage is applied via $R4$, it is evident that a short circuit in $C3$ is a probable cause. If $C3$ checks out normally, the technician turns his attention to $R4$ and $L1$. An open circuit in either of these components will result in loss of bias voltage.

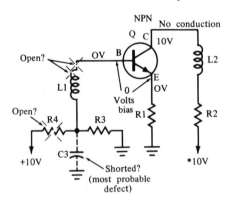

**Figure 1-26**  Component failure can cause loss of bias voltage.

From the standpoint of probability, capacitor defects are more likely to occur than are resistor or inductor defects. Circuit analysis indicates in this situation that if there were a base-emitter short circuit in the transistor, the base-emitter bias voltage would be zero, but the emitter voltage would measure above ground potential. In other words, with a base-emitter short circuit, there will still be current flow through $R1$, and the resulting voltage drop across $R1$ will raise the emitter potential above ground. Note that since the emitter is connected to ground through $R1$, when the base voltage is brought to zero for any reason, the transistor will normally be cut off and no collector current will flow. Consequently, there will be zero current flow through $R1$ and the emitter terminal will rest at 0 V. With the transistor cut off, its collector potential will rise to practically the supply-voltage value.

The most probable transistor defect is leakage from collector to base through the collector junction. Collector-junction leakage changes the DC voltage distribution in typical *PNP* and *NPN* bipolar transistor circuitry, as shown in Fig. 1-27. Note that collector leakage has the effect of increasing the leakage current through the transistor from collector to emitter. Therefore, collector leakage causes an increase in the voltage drops across $R1$ and $R2$. This increased voltage drop across $R1$ causes the emitter voltage to become abnormal in the configuration of Fig. 1-27(a). In addition, the increased voltage drop across $R2$ causes the collector voltage to become subnormal. However, when the configuration in Fig. 1-27(b) is being checked, observe that an increased voltage drop across $R1$ causes the emitter voltage to become subnormal; the increased voltage drop across $R2$ causes the collector voltage to become abnormal.

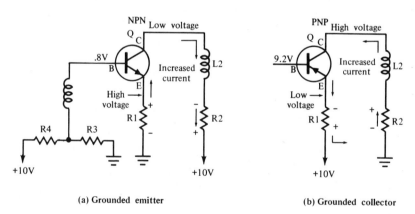

(a) Grounded emitter                    (b) Grounded collector

**Figure 1-27**   Collector leakage changes the DC voltage distribution. All voltages measured with respect to ground.

In the foregoing configurations, when collector leakage is quite serious, the transistor can become zero-biased or reverse-biased, although the collector current is abnormal. Note that some of the collector leakage current is diverted into the base circuit. This diversion current has a tendency to produce a reversed base-emitter bias. Consequently, whenever the technician observes reversed bias polarity on a transistor that normally operates in class A, collector leakage should be suspected at the outset. If the collector-base junction is short-circuited, it is evident that the same DC voltage value will be measured at the base and collector terminals. Or, if the base-collector junction becomes open-circuited, the collector voltage will either measure zero or practically the supply-voltage value, depending upon the circuit arrangement.

Two useful quick checks can often be made of transistor control action. These are called "turn-off" and "turn-on" tests. A turn-off test is made by bringing the transistor's base-emitter bias to zero while the collector-emitter voltage is monitored. In circuits such as that shown in Fig. 1-28, a turn-off test is made by temporarily short-circuiting the base and emitter terminals together, with a DC voltmeter connected between collector and ground. When the base and emitter terminals are connected together in the configuration of Fig. 1-28(a), the collector voltage jumps up to the supply-voltage value, if the transistor has normal control action. However, in the configuration of Fig. 1-28(b), the collector voltage drops to zero, if the transistor has normal control action.

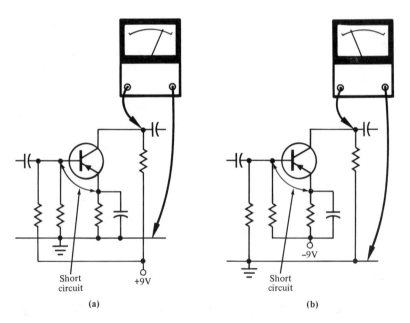

**Figure 1-28** Basic transistor "turn-off" test procedure: **(a)** grounded emitter; **(b)** grounded collector.

Typical "turn-on" tests are depicted in Fig. 1-29. This test is made by increasing the forward bias on a transistor while the collector voltage or emitter voltage is monitored. A 50-kilohm bleeder resistor is temporarily applied to increase the forward bias voltage. If the transistor has normal control action, the collector current increases when the forward bias is increased. This condition results in a decrease of collector voltage in the configuration of Fig. 1-29(a). On the other hand, increased forward bias results in an increase of emitter voltage in the configuration of Fig. 1-29(b), if the transistor has normal control action. In-circuit transistor tests are very useful, because transistors are usually soldered into printed-circuit boards.

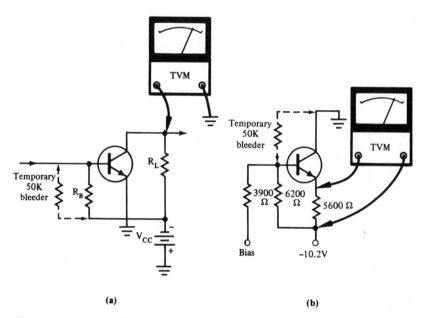

(a)                                    (b)

**Figure 1-29** Examples of "turn-on" test procedure: **(a)** grounded emitter; **(b)** grounded collector.

Various modern TVM's are provided with a low-power ohm-meter function, in addition to a conventional ohmmeter function. A low-power resistance-measuring function has an advantage over a conventional ohmmeter in that it applies a test potential of less than 0.1 V between the points under measurement in an electronic circuit. Accordingly, the test voltage is less than the threshold value required to turn a normal transistor or diode "on." Accordingly, many resistors in solid-

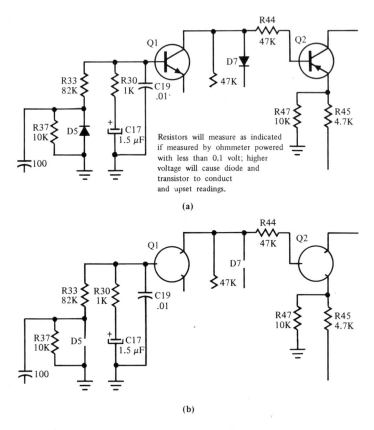

Resistors will measure as indicated
if measured by ohmmeter powered
with less than 0.1 volt; higher
voltage will cause diode and
transistor to conduct
and upset readings.

(a)

(b)

**Figure 1-30**   Resistance measurement in solid-state circuitry: **(a)** device junctions will conduct when forward-biased by test voltage from conventional ohmmeter; **(b)** how the circuit "looks" to a low-power ohmmeter.

state circuitry can be checked without disconnection. With reference to Fig. 1-30, a low-power ohmmeter will check the resistance values of R37, R33, R30, and R44 accurately in circuit. Of course, if a capacitor, diode, or transistor happens to be defective, an inaccurate resistance measurement will result. Therefore, the technician must occasionally analyze and interpret a pattern of incorrect resistance values that are measured in circuit.

A conventional, or high-power, resistance function is required, in addition to a low-power ohms function, in order to check the front-to-back ratios of semiconductor devices. Resistance values measured in a front-to-back ratio test of a device junction can vary considerably, depending upon the particular ohmmeter that is used, and upon the resistance range that is used. In other words, the junction is characterized by nonlinear resistance, and the resistance value that is indicated by an ohmmeter depends upon the value of test voltage that is applied to the junction. Nevertheless, a simple front-to-back ratio test with an ohmmeter is adequate to "weed out" junction devices that are definitely defective. Forward-resistance readings should be quite low, and reverse-resistance readings should be quite high.

Audio signal tracing can be accomplished with either an AC voltmeter or with an oscilloscope. However, an oscilloscope is more informative, in that it shows the signal waveform that is present at the test point. The basic principle of signal tracing is exemplified in Fig. 1-31. In this example, the first stage exhibits a voltage gain from input to output, but the second stage stops signal passage completely. Because there is no signal input to the third stage, its condition cannot be determined without further tests. After a failure has been traced to a particular stage, the technician ordinarily proceeds to make DC-voltage tests to close in on the defective component or device. In various cases, DC-voltage measurements are supplemented by resistance measurements.

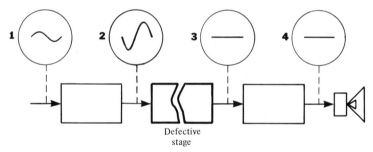

**Figure 1-31** Basic principle of signal tracing.

Signal-tracing tests in negative-feedback circuits can be misleading, unless the technician takes the normal circuit action into account. As an illustration, Fig. 1-32 depicts a three-stage audio amplifier with 20 dB of negative feedback. Although the preamplifier seems to be the distorting stage, this is not so. The fault will be found in the driver stage. This deceptive conclusion results from the fact that negative feedback operates by predistorting the total input signal to the preamplifier. In turn, the output signal from the preamplifier is distorted; it is distorted in a manner that compensates for the nonlinearity of a following stage. Therefore, when a distorted waveform is displayed in an audio-amplifier circuit, the distortion must be evaluated with respect to any negative-feedback loop that may be present.

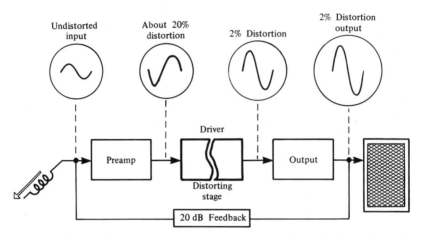

**Figure 1-32**   Feedback loop makes the preamplifier "look like" the distorting stage.

When one is signal-tracing waveforms in power-amplifier circuitry, it sometimes appears that a power stage has no gain (see Fig. 1-33). In some cases, it may seem that a power stage imposes a signal loss. However, the technician must keep in mind that an oscilloscope displays voltage waveforms only. On the other hand, the power gain of a stage is equal to the product of its voltage gain and its current gain. Thus, a power-amplifier stage may develop high power gain on the basis of a high current gain, whereas its voltage gain may be unity, or even less. Current waveforms can be checked with an oscilloscope with a current probe, or often by means of a suitable expedient. For example, if a series resistor happens to be available in the line of signal flow, the waveform across the resistor will represent the current waveform in the circuit. In turn, Ohm's law may be applied (if the value of the resistor is known) to calculate the current value. In general, technicians avoid current measurements as often as possible, and concentrate upon voltage and resistance checks.

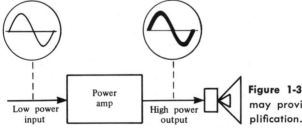

**Figure 1-33**   Power amplifier may provide no voltage amplification.

## 1-5 DECIBEL MEASUREMENTS

Since the response of the eye and ear to signal levels is logarithmic, audio gains and losses are measured to advantage in decibel units. Although most AC voltmeters have decibel scales, it is important to note that the decibel is a power ratio, and not a voltage ratio. Voltage ratios correspond to power ratios, if the voltages are measured across equal load resistances. However, if the load resistances are unequal, voltage values do not correspond directly to power values. Decibel units are additive and subtractive. For example, if there is a 20-dB loss in a volume control, followed by a gain of 30 dB in an amplifier, the overall gain is 10 dB. In terms of loudness units at moderate sound levels, a gain of 10 dB is generally judged to be approximately twice as loud as the original level, and a loss of 10 dB is generally judged to be about half as loud as the original level.

All dB values are referenced to some chosen power value, to which the level of 0 dB is assigned. Some dB scales are referenced to 1 mW in 600 ohms (see Fig. 1-34). Various other reference levels will be encountered. The dB scales of an AC voltmeter read directly only when the measurements are made across a value of load resistance for

**Figure 1-34** The zero-dB level is referenced to 1 mW in 600 Ω in this example. (*Courtesy of Heath* Co.)

which the scales have been referenced. However, calculations can always be made to correct indicated dB values both for nonstandard load-resistance values, and for a zero-dB reference level other than that for which the meter is rated. A simple example of a dB measurement across 600-$\Omega$ loads with AC voltmeters designed to indicate dB values across 600-$\Omega$ loads is shown in Fig. 1-35. A good sine waveform should be utilized for dB measurements, or the indicated values will be subject to waveform error. In this example, the audio oscillator supplies a signal level of 2 dB to the 600-$\Omega$ volume control, and the amplifier increases the signal level 12 dB. In turn, the overall gain is the difference between these two values, or 10 dB.

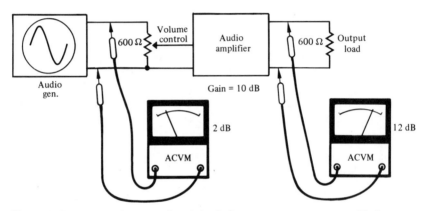

**Figure 1-35**    A simple example of decibel measurements across 600 $\Omega$ resistive loads.

Note that many AC voltmeters have only one decibel scale, which is usually applicable directly to the lowest AC-voltage range of the instrument. Accordingly, when the meter is operated on a higher AC-voltage range, it is necessary to add a corresponding number of decibels to the indicated value. This is called the *scale factor,* and it is usually printed on the meter scale plate, or in the instruction manual for the instrument. In any case, the technician can calculate the required scale factor on the basis of the range ratio. As a practical note, although two meters are shown in Fig. 1-35, only one meter is necessary; in practice, the test leads are simply moved from the input terminals to the output terminals of the unit or system under test. The basic relation between dB values, power ratios, and voltage ratios is seen in Table 1-1. Note that dB measurements are valid across resistive loads only;

TABLE 1-1
Power Ratios, Voltage Ratios, and Decibel Values
(Voltage ratios based on equal load resistances)

| Power Ratio | Voltage Ratio | dB<br>$\rightarrow$ +<br>$\leftarrow$ $\rightarrow$ | Voltage Ratio | Power Ratio |
|---|---|---|---|---|
| 1.000 | 1.0000 | 0 | 1.000 | 1.000 |
| .9772 | .9886 | .1 | 1.012 | 1.023 |
| .9550 | .9772 | .2 | 1.023 | 1.047 |
| .9333 | .9661 | .3 | 1.035 | 1.072 |
| .9120 | .9550 | .4 | 1.047 | 1.096 |
| .8913 | .9441 | .5 | 1.059 | 1.122 |
| .8710 | .9333 | .6 | 1.072 | 1.148 |
| .8511 | .9226 | .7 | 1.084 | 1.175 |
| .8318 | .9120 | .8 | 1.096 | 1.202 |
| .8128 | .9016 | .9 | 1.109 | 1.230 |
| .7943 | .8913 | 1.0 | 1.122 | 1.259 |
| .6310 | .7943 | 2.0 | 1.259 | 1.585 |
| .5012 | .7079 | 3.0 | 1.413 | 1.995 |
| .3981 | .6310 | 4.0 | 1.585 | 2.512 |
| .3162 | .5623 | 5.0 | 1.778 | 3.162 |
| .2512 | .5012 | 6.0 | 1.995 | 3.981 |
| .1995 | .4467 | 7.0 | 2.239 | 5.012 |
| .1585 | .3981 | 8.0 | 2.512 | 6.310 |
| .1259 | .3548 | 9.0 | 2.818 | 7.943 |
| .10000 | .3162 | 10.0 | 3.162 | 10.00 |
| .07943 | .2818 | 11.0 | 3.548 | 12.59 |
| .06310 | .2512 | 12.0 | 3.981 | 15.85 |
| .05012 | .2293 | 13.0 | 4.467 | 19.95 |
| .03981 | .1995 | 14.0 | 5.012 | 25.12 |
| .03162 | .1778 | 15.0 | 5.623 | 31.62 |
| .02512 | .1585 | 16.0 | 6.310 | 39.81 |
| .01995 | .1413 | 17.0 | 7.079 | 50.12 |
| .01585 | .1259 | 18.0 | 7.943 | 63.10 |
| .01259 | .1122 | 19.0 | 8.913 | 79.43 |
| .01000 | .1000 | 20.0 | 10.000 | 100.00 |
| $10^{-3}$ | $3.162 \times 10^{-2}$ | 30.0 | $3.162 \times 10$ | $10^3$ |
| $10^{-4}$ | $10^{-2}$ | 40.0 | $10^2$ | $10^4$ |
| $10^{-5}$ | $3.162 \times 10^{-3}$ | 50.0 | $3.162 \times 10^2$ | $10^5$ |
| $10^{-6}$ | $10^{-3}$ | 60.0 | $10^3$ | $10^6$ |
| $10^{-7}$ | $3.162 \times 10^{-4}$ | 70.0 | $3.162 \times 10^3$ | $10^7$ |
| $10^{-8}$ | $10^{-4}$ | 80.0 | $10^4$ | $10^8$ |
| $10^{-9}$ | $3.162 \times 10^{-5}$ | 90.0 | $3.162 \times 10^4$ | $10^9$ |
| $10^{-10}$ | $10^{-5}$ | 100.0 | $10^5$ | $10^{10}$ |

because an impedance load develops both real power and reactive power, dB indications across impedances are not fully informative. The power ratio corresponding to a dB value is ordinarily understood to be a ratio of two real-power values. Note that no decibel table can be completely comprehensive, and that some dB values may have to be calculated in various situations. Such calculations in the range from 0.01 to 990 ratios of power can be made with minimum effort by referring to Table 1-2.

TABLE 1-2

Decibel Calculations for Power Ratios from 0.01 to 990

Power ratios expressed in + dB.

| Power Ratio | .0 | .1 | .2 | .3 | .4 | .5 | .6 | .7 | .8 | .9 |
|---|---|---|---|---|---|---|---|---|---|---|
| 1 | .000 | .414 | .792 | 1.139 | 1.461 | 1.761 | 2.041 | 2.304 | 2.553 | 2.788 |
| 2 | 3.010 | 3.222 | 3.424 | 3.617 | 3.802 | 3.979 | 4.150 | 4.314 | 4.472 | 4.624 |
| 3 | 4.771 | 4.914 | 5.051 | 5.185 | 5.315 | 5.441 | 5.563 | 5.682 | 5.798 | 5.911 |
| 4 | 6.021 | 6.128 | 6.232 | 6.335 | 6.435 | 6.532 | 6.628 | 6.721 | 6.812 | 6.902 |
| 5 | 6.990 | 7.076 | 7.160 | 7.243 | 7.324 | 7.404 | 7.482 | 7.559 | 7.634 | 7.709 |
| 6 | 7.782 | 7.853 | 7.924 | 7.993 | 8.062 | 8.129 | 8.195 | 8.261 | 8.325 | 8.388 |
| 7 | 8.451 | 8.513 | 8.573 | 8.633 | 8.692 | 8.751 | 8.808 | 8.865 | 8.921 | 8.976 |
| 8 | 9.031 | 9.085 | 9.138 | 9.191 | 9.243 | 9.294 | 9.345 | 9.395 | 9.445 | 9.494 |
| 9 | 9.542 | 9.590 | 9.638 | 9.685 | 9.731 | 9.777 | 9.823 | 9.868 | 9.912 | 9.956 |

For power ratios between 0.01 and 0.099, use above table to find dB for 100 times the ratio and subtract 20 dB. ·

For power ratios between 0.1 and 0.99, use above table to find dB for 10 times the ratio and subtract 10 dB.

For power ratios between 1 and 9.9, use above table directly.

For power ratios between 10 and 99, use above table to find dB for 1/10 of the ratio and add 10 dB.

For power ratios between 100 and 990, use above table to find dB for 1/100 of the ratio and add 20 dB.

Two basic situations are encountered in the measurement of dB values across resistive loads that have different values from that for which the dB meter scale has been calibrated. In the first situation, the load resistances are different from the reference value for the dB meter, but these load resistances are equal in value as exemplified in Fig. 1-36(a). In this situation, the technician can determine the dB gain or loss of the system by merely taking the difference between the two readings. For example, the reference value for the dB meter might be 600 Ω.

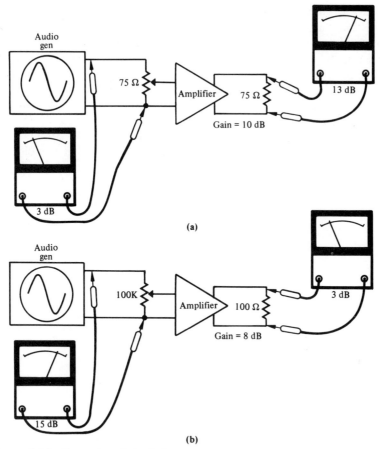

**Figure 1-36** Examples of decibel measurements: (a) across equal resistances;
(b) across unequal resistances.

If the input and output resistances of an amplifier should both be 75
Ω, the technician can still use the dB meter that has a 600-Ω reference
value. With reference to Fig. 1-36(a), neither the 3-dB nor the 13-dB
reading is correct in itself. Nevertheless, the difference between these
two readings, or 10 dB, is a correct calculation, inasmuch as the two
readings were made across equal load resistances. Thus, the gain of
the system in this example is 10 dB.

Next, with reference to Fig. 1-36(b), these dB measurements
are made across unequal load resistances. Neither of these resistance
values corresponds to the 600-Ω reference value of the dB meter. In
turn, neither the 15-dB reading nor the 3-dB reading is correct in itself,

nor is the difference between these two readings correct. It may be noted that this system provides gain, although the dB meter readings seem to indicate that there is a loss. In order to evaluate these dB readings correctly, they must be converted to suitable resistive reference values. In other words, a corrective factor must be applied to determine the true dB gain or loss. The chart shown in Figure 1-37 is suitable for this purpose. For example, if the first measurement is made across 100,000 Ω, and the second measurement is made across 1000 Ω, this resistance ratio is 100. In turn, the chart shows that 20 dB must be added to or subtracted from the apparent gain or loss that is indicated by the measured values.

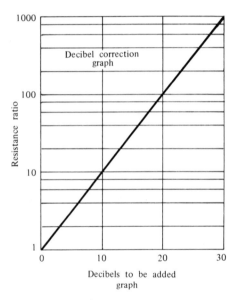

**Figure 1-37**   Decibel correction chart.

Consider the distinction between relative and absolute dB levels. Any dB scale has a certain power ratio specified as its zero-dB level. In turn, all dB values below this reference level are negative dB values, and all above zero dB are positive values. Red and black numerals may be printed on the dB scale, to call attention to this difference in sign. Positive and negative signs must be taken into account when one is comparing dB levels on either side of zero. For example, the difference between −5 dB and +3 dB is 8 dB. When dB values are measured across a resistance that has the reference value for the meter, these values can be interpreted directly as power ratios by consulting a dB table, or by calculation. On the other hand, when dB values are measured across a resistance that has some value other than the meter's reference value, these values are only indirectly related to power values and power ratios. As noted previously, if the technician takes a pair of dB readings across 1000-Ω loads with a 600-Ω dB meter, the difference between these two readings will be the true difference in decibels between the two levels, although neither reading is correct in itself. These readings are called relative dB values.

Consider next the dBm unit and its measurement. This is an abbreviation for decibels above (or below) a power level of 1 mW. In turn, a dBm value corresponds to a quantity of power expressed in terms of its ratio to 1 mW. It is standard practice to reference dBm values to 1 mW in 600 Ω. The graph in Fig. 1-38 relates dBm values to rms AC values. Although dBm measurements are customarily made at 1000 Hz, as are other basic audio measurements, this test frequency is arbitrary. Zero dBm indicates a power level of 1 mW in 600 ohms; 10 dBm indicates a power level of 10 mW, and so on. If an AC voltmeter with a dBm scale is used to measure dBm values across a resistive load other than 600 ohms, the correction factors shown in Table 1-3 must be algebraically added to a dBm value found from the chart in Fig. 1-38. As noted in Fig. 1-38, zero dBm corresponds to 0.775 V rms across 600 Ω. Similarly, 20 dBm corresponds to 7.75 V rms across 600 Ω.

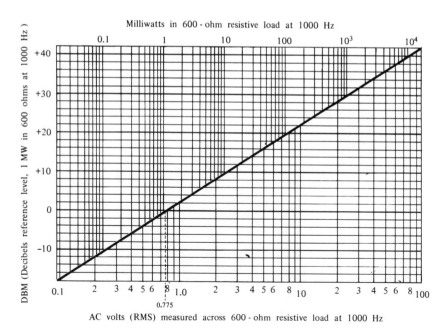

**Figure 1-38**  Graph for conversion of rms voltages to dBm values.

**Table 1-3**

List of dBm correction factors.

| Resistive load at 1000 Hz | DBM* |
|:---:|:---:|
| 600 | 0 |
| 500 | +0.8 |
| 300 | +3.0 |
| 250 | +3.8 |
| 150 | +6.0 |
| 50 | +10.8 |
| 15 | +16.0 |
| 8 | +18.8 |
| 3.2 | +22.7 |

*DBM is the increment to be added algebraically to the DBM value read from the graph.

A volume unit (VU) is a power ratio that indicates the level of a complex wave above a reference volume. A typical VU meter is illustrated in Fig. 1-39. Thus, a VU measurement indicates the relative power level of a speech or music waveform. Volume units are not used to indicate the power level of a sine-wave signal; dBm units are utilized for this purpose. If the power level of a sine-wave signal is measured with a VU meter, a reading will be obtained in dBm units. A VU measurement implies the application of a voice or music waveform, which is characterized by high peak values and a low average value. As a rule of thumb, it is commonly assumed that the average peak value in a program waveform is 10 dB above a sine-wave peak level. In practice, an audio system operating at a level of +12 VU will be tested for percentage of distortion at a sine-wave level of +22 dBm.

**Figure 1-39**   A typical VU meter. (*Courtesy of Simpson Electric Company.*)

In VU measurements, the reference volume is specified as a strength of program wave that produces a reading of zero VU on a meter such as that described above. This type of meter has specified damping, and is calibrated to indicate 0 VU on a 1-kHz sine-wave input with a power level of 1 mW in 600 Ω. Thus, reference volume is not a precise concept, and it cannot be defined in fundamental terms. However, volume-unit measurements are of basic importance in the monitoring of audio systems in radio broadcast operations.

Next, note that the phon is a loudness unit. Thus, it is distinguished from the dBm, which is a power unit. The loudness unit is of basic importance in audio systems, because the ear is not equally responsive to a given power level at various frequencies. Thus, the phon is a function of frequency, and represents different power levels at different frequencies—a phon unit has the same loudness at any chosen frequency. The phon relation to frequency and to decibels is depicted in Fig. 1-40. By definition, a frequency of 1 kHz is taken as a common reference point, so that at this frequency the phon level is equal to the decibel level (provided that the same reference level is used for both measurements). Zero reference level for the loudness unit is standardized at 0.0002 dyne/cm². With reference to Fig. 1-40, a loudness control in a high-fidelity amplifier is frequency-compensated to conform to the curves of constant-phon values at corresponding power levels.

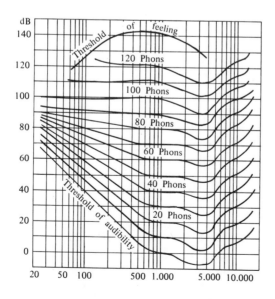

**Figure 1-40** Relation of loudness units (phons) to frequency and to decibels.

**Wow, Flutter, and Rumble**    Wow is a type of distortion in sound reproduction caused by variation in speed of a turntable or tape (see Fig. 1-41). This distortion is measured by a wow meter that indicates the instantaneous speed variation of a turntable. A related type of distortion is termed *flutter,* or *drift.* It is caused by frequency deviations resulting from irregular motion of a turntable or tape transport during recording, duplication, or reproduction. Flutter has a typical repetition rate of 10 Hz, whereas wow generally has a lower repetition rate, such as ⅓ Hz. In the strict sense of the term, drift distortion has a lower repetition rate than wow. Flutter is measured with an instrument termed a *flutter bridge.* Rumble, also called turntable rumble, denotes a low-frequency type of interference caused by mechanical vibration (often from a driving motor) which affects the recording or reproducing turntable. Rumble interference may be encountered in tape recorders also (see Fig. 1-42).

**Basic Definitions**    For any underdamped motion during any complete oscillation, the quotient of the logarithmic decrement and the time required by the oscillation is defined as the *damping factor.* This factor is a fundamental characteristic of speaker response. In other words, it is a numerical value that indicates the ability of an amplifier-speaker arrangement to operate properly. Values over 4 are generally considered to be satisfactory. The damping factor is equal to the ratio of the rated load impedance of an amplifier to the internal (output) impedance of the amplifier. The *logarithmic decrement* of an exponentially damped waveform is defined as the natural logarithm of the ratio of the first to the second of two successive amplitudes that have the same polarity.

Tracking force (stylus force) is also termed the vertical stylus force, needle pressure, or stylus pressure. It is equal to the downward force, in gram or ounce units, that is exerted on the disc by the reproducing stylus. A stylus tip becomes progressively worn (see Fig. 1-43). In the same category, *compliance* is defined as the reciprocal of stiffness, or the capability to yield or flex. It denotes the ease with which a stylus responds to an outside force. Thus, it is the mechanical and acoustical equivalent of electrical capacitance. A malfunctioning pickup may be prone to groove *skipping,* also called hopping, or skating. This fault can be the result of insufficient stylus pressure. However, lack of dynamic balance can make the tone arm responsive to vibration and resultant skating, although the stylus pressure is correct.

Quieting denotes the decrease in noise voltage at the output of an FM receiver in the presence of an unmodulated carrier. In an FM receiver, the *quieting sensitivity* is defined as the minimum input signal that will provide a specified output signal-to-noise ratio. The *amplitude*

**Figure 1-41** Uneven turntable speed can be indicated by a stroboscopic (strobe) disc.

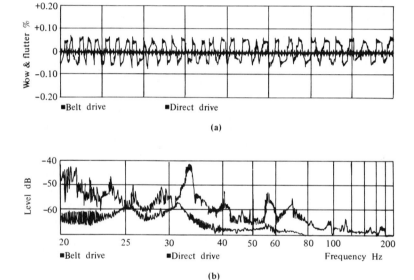

(a)

(b)

**Figure 1-42** Typical wow, flutter, and rumble patterns: **(a)** wow and flutter patterns for belt-drive and direct-drive turntables; **(b)** frequency spectrum of rumble interference for belt-drive and direct-drive turntables.

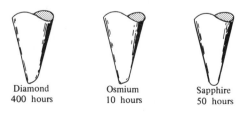

Diamond
400 hours

Osmium
10 hours

Sapphire
50 hours

**Figure 1-43** Examples of wear on stylus tips.

*suppression ratio,* in frequency modulation technology, is defined as the ratio of the magnitude of the undesired output to the magnitude of the desired output from the receiver when the applied signal is simultaneously amplitude- and frequency-modulated. In general, this factor is measured with an applied signal that is amplitude-modulated 30 percent at a 400-Hz rate, and that is frequency-modulated at 30 percent of the maximum system deviation at a 1000-Hz rate.

*Image rejection* denotes the suppression of image-frequency signals in a superheterodyne receiver. An image-frequency signal is an input signal that causes interference with the signal to which the receiver is nominally tuned. This image-frequency signal beats with the local-oscillator frequency to produce a spurious IF frequency. Image rejection is improved by increased tuning selectivity. The *capture effect* denotes the capability of an FM receiver to select the stronger of two FM input signals that have the same carrier frequency, with resultant complete rejection of the weaker signal. If both of the input signals have the same strength, both may be processed, but the detector output will then be unintelligible. The *capture ratio* is a measure of the capability of an FM tuner to reject unwanted FM station signals or interference that has the same frequency but a smaller amplitude, as the desired signal. This capture ratio is stated in dB units. Thus, the lower the capture-ratio value, the better is the performance of the FM tuner.

The *sensitivity* of a radio receiver is equal to the minimum value of input signal that is required to produce a specified output-signal amplitude with a specified signal-to-noise ratio. This signal input value may be expressed as a power value or as a voltage value at a stipulated input network impedance. A *sensitivity adjustment,* also called a span adjustment, denotes provision of a control for the ratio of output signal excitation voltage per unit measured. This is usually accomplished in a system by changing the gain of one or more of the amplifiers. This placement of excitation control components, such as potentiometers or rheostats in series with the excitation of a transducer provides a sensitivity adjustment for the system. Note that in the latter case, no significant change is introduced in the output-to-input ratio of the transducer.

The *signal-to-noise ratio* is also called signal/noise ratio, or SN ratio. It is defined as the ratio of the magnitude of the signal to that of the noise, generally expressed in dB units. It is the ratio of the amplitude of a signal after demodulation to the amplitude of the noise accompanying the signal. The signal-to-noise ratio can also be considered as the ratio, at any specified point in a circuit, of signal power to total circuit-noise power. Other abbreviations for this unit are s/n ratio, and snr.

# Audio Preamplifiers

## 2-1  GENERAL CONSIDERATIONS

Audio preamplifiers are sometimes fabricated as individual units, but they are usually combined with power amplifiers, as exemplified in Fig. 2-1. This amplifier provides a magnetic phono input, tuner and two auxiliary inputs, tape recording outputs, and tape monitor button and jack. A quadraphonic synthesizer is included to process stereo signals into synthetic quadraphonic signals. Bass, treble, and midrange tone controls are provided, with a loudness button that operates with high-pass and low-pass filters. The power-amplifier section develops 25 watts rms per channel over a frequency range from 20 Hz to 20 kHz, with less than 0.5 percent harmonic distortion. It is rated for less than 0.2 percent intermodulation distortion at 15 W output. A frequency response from 20 Hz to 70 kHz is provided within ±2 dB at 1 W output. Signal-to-noise ratio at the phono input is 60 dB, and 75 dB at auxiliary inputs. The phono overload capability is 150 mV.

A configuration for a typical hi-fi preamplifier is shown in Fig. 2-2. It provides inputs for a radio tuner or FM decoder, magnetic phono cartridge, and a tape head or a microphone. Four equalization switch positions enable the operator to obtain flat frequency response from any of the inputs. Treble equalization and bass-boost controls are also provided. The output is taken from a conventional volume control. Two stages of amplification are provided in the common-emitter mode, with regulated DC supply voltage. The third stage operates in the common-collector mode. Frequency-selective negative feedback is employed to obtain the required equalization characteristics. An output

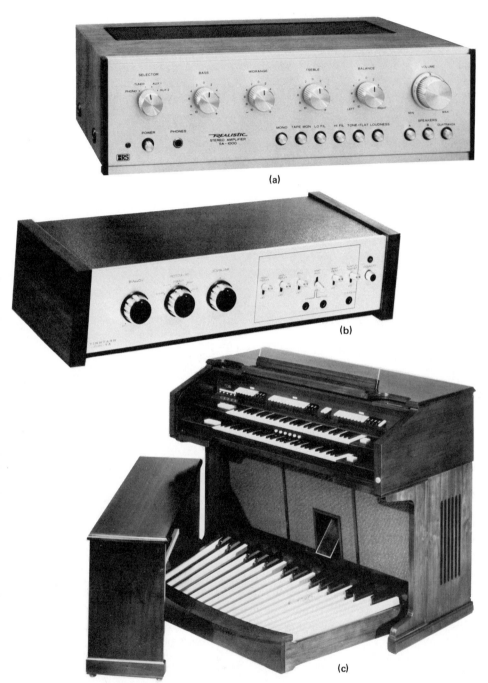

**Figure 2-1** Typical high-fidelity amplifiers: **(a)** preamplifier/power-amplifier (*Courtesy of Radio Shack, a Tandy Corp. Company*); **(b)** preamplifier (*Courtesy of Heath Co.*); **(c)** amplifiers are used in electronic organs. (*Courtesy, Conn*)

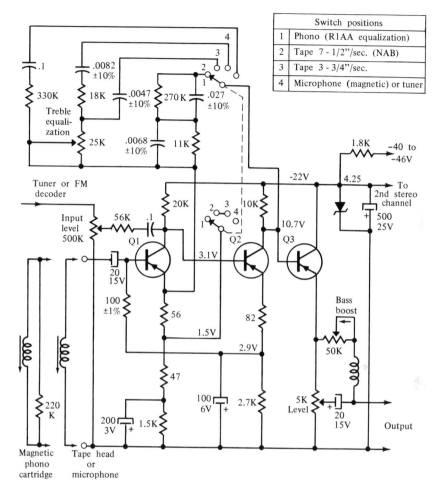

| Switch positions | |
|---|---|
| 1 | Phono (RIAA equalization) |
| 2 | Tape 7 - 1/2"/sec. (NAB) |
| 3 | Tape 3 - 3/4"/sec. |
| 4 | Microphone (magnetic) or tuner |

**Figure 2-2**  Configuration of a typical hi-fi preamplifier.

level of 1 V rms is provided when the preamp is driven by standard transducers.

## 2-2  AUDIO AMPLIFIER PRINCIPLES

Basic amplifier parameters for small-signal bipolar transistors in the common-emitter, common-base, and common-collector configurations are noted in Fig. 2-3. A load resistance of 10,000 Ω and a source resistance of 1000 Ω are stipulated in each case. It will be shown that

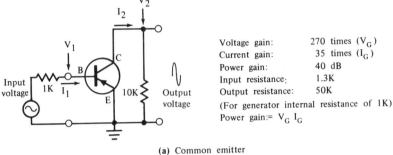

Voltage gain:        270 times ($V_G$)
Current gain:        35 times ($I_G$)
Power gain:         40 dB
Input resistance:    1.3K
Output resistance:   50K
(For generator internal resistance of 1K)
Power gain:= $V_G\, I_G$

(a) Common emitter

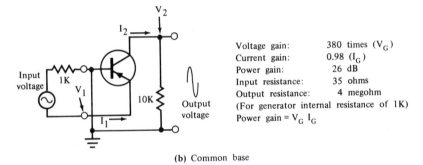

Voltage gain:        380 times ($V_G$)
Current gain:        0.98 ($I_G$)
Power gain:         26 dB
Input resistance:    35 ohms
Output resistance:    4 megohm
(For generator internal resistance of 1K)
Power gain = $V_G\, I_G$

(b) Common base

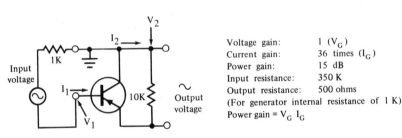

Voltage gain:        1 ($V_G$)
Current gain:        36 times ($I_G$)
Power gain:         15 dB
Input resistance:    350 K
Output resistance:   500 ohms
(For generator internal resistance of 1 K)
Power gain = $V_G\, I_G$

(c) Common collector

**Figure 2-3**  Basic amplifier parameters for small-signal bipolar transistors: (a) common emitter; (b) common base; (c) common collector.

various amplifier parameters are a function of source and load resistance values. The common-base (CB) configuration has the highest voltage gain; the common-collector (CC) configuration has the highest current gain; the common-emitter (CE) configuration has the highest power gain; the CC configuration has the highest input resistance; the CB configuration has the highest output resistance. These input-resistance and output-resistance values denote AC resistance—

not DC resistance. An AC resistance is also termed a *dynamic resistance,* or an *incremental resistance.*

The common-emitter configuration has the least difference in its input- and output-resistance values, and is the most widely used configuration. With reference to Fig. 2-4, the basic CE amplifier arrangement is forward-biased. In this example, an increase in base current of 1 $\mu$A causes a collector-current increase of 49 $\mu$A. In turn, the current amplification (beta) of the stage is 49 times. Observe that the emitter current is the sum of the collector current and the base current. Operating parameters noted in Fig. 2-3 are based on a source resistance of 1000 $\Omega$ and a load resistance of 10,000 $\Omega$. If the load resistance is decreased, the stage voltage gain decreases, as tabulated in Table 2-1. On the other hand, if the load resistance is increased, the stage gain increases. Reverse relations occur for the stage current gain. Consequently, the stage power gain has a maximum value for a load resistance of approximately 50,000 $\Omega$.

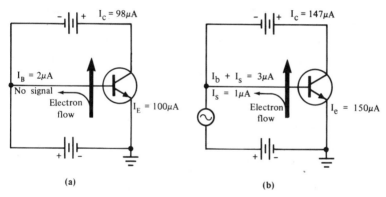

(a)                    (b)

**Figure 2-4**   Electrode currents in the CE configuration: **(a)** no-signal current distribution; **(b)** input-signal current distribution.

Small-signal operation of a bipolar transistor denotes an input signal level in the range from 1 $\mu$V to 10 mV. Thus, a preamplifier that develops an output of 1 V operates at least one of its transistors above the small-signal range. Preamplifier transistors are operated in class A. Although this is an inefficient mode of operation, the small currents that are involved correspond to a comparatively small loss of power. Small-signal operation is associated with a very small percentage of distortion, because only a limited interval of the transistor's transfer characteristic is traversed by the signal swing. However, even this low distortion can be further reduced by employment of negative feedback.

TABLE 2-1

Common-emitter Amplifier Parameters for Various
Load-resistance Values

Common-Emitter Configuration

| | Collector Load Resistance | | |
|---|---|---|---|
| Parameter | 1 k | 10 k | 100 k |
| Voltage gain | 30 | 270 | 1000 |
| Current gain | 50 | 35 | 20 |
| Power gain | 30 dB | 40 dB | 43 dB |
| Input resistance | 1.3 k | 1.3 k | 1.2 k |
| Output resistance | 60 k | 50 k | 40 k |

For generator internal resistance of 1 k.

Component and device noise levels are an important consideration for the input stage of a preamplifier. Negative feedback assists in reduction of the noise level.

Although the CB configuration has a very large difference between its input-resistance and output-resistance values, this relation can be useful in some situations for impedance-matching requirements in circuits or systems. The CC configuration also has a large difference in input-resistance and output-resistance values, and this difference has an inverse relation to that of the CB configuration. Thus, the CC arrangement is widely used for impedance matching, also. With reference to Fig. 2-5(a), it is seen that both the CE and the CB configurations have low voltage gain for low values of load resistance, whereas the CC configuration has practically constant voltage gain (unity) until the load-resistance value approaches a short-circuit condition. Referring to Fig. 2-5(b), observe that both the CE and the CC arrangements have high current gain for high values of load resistance, with decreasing current gain for low values of load resistance. However, the common-base circuit maintains a practically constant current gain (unity) until the load resistance is increased to very high values.

Note in Figure 2-5(c) that the CE configuration has the highest power gain, which peaks at a load resistance of approximately 50,000 Ω. Next in order, the common-base arrangement has a power gain that peaks at a load resistance of about 0.5 MΩ. Finally, the CC configuration has a power gain that peaks at a load resistance of approximately 1000 Ω. With reference to Fig. 2-6(a), note that the CB and CC arrangements have essentially the same value of output resistance (dy-

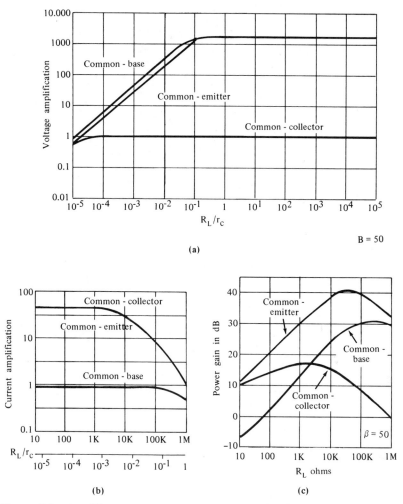

**Figure 2-5** Amplifier parameter variation versus load-resistance values: **(a)** voltage gain versus load resistance; **(b)** current gain versus load resistance; **(c)** power gain versus load resistance.

namic resistance) for load values up to approximately 1000 Ω. For higher values of load resistance, the CE configuration maintains a comparatively constant value of output resistance, whereas the CB arrangement develops a higher plateau of output resistance. With reference to Fig. 2-6(b), observe that the input (dynamic) resistance of a stage is relatively independent of the load-resistance value in the CE configuration. On the other hand, a CB arrangement has a low value of

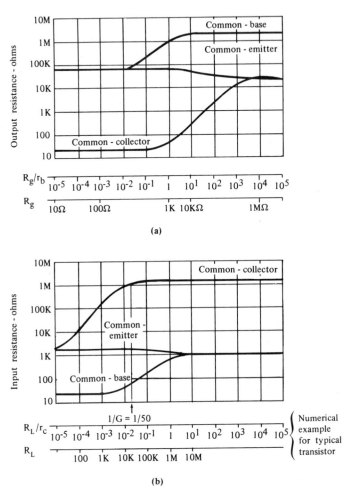

**Figure 2-6** Variation of input resistance and output resistance with load resistance: **(a)** output resistance versus load resistance; **(b)** input resistance versus load resistance.

input resistance for low values of load resistance, and attains a higher plateau of input resistance for increasingly great values of load resistance. The CC configuration shows a roughly similar trend, which attains its higher plateau at somewhat lower values of load resistance.

Some preamplifiers employ field-effect transistors. Sometimes an input FET is followed by bipolar transistors. Symbols for the two basic types of FETs are shown in Fig. 2-7 with bipolar transistor symbols for comparison. Because the gate electrode of a metallic-oxide

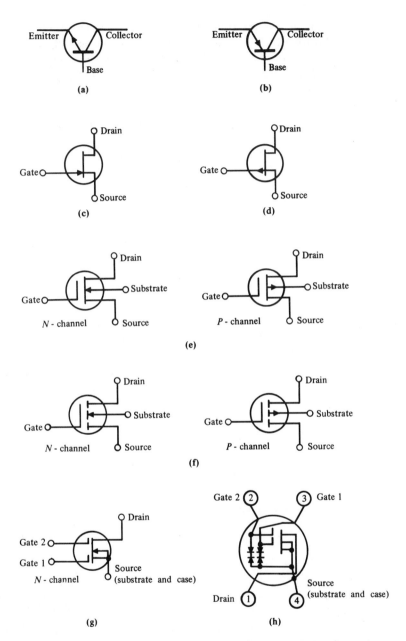

**Figure 2-7** Transistor symbols: **(a)** *NPN* bipolar; **(b)** *PNP* bipolar; **(c)** *N*-channel JFET; **(d)** *P*-channel JFET; **(e)** depletion-type MOSFET's; **(f)** enhancement-type MOSFET's **(g)** dual-gate, *N*-channel, depletion-type MOSFET; **(h)** dual-gate-protected, *N*-channel, depletion-type MOSFET.

semiconductor field-effect transistor (MOSFET) is easily damaged by accidental overload, there is a marked trend to the use of zener-diode gate-protected types of MOSFETs. A MOSFET is an example of an insulated-gate field-effect transistor (IGFET). Note that a junction field-effect transistor (JFET) has essentially the same characteristics as a MOSFET, except that the former can conduct forward-bias current. Basic characteristics for depletion-type and enhancement-type FETs are shown in Fig. 2-8. Preamplifiers generally employ the depletion type of FET. Enhancement-type FETs are utilized chiefly in digital circuitry.

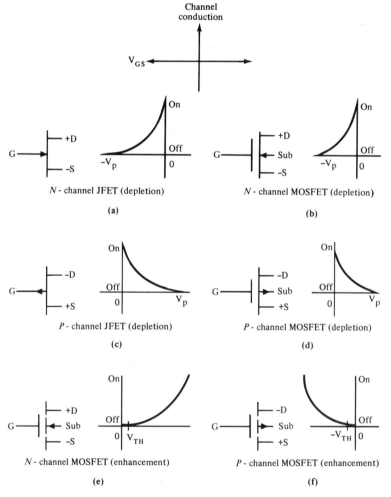

**Figure 2-8** Drain-source conduction characteristics for depletion-type and enhancement-type FET's.

Basic FET amplifier configurations and parameters are shown in Fig. 2-9. As the common-emitter configuration is most often utilized in bipolar transistor amplifier circuits, so is the common-source configuration most often employed in unipolar transistor amplifier circuits. The chief advantage of the common-source arrangement is its extremely high input resistance. In turn, it is suitable for use as an input stage that is energized by a high-impedance transducer. Whenever an FET without gate protection is removed from or inserted into a circuit,

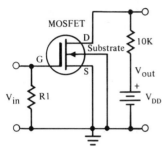

Voltage gain: 50 times
Transconductance: 5,000 $\mu$mhos
Power gain: 17 dB (50 times)
Input resistance: Very high
Output resistance: 20K
(For generator internal resistance
of 500 ohms)

(a) Common source

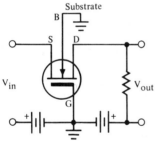

Voltage gain: 1.8 times
Input resistance: 240 ohms
Output resistance: High
(For generator internal resistance
of 500 ohms)

(b) Common gate

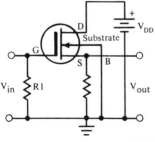

Voltage gain: 0.5
Input resistance: 2 meg
Output resistance: 240 ohms
(For generator internal resistance
of 500 ohms)

(c) Common drain

**Figure 2-9**  Basic FET amplifier configurations and parameters: **(a)** common source; **(b)** common gate; **(c)** common drain.

it is essential to provide a short circuit from its gate to its source while the device is disconnected, and while it is being handled. Otherwise, static electricity is very likely to puncture the extremely thin gate insulation inside the transistor, and cause catastrophic failure. Also, it is essential that the tip of a soldering iron be connected to a good earth ground whenever gate circuitry is being soldered.

Consider next the comparative device parameters noted in Table 2-2. A MOSFET transistor provides the highest input impedance;

TABLE 2-2
Comparative Device Parameters

| Parameter | Bipolar Transistor | JFET Transistor | MOSFET Transistor |
|---|---|---|---|
| Input impedance | Low | High | Very high |
| Noise | Low | Low | Unpredictable |
| Aging | Not noticeable | Not noticeable | Noticeable |
| Bias voltage temperature coefficient | Low and predictable | Low and predictable | High and unpredictable |
| Control electrode current | High | 0.1 nA | 10 pA |
| Overload capability | Comparatively good | Comparatively good | Poor |

both bipolar and JFET transistors have comparatively low noise levels, whereas the noise level of a MOSFET is somewhat unpredictable; MOSFETs are more subject to deterioration with age than are bipolar and JFET transistors; a MOSFET has a relatively high and unpredictable bias-voltage temperature coefficient; a MOSFET provides the lowest control-electrode current demand; both bipolar and JFET transistors have better overload capability than a MOSFET transistor.

## 2-3  TOLERANCE CONSIDERATIONS

Components and devices have manufacturing tolerances that are often of central importance to the design engineer. For example, the current gain (beta) of bipolar transistors in a production lot may vary extensively, unless a premium price is paid for 100 percent testing and power output from an amplifier stage. Beta tolerances produce a wide tolerance on signal-output power from a stage. For example, a doubling of the current gain and of the voltage gain results in quadrupling of the power output from an amplifier stage. As detailed subsequently, wide tolerances of this kind can be controlled and minimized by suitable negative-feedback action. Reference to Fig. 2-5(c) shows that a ±20 percent tolerance on a 10,000-Ω load resistor will not cause a large variation on signal-power output in the CE configuration.

All transistors are nonlinear to some extent. This nonlinearity is subject to tolerances in a production lot; in turn, the percentage distortion developed by a simple amplifier stage will not be exactly the same from one unit to the next. The transfer characteristic for one kind of small-signal transistor is shown in Fig. 2-10. This is a design-center characteristic, and it is subject to tolerances in production. To minimize amplifier distortion by reduction of inherent nonlinearity in transistor characteristics, designers utilize some form of negative feedback. An additional advantage of negative feedback is that it makes an amplifier less responsive to the characteristics of replacement transistors. Negative feedback functions by conducting a portion of the amplifier output signal back to the input circuit, where it is mixed with the input signal and partial cancellation occurs. This mixture of the source waveform with the negative-feedback waveform serves to predistort the total input signal, so that the nonlinear characteristic of the amplifier is compensated, at least in part. If a very large amount of negative feedback is employed, even a very nonlinear amplifier can be made highly linear.

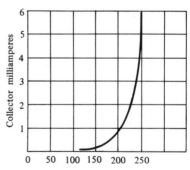

**Figure 2-10** Transfer characteristic for a small-signal transistor.

Refer to Fig. 2-11. This diagram illustrates negative-feedback action. Since a 10-mV input to the amplifier produces a 2-V output, the gain of the amplifier alone is 200 times. Next, observe that the output voltage drives the negative-feedback circuit. The output from the feedback network is 90 mV. This feedback voltage opposes the source voltage of 100 mV, leaving 10 mV at the input terminals of the amplifier.

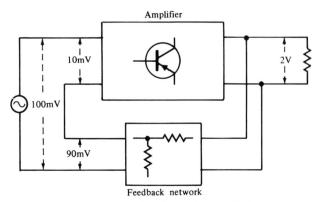

**Figure 2-11**    Example of negative-feedback circuit relations.

Accordingly, the end result is that a generator voltage of 100 mV produces a 2-V output from the amplifier. In other words, the gain of the stage is 20 times. Negative feedback in this example has reduced the stage gain from 200 to 20 times. Although this is a large reduction in gain, it represents an essential tradeoff for reduction of distortion. In a theoretically limiting situation, with 100 percent negative feedback, the transfer characteristic of the transistor would be completely linearized, and the amplifier would develop zero percent distortion.

Consider the tolerance on transistor gain. If the transistor in Fig. 2-11 is replaced by another transistor that provides only one-half the gain of the original transistor, the output signal voltage would drop to one-half of its original value if negative feedback were not used. On the other hand, the action of negative feedback in this arrangement is seen to be such that the output voltage will drop to merely 90 percent of its original value. In other words, the negative-feedback action has reduced a 50 percent tolerance on transistor beta value to an effective tolerance of 10 percent. It is evident that negative-feedback action will also reduce the noise level in an amplifier. As an illustration, suppose that the transistor depicted in Fig. 2-11 produces noise pulses as a result of marginal collector-junction leakage. A noise pulse then appears at the output of the stage, but simultaneously, a cancellation pulse is fed back to the input of the transistor, thereby greatly attenuating the amplitude of the output noise pulse.

Observe that the negative-feedback arrangement shown in Fig. 2-11 is said to have significant feedback. This term means that sufficient negative feedback is employed to reduce the gain of the amplifier to 25 percent or less of its original value. In this example, the amplifier gain is reduced to 10 percent of its original value. A voltage gain reduction to 10 percent is also called 20 dB of negative feedback. With reference to Fig. 2-12, negative feedback also improves the frequency response of an amplifier. For example, suppose that the transistor in Fig. 2-11 has a beta cutoff frequency of 10 kHz. In turn, if no negative feedback were utilized, the frequency response of the amplifier would be as shown by the solid curve in Fig. 2-12. On the other hand, if 20 dB of negative feedback is utilized, the amplifier frequency response is improved as depicted by the dashed curve. This is a 27 percent improvement in gain at the −3-dB cutoff point.

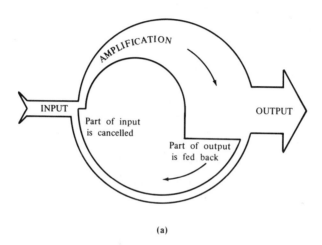

(a)

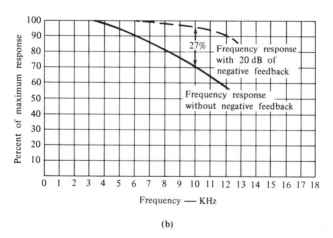

(b)

**Figure 2-12** Negative feedback action: **(a)** plan of a negative feedback system; **(b)** improvement of frequency response by 20 dB of negative feedback.

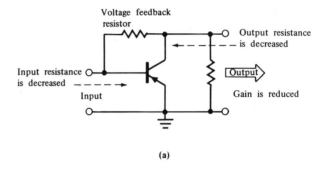

(a)

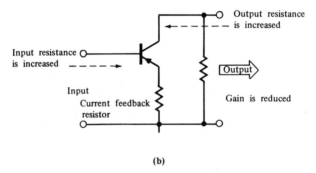

(b)

**Figure 2-13** Skeleton circuits of basic feedback arrangements: **(a)** voltage feedback; **(b)** current feedback.

There are two basic negative-feedback arrangements, called the voltage-feedback configuration and the current-feedback configuration, as shown in the skeleton circuits of Fig. 2-13. Voltage feedback is provided by a resistor connected from the collector to the base of the transistor. Current feedback is provided by a resistor connected in series with the emitter lead. Voltage feedback decreases the input resistance and decreases the output resistance of a stage. Current feedback increases the input resistance and increases the output resistance of a stage. Both current and voltage feedback operate by opposing the source voltage to the amplifier by a certain fraction of the output voltage. The fraction of the output voltage that is mixed (in phase opposition) with the source voltage is often termed $B$. The amplification of the stage without negative feedback is often termed $A$. In turn, the reduction in harmonic distortion that results from the use of negative feedback is given by the equation

$$D_n = \frac{D_o}{1 + AB}$$

where $D_n$ is the percentage distortion with negative feedback.
$D_o$ is the percentage distortion without negative feedback.
$A$ and $B$ are defined as above.

As shown in Fig. 2-14, there are four prototype negative-feedback arrangements. In the series-parallel configuration, the amplifier input and the feedback network are connected in series, whereas the amplifier output and the feedback network are connected in parallel. In the parallel-parallel configuration, the amplifier input and the feedback network are connected in parallel, and the amplifier output and the feedback network are also connected in parallel. In the series-series configuration, the amplifier input and the feedback network are connected in series, and the amplifier output and the feedback network are also connected in series. In the parallel-series configuration, the amplifier input and the feedback network are connected in parallel, whereas the amplifier output and the feedback network are connected in series.

Voltage feedback is exemplified in Fig. 2-14(a) and (b); the output voltage tends to remain independent of the value of $R_L$. Current feedback is exemplified in Fig. 2-14(c) and (d); the output current tends to remain independent of the value of $R_L$. In other words, parallel-output connection tends to make the amplifier "look like" a constant-voltage source, whereas the series-output connection tends to make the amplifier "look like" a constant-current source. This is just another way of saying that the parallel-output connection decreases the amplifier output resistance, whereas the series-output connection increases the amplifier output resistance. In addition to the extension of high-frequency response that results from the use of basic negative feedback, additional extension can be obtained by the use of a frequency-compensated negative-feedback loop, as exemplified in Fig. 2-15. Capacitor $C$ has less reactance with increasing frequency, thereby decreasing the amount of negative feedback at higher frequencies by development of increasing gain. A tradeoff is involved, in that the percentage of distortion will increase at higher frequencies.

As an illustration of harmonic distortion reduction by employment of negative feedback, suppose that the amplifier depicted in Fig. 2-11 develops 5 percent harmonic distortion without negative feedback. In this example, $A = 200$ and $B = 45$. The percentage of distortion with negative feedback will be approximately 0.5 percent. Otherwise stated, 20 dB of negative feedback provides a 90 percent reduction in harmonic distortion in this situation. A generator voltage of 100 mV

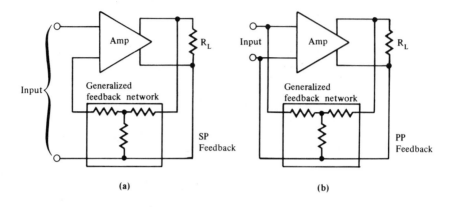

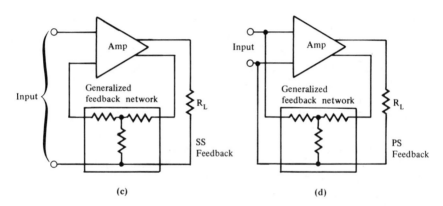

**Figure 2-14** Four prototype negative-feedback arrangements: **(a)** series-parallel; **(b)** parallel-parallel; **(c)** series-series; **(d)** parallel-series.

results in an output voltage of 2 V from the stage. If no negative feedback is utilized, a generator voltage of 10 mV will result in an output of 2 V. Thus, when negative feedback is used, the input signal level may be increased to obtain the same output level that would prevail with no negative feedback. On the other hand, it can happen that the input signal level cannot be increased. Therefore, one or more additional stages must be included to bring up the output level as required.

**Transistor Worst-case Factors**   As noted previously, transistors are often subject to comparatively wide tolerances. Various other characteristics, limitations, and operating factors should be taken into consideration, as follows:

1. *Deterioration with time.* Conservative ratings of transistor parameters should be assigned to allow for reasonable deterioration in operating characteristics with time. This allowance is of particular importance in high-reliability designs and in uncompromising design procedures.
2. *Current gain versus temperature.* At collector-current levels above a few mA, the alpha or beta value of a transistor decreases at a greater rate as the temperature increases.
3. *Power dissipation versus temperature.* Circuit-design provisions may be required to avoid excessive power dissipation by a transistor at higher operating temperatures.
4. *Frequency limitations.* Frequency cutoff limits in CE or CC configurations depend on forward current-gain values. Collector capacitance is a contributing factor in the high-frequency response limit.
5. *Collector leakage currents.* Collector leakage current will double for each 8-deg to 10-deg increase in operating temperature. It is good practice to minimize the circuit resistance between base and emitter, insofar as stage gain is not adversely affected.
6. *Power considerations.* Apply a suitable thermal derating factor for operating temperatures above 25°C. This is approximately 1 to 10 mW/°C for small-signal transistors, and 0.25 to 1.5 W/°C for power-type transistors. Include an emitter swamping resistance whenever this is practical, to avoid the possibility of thermal runaway.
7. *Temperature considerations.* Excessive leakage currents can be avoided by limiting the maximum junction temperature. Bias variation can be reduced by limiting the minimum junction temperature; both germanium and silicon transistors have a negative temperature coefficient of 2 mV/°C. Large values of collector current $I_c$ assist in reduction of collector-current variation owing to temperature changes. Low values of source resistance in driving a base circuit contribute to a low stability factor. Note that a low stability factor will not improve the performance of a DC amplifier.
8. *Operating voltage precautions.* Do not exceed $V_{CB}$ maximum, $V_{CE}$ maximum, or $V_{BE}$ maximum (reverse breakdown voltage) ratings under any condition of circuit operation. Keep in mind that the reverse breakdown voltage of a silicon transistor decreases with increasing temperature.

With reference to Fig. 2-15(b), an alternative form of fre-

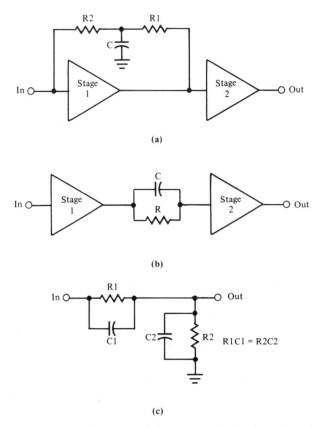

**Figure 2-15**  Frequency-selective and frequency-independent RC circuits: (a) frequency-selective negative-feedback loop; (b) frequency-selective amplifier coupling circuit; (c) frequency-independent RC voltage divider.

quency-selective circuitry is shown. This method does not employ negative feedback; instead, the amplifier coupling circuit is made frequency-selective. Its frequency characteristics depend upon the input capacitance and resistance of the second stage. When $R$ and $C$ have suitable values, an extension of the amplifier's high-frequency response is obtained, owing to the decreasing reactance of $C$ with increasing frequency. A tradeoff is also involved in this arrangement, inasmuch as the RC coupling network reduces the amplifier gain at lower frequencies. Next, observe the frequency-independent RC voltage divider depicted in Fig. 2-15(c). This configuration is used in an amplifier network to reduce the signal level without introducing any frequency distortion. In other words, if the time constant of the first section is equal to the time constant of the second section, the output voltage will be a specified fraction of the input voltage at any frequency.

## 2-4 TROUBLESHOOTING TECHNIQUES

As noted in the first chapter, DC-voltage measurements are basic in amplifier troubleshooting procedures. In direct-coupled circuitry, interpretation of incorrect voltage values may or may not be straightforward. As an illustration, consider the arrangement shown in Fig. 2-16. A typical trouble symptom is no audio output, with zero emitter bias voltage on the output transistor. This measurement throws immediate suspicion on the transistor, and it is likely that the base-emitter junction will be found open-circuited. Although the collector voltage on the second transistor will measure abnormally high, this does not throw suspicion on the driver transistor, because of the direct-coupled configuration. On the other hand, if the driver transistor were RC-coupled to the output transistor, the abnormal driver collector voltage would cast suspicion on the driver transistor.

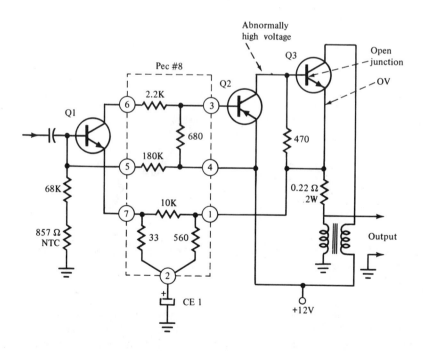

**Figure 2-16**   An open emitter junction results in zero emitter voltage.

Sometimes incorrect DC-voltage values occur intermittently; the intermittent condition may be responsive to a slight flexing of a circuit board, for example. In such a case, a microscopic break may be found in a printed-circuit conductor. When double-sided circuit boards are employed, as exemplified in Fig. 2-17, poor through-connections are ready suspects. In this situation, it is advisable to insert a short copper-wire jumper through the eyelet, and to add solder at each end of the eyelet. Another typical fault is depicted in Fig. 2-18; because of mechanical damage, a break has occurred in a foil conductor. In this situation, the technician usually runs a copper-wire jumper between the associated eyelets and solders the ends of the jumper to the eyelets.

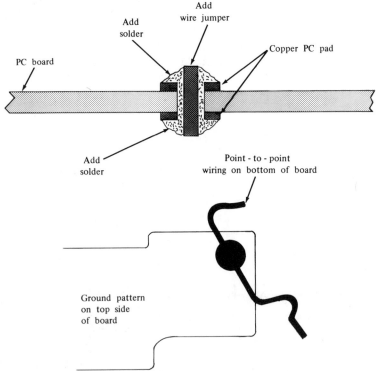

**Figure 2-17**  Intermittent operation can be caused by poor connections through double-sided circuit boards.

In-circuit tests are very useful, because transistors are usually soldered into PC boards. Sometimes it is desirable or necessary to make a direct measurement of current in a transistor circuit, as shown in Fig. 2-19. When a PC conductor is to be opened, the technician generally

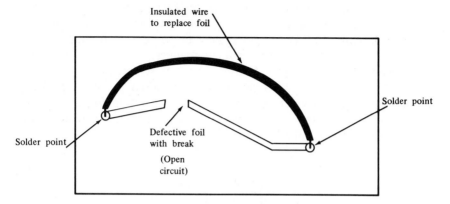

**Figure 2-18**   Repairing a defective circuit-board conductor.

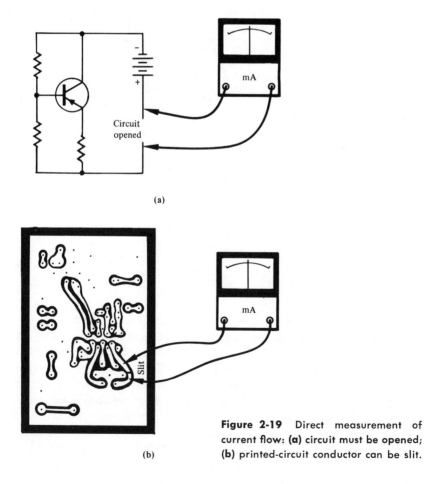

**Figure 2-19**   Direct measurement of current flow: **(a)** circuit must be opened; **(b)** printed-circuit conductor can be slit.

uses a sharp knife or a razor blade to slit through the conductor. Then sharp-pointed test prods can be pressed on the conductors to penetrate the varnish or other coating that may be present. After the current measurement is completed, the printed conductor is restored to normal condition by bridging the slit with a drop of solder. Direct measurements of current flow will be inaccurate if the internal resistance of the meter disturbs circuit action. An example is shown in Fig. 2-20. The 2000-Ω meter resistance inserted in series with the base lead causes the measurement to be quite inaccurate.

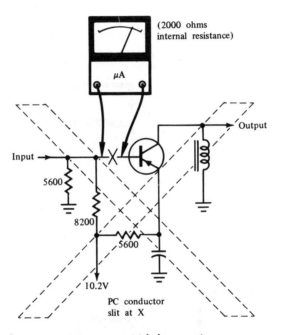

**Figure 2-20**    Base current measurement is inaccurate.

Whenever a current meter is inserted in series with a circuit, there is more or less voltage drop across the terminals of the current meter. This is called the *voltage burden* of the current meter; the voltage burden can easily be checked, as depicted in Fig. 2-21. It is evident that a voltmeter has a current burden; if this burden is excessive, circuit action will be disturbed and the indicated voltage value will be incorrect. The voltage burden of a current meter is minimized if a sensitive movement is used, because the resistance of the meter shunt is accordingly less. Similarly, the current burden of a voltmeter is minimized if a

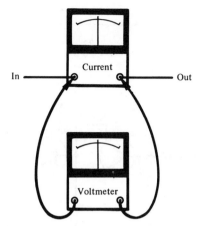

**Figure 2-21** Measuring the voltage burden of a current meter.

sensitive movement is used, because the resistance of the meter multiplier is accordingly greater.

If a transistor is operating nonlinearly and developing appreciable distortion, this fact can often be established by making a suppressed-zero measurement of collector voltage with and without an input signal, as shown in Fig. 2-22. This test is based on the principle that, if a transistor is operating strictly in class A, no DC voltage component will be produced by application of the AC signal. In other words, the DC-voltage value at the collector of $Q2$ will normally remain the same in the presence or absence of signal. A more sensitive test is provided by suppressed-zero operation. This consists of applying a bucking voltage to the voltmeter from a bench power supply, so that the meter indicates zero (or a very low voltage) in the absence of signal. In turn, the voltmeter can be operated on its lowest range, and a more sensitive indication is thereby obtained when the signal is applied. Note that any amplifier will operate nonlinearly if it is driven beyond its rated output.

Although the foregoing distortion test is valid in most cases, there is one type of nonlinearity that it cannot indicate. In other words, if the amplifier is energized by a sine wave, and if the sine wave is compressed or clipped by equal amounts on both peaks, no DC component will be produced. In turn, the collector voltage will not change from the no-signal condition to the signal condition. However, this type of nonlinearity is the exception, and not the rule. A more critical test can be made by observing the waveform at the collector of the transistor with an oscilloscope. In turn, if symmetrical peak distortion happens to occur, this fact will be apparent in the screen pattern. Note, however, that the vertical amplifier of the oscilloscope must have better linearity

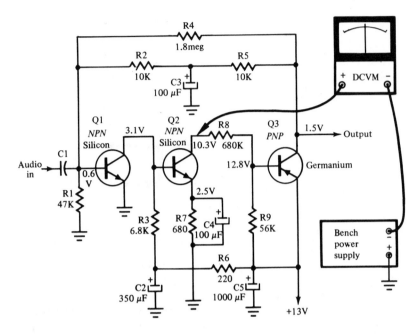

**Figure 2-22**    Suppressed-zero method of checking for nonlinear operation.

than the audio amplifier under test. If the distortion in the audio amplifier is not substantial, it is difficult to interpret the screen pattern mean-
ingfully. In such a case, the technician should use a specialized distortion
meter that can measure small percentages of distortion.

When the signal is being stopped somewhere in an amplifier,
the technician may quick-check successive stages by means of "click"
tests, as shown in Fig. 2-23. A jumper is applied between the base and
emitter terminals of each transistor in turn. For example, it may be
observed that, when a "click" test is made at Q3, a sound output is
obtained from the speaker (or headphones). Then, when a "click"
test is made at Q2, it may be observed that no sound output is obtained.
This result indicates either that Q2 is defective, or that, if Q2 is normal,
some circuit defect has occurred that removes the forward bias from
Q2. Accordingly, the technician proceeds to make DC voltage measurements. If necessary, supplementary resistance measurements are made
to close in on the defective component. Note in passing that it is
hazardous to make "click" tests from the base of a transistor to ground.
In some configurations, grounding of the base will cause excessive
emitter-base current flow, and will burn out the transistor.

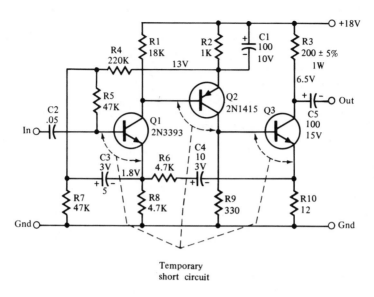

Temporary
short circuit

**Figure 2-23** "Click" tests in an audio amplifier network.

**Noise Quick Checks**   Noise can originate anywhere in an audio system. However, the most disturbing noise sources are usually in the preamplifier section. The input stage, in particular, falls under suspicion, because any noise generated in this stage is amplified by all of the following stages. Transistors for input stages may be selected for minimum noise level. Although collector leakage is often a noise source, resistors that have deteriorated, leaky capacitors, and marginal diodes can also generate objectionable noise. Coupling transformers occasionally become noisy. In addition, poor connections often generate noise. An imperfect connection can often be localized by tapping various components and devices, or by gently flexing a circuit board. To close in on any type of noise source, the quick check depicted in Fig. 2-24 is very helpful. A $0.1\mu F$ capacitor is shunted step by step across each component and device in the preamplifier circuit. If a resistor is noisy, for example, the noise output from the speaker will stop, or will be reduced to a low level, when the test capacitor is shunted across the faulty resistor. Note that the test capacitor should be connected and disconnected only with the power turned off. Also, the test capacitor should be discharged before it is reconnected into the circuit. This precaution will avoid possible surge damage to semiconductor devices. Narrow-band and wide-band noise patterns appear on a scope screen as shown in Figure 2-25.

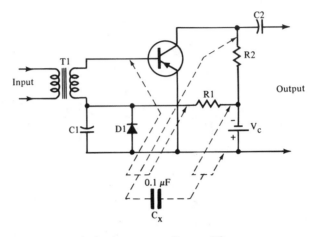

**Figure 2-24** Noise quick checks in an audio amplifier.

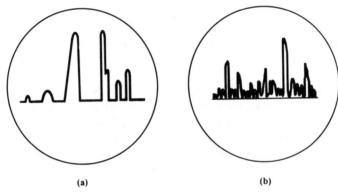

(a)                             (b)

**Figure 2-25** Random noise patterns: **(a)** narrow-band noise; **(b)** wide-band noise.

**In-circuit Transistor Testing** Prior explanation has been made concerning in-circuit transistor tests by means of turn-off and turn-on quick checks. More extensive test data can be obtained by the use of an in-circuit transistor tester, such as that illustrated in Fig. 2-26. This instrument provides in-circuit or out-of-circuit good-bad tests for either bipolar transistors or field-effect transistors. The test leads are connected to the terminals of the transistor in question; in turn, the meter provides a good-bad indication, and a "chirp" with a built-in audible tone when the control switch is set to the correct test position for the particular transistor. Current gain (beta) and leakage currents can be measured in out-of-circuit tests.

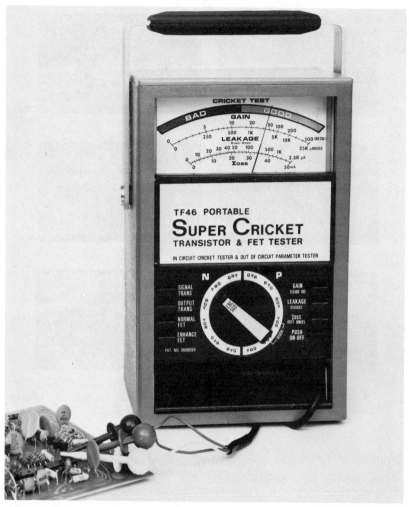

**Figure 2-26** An in-circuit transistor tester and out-of-circuit parameter tester. (*Courtesy of Sencore, Inc.*)

**Audio Waveform Distortion** Large percentages of distortion in audio waveforms are readily apparent. On the other hand, small percentages of distortions are difficult to "see," as exemplified in Fig. 2-27. Therefore, the oscilloscope has limited capability to track down distortion in a high-fidelity system. However, the technician can improve the effectiveness of oscilloscope indication by utilizing Lissajous patterns. When the input signal of a stage is fed to the vertical amplifier of an oscilloscope, and the output signal of the same stage is fed to the horizontal

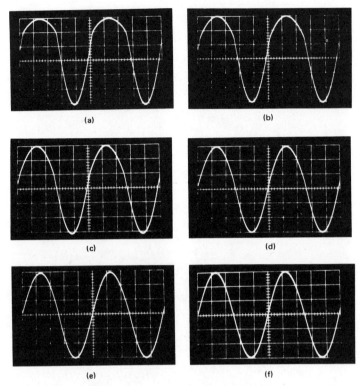

(a)

(b)

(c)

(d)

(e)

(f)

**Figure 2-27**  Examples of distortion percentages: **(a)** 20 percent; **(b)** 15 percent; **(c)** 10 percent; **(d)** 5 percent; **(e)** 3 percent; **(f)** 1 percent.

amplifier of the oscilloscope, a straight diagonal line is normally displayed at a test frequency of 1 kHz. However, any small percentage of harmonic distortion causes the line display to become more or less curved. Although it is impractical to make a quantitative measurement of the percentage of distortion, this method provides a reasonably sensitive indicator of distortion. Note that the vertical and horizontal amplifiers must have better linearity than the audio stage under test. As a rough rule of thumb, percentage-of-distortion values typical of various audio systems and subsystems are as follows:

**Frequency-modulated Transmitters**
100% modulation—5 to 7%
80% modulation—2 to 3%

**Disc-recording Systems**
Record/playback—2.5 to 4%

**Audio Amplifiers**
>High quality—0.10 to 1%
>Medium quality—2 to 5%

**Magnetic Recorders and Reproducers**
>Record/playback—2 to 4%

**Troubleshooting Integrated Circuitry** Preamplifiers may be designed with integrated circuits, as exemplified in Fig. 2-28. A basic audio preamplifier configuration is depicted in Fig. 2-29. An integrated circuit may be plugged into a socket, or its leads may be soldered into the printed-circuit board. If a socket is provided, a simple substitution test may be made in case the IC falls under suspicion. However, if the IC leads are soldered into the amplifier circuitry, in-circuit tests should be made to determine the cause of amplifier malfunction. One of the most important tests is a measurement of source-current drain. For example, if a milliammeter is connected across the on-off switch terminals in Fig. 2-29, a current drain of 2.2 mA, approximately, is normally measured both in the presence and in the absence of applied signal. If a substantially lower or higher value of current is measured, it is indicated that the IC or an associated component is defective.

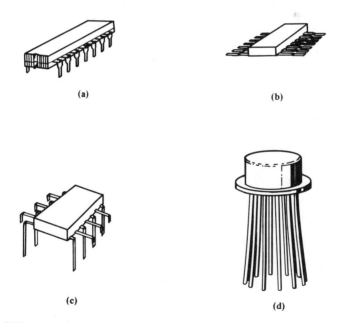

(a)

(b)

(c)

(d)

**Figure 2-28** Appearance of typical integrated circuits: (a) dual in-line; (b) flat-pack; (c) staggered-lead; (d) TO-5 housing.

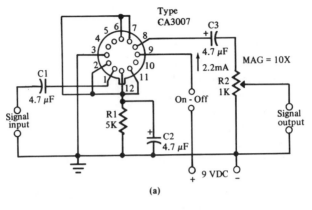

(a)

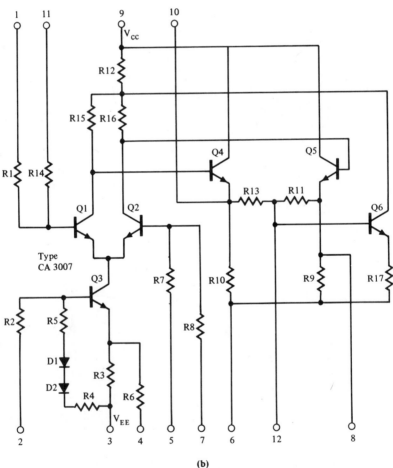

(b)

**Figure 2-29** A basic IC audio preamplifier configuration: **(a)** external circuitry; **(b)** internal circuitry of IC.

With reference to Fig. 2-29, it is evident that the value of $R1$ can be measured in circuit with a low-power ohmmeter. If its apparent value happens to be substantially less than 5 kilohms, it is indicated that either $C2$ is defective, or that the IC is defective. Although the value of $R1$ could drift to a lower value, this defect is less probable. Similarly, the value of $R2$ can be measured in circuit with a low-power ohm-meter. To check the condition of $C1$, $C2$, and $C3$, the most expedient approach is to slit a PC conductor at one terminal of the capacitor under test, and to make a "bridging" check with a known good capac-itor. Integrated-circuit terminal voltages may be specified in amplifier servicing data. In such a case, off-value terminal voltages can provide clues to amplifier defects. Note that these voltages are subject to a tolerance, such as ±10 percent.

**Troubleshooting Modularized Circuitry**   Some audio amplifiers are de-signed in modular form, as exemplified in Fig. 2-30. The advantage of this design is that a substitution test can be made of a suspected module. If the module happens to be faulty, it can then be repaired at leisure, and down time is minimized. Analysis of module malfunction is based on DC voltage measurements. Observe the table of specified terminal voltages for $Q501$, $Q502$, $Q503$, and IC501 in Fig. 2-30. These voltages are subject to reasonable tolerances, such as ±10 percent, or ±20 percent. (Tolerances may be stated by the amplifier manufacturer.) Out-of-tolerance voltages direct attention to the associated components and devices. Resistance measurements with a low-power ohmmeter are often helpful in pinpointing faults. Transistors can be quick-checked in circuit with suitable semiconductor testers, such as those described previously in this chapter.

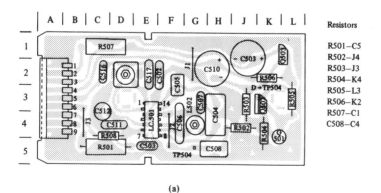

(a)

**Figure 2-30**   Typical audio module arrangement: (a) component side. (Cour-tesy of GE.)

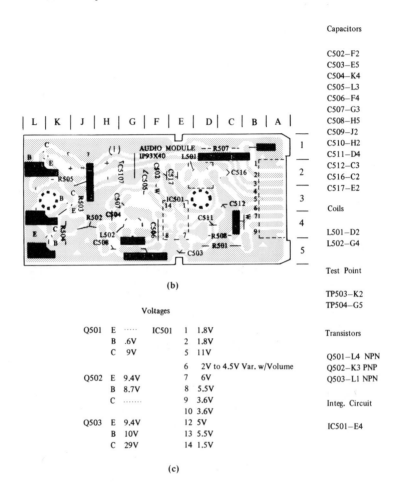

(b)

Voltages

| Q501 | E | ..... | IC501 | 1 | 1.8V |
|------|---|-------|-------|---|------|
|      | B | .6V   |       | 2 | 1.8V |
|      | C | 9V    |       | 5 | 11V  |
|      |   |       |       | 6 | 2V to 4.5V Var. w/Volume |
| Q502 | E | 9.4V  |       | 7 | 6V   |
|      | B | 8.7V  |       | 8 | 5.5V |
|      | C | ......  |       | 9 | 3.6V |
|      |   |       |       | 10 | 3.6V |
| Q503 | E | 9.4V  |       | 12 | 5V  |
|      | B | 10V   |       | 13 | 5.5V |
|      | C | 29V   |       | 14 | 1.5V |

(c)

**Capacitors**

C502–F2
C503–E5
C504–K4
C505–L3
C506–F4
C507–G3
C508–H5
C509–J2
C510–H2
C511–D4
C512–C3
C516–C2
C517–E2

**Coils**

L501–D2
L502–G4

**Test Point**

TP503–K2
TP504–G5

**Transistors**

Q501–L4 NPN
Q502–K3 PNP
Q503–L1 NPN

**Integ. Circuit**

IC501–E4

**Figure 2-30** *Continued*   **(b)** solder side; **(c)** specified operating voltage. *(Courtesy of GE.)*

# 3

***

# Audio Power Amplifiers

## 3-1 GENERAL CONSIDERATIONS

There is no sharp dividing line between small-signal amplifiers and power amplifiers. Driver amplifiers, for example, occupy an intermediate position between preamplifiers and power amplifiers, or between a buffer amplifier and an output power amplifier, as exemplified in Fig. 3-1. The arrangement shown in Fig. 3-1(a) is representative of high-fidelity design, and the sequence depicted in Fig. 3-1(b) is typical of electronic organs. As noted in the diagrams, a power output amplifier may operate in class AB or in class B. This class of operation is always designed as a push-pull or equivalent configuration. Some form of negative feedback is generally included to minimize distortion. Because a class B amplifier inevitably introduces crossover distortion to some extent, designers often supplement negative-feedback action with a slight forward bias on the output transistors. In turn, this arrangement is called class AB amplification.

A high-fidelity power amplifier was illustrated previously. Instrument amplifiers, as exemplified in Fig. 3-2, comprise another class of power amplifiers. An instrument amplifier may be supplemented by a microphone mixer, such as that illustrated in Fig. 3-3. This is a stereo unit that can be used with two power amplifiers. The mixer in this example has a frequency response from 40 Hz to 20 kHz ±1 dB, and harmonic distortion less than 0.5 percent. Each of the two outputs has its individual master level control and VU meter, which can be switched for either mono or stereo operation. The console provides four microphone and two auxiliary inputs. The fourth microphone input has a

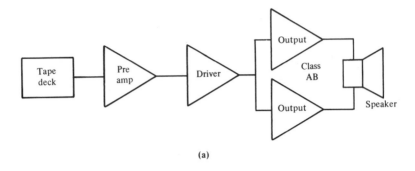

(a)

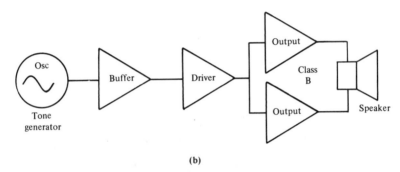

(b)

(c)

**Figure 3-1** Examples of power-amplifier and driver arrangements: **(a)** tape deck, preamplifier, driver amplifier, and output power amplifier; **(b)** oscillator, buffer amplifier, driver amplifier, and output power amplifier; **(c)** illustration of a stereo amplifier. (*Courtesy of Kenwood.*)

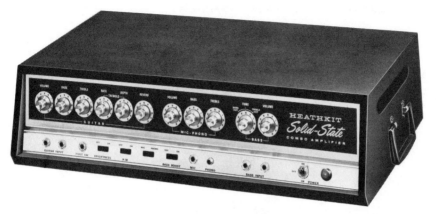

**Figure 3-2** A solid-state combo guitar amplifier. (*Courtesy of Heath* Co.)

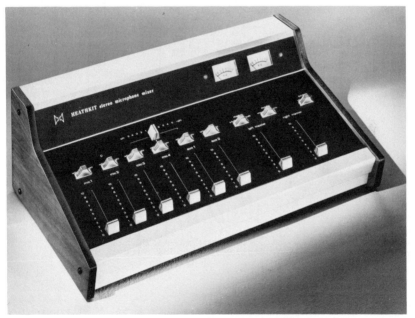

**Figure 3-3** A microphone mixer console. (*Courtesy of Heath* Co.)

"pan" control to adjust its apparent location from left to right, or any-where in between. Backlighted VU meters are provided, with two switch-selected ranges supplemented by a pair of light-emitting diodes (LED's) with adjustable thresholds of 80 mV to 5.5 mV. These devices display instantaneous audio peaks, to assist the operator in riding gain.

## 3-2   COMPLEMENTARY SYMMETRY AMPLIFIERS

Many circuit designers prefer the complementary-symmetry type of audio power amplifier. It has the advantages of reduced circuit complexity, elimination of a separate phase-inverter stage, and provides extended frequency response owing to reduced common-mode conduction. A skeleton circuit diagram for a complementary-symmetry amplifier is shown in Fig. 3-4. Observe that $Q1$ and $Q2$ operate in the CC mode.

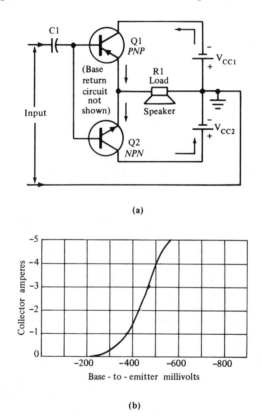

(a)

(b)

**Figure 3-4** A zero-bias complementary-symmetry configuration: **(a)** skeleton circuit diagram; **(b)** typical power-transistor transfer characteristic.

Each transistor conducts over one-half of an input cycle, because $Q1$ is a *PNP* type, whereas $Q2$ is an *NPN* type. Resultant output circuit action can be followed by observing the simplified circuit depicted in Fig. 3-5. The internal emitter-collector circuit of $Q1$ is represented by variable resistor $R1$, and that of $Q2$ is represented by variable resistor

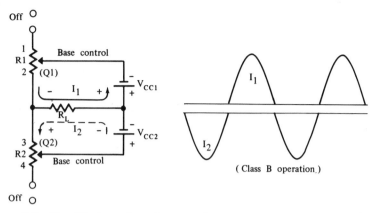

**Figure 3-5**    Simplified version of a complementary symmetry output circuit.

$R2$. While the arm of one resistor is in its "off" position, the other resistor arm varies through its range. Next, these relations are reversed. Note that $Q1$ and $Q2$ must have closely matched characteristics, or the output waveform will contain amplitude distortion.

Power amplifiers usually require transistor operation at power levels that are near the thermal runaway conditions. This hazard is aggravated by biasing networks that have marginal stability, but which may be used by the designer because of increased operating efficiency. Inasmuch as thermal runaway in power stages is almost certain to damage or destroy the transistors, the designer must give careful attention to worst-case principles in order to eliminate, or at least to minimize, the possibility of thermal runaway. Worst-case conditions include the onset of indefinite increase in current gain $h_{fe}$, zero base-emitter voltage, minimal load impedance, and saturation current $I_{co}$ at a maximum value. In a class B power amplifier, the maximum transistor power dissipation occurs at the time when the signal power output is 40 percent of its maximum value; at this time, the power dissipated by each transistor is 20 percent of the maximum power output. By way of comparison, in a class A amplifier, maximum transistor power dissipation occurs in the absence of an input signal.

The arrangement shown in Fig. 3-4 is one of the basic output-transformerless (OTL) types of audio-output configurations. Most complementary-symmetry stages are operated in class AB. Sufficient forward bias is applied to the transistors to minimize crossover distortion. With reference to Fig. 3-6, a small forward bias is employed; it is an emitter-follower configuration in which $R1$, $R2$, and $R3$ provide forward bias for $Q1$ and $Q2$. Bias resistor $R1$ is connected in series with

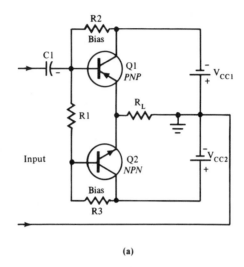

(a)

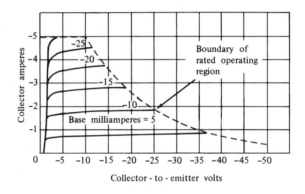

(b)

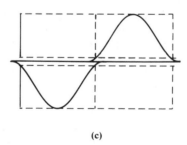

(c)

**Figure 3-6** Forward-biased CE complementary symmetry configuration: **(a)** schematic diagram; **(b)** maximum power dissipation rating for a typical power transistor; **(c)** small forward bias minimizes crossover distortion.

the base-emitter junctions of $Q1$ and $Q2$. If the two junctions have equal resistance values, the voltage drop across each junction will be one-half of the total voltage drop across $R1$. In practice, the value of $R1$ is very small, and its unbalancing effect on the input signal to $Q2$ is negligible. Optimal class AB operation will be obtained only if the characteristics of $Q1$ and $Q2$ are reasonably matched. Mismatch of the transistors can result in a combination of crossover distortion and stretching distortion, as exemplified in Fig. 3-7. Note that if the transistors are matched, and too much forward bias is used, both of the transistors will develop stretching distortion.

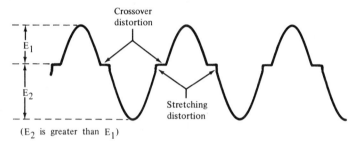

**Figure 3-7** Alternate crossover and stretching distortion.

**Cascaded Complementary-symmetry Audio Power Amplifiers** Many audio power amplifiers are designed with complementary-symmetry circuitry in the common-emitter mode. Direct coupling is generally utilized with an OTL arrangement, as exemplified in Fig. 3-8. One CE complementary-symmetry stage ($Q3$ and $Q4$) is directly driven by another CE complementary-symmetry stage ($Q1$ and $Q2$). A single-ended input signal is utilized. When the input signal goes positive, $Q1$ conducts and $Q2$ remains nonconducting. Because of the 180-deg phase reversal that occurs from input to output in the CE configuration, the collector of $Q1$ goes in the negative direction; this causes $Q3$ to conduct, and $Q3$'s collector goes in the positive direction. When the input signal goes negative, $Q2$ conducts, and its collector goes in the positive direction. This causes $Q4$ to conduct, and its collector goes in the negative direction. Transistors $Q1$ and $Q3$ are nonconducting during this interval. Battery $V_{EE1}$ supplies the required biasing voltages for $Q1$ and $Q3$; battery $V_{EE2}$ supplies the required biasing voltages for $Q2$ and $Q4$.

Note that the emitter-base junction of $Q3$ is connected in series with the collector-emitter circuit of $Q1$ and $V_{EE1}$. Consequently, the emitter of $Q3$ is positive with respect to its base (forward bias), and the collector of $Q1$ is positive with respect to its emitter, as required for

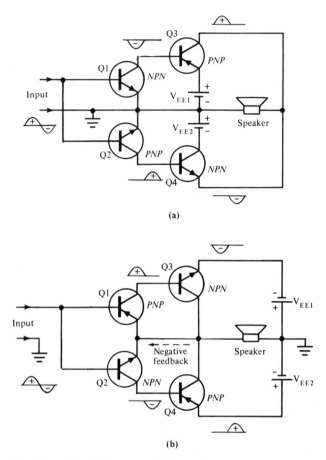

(a)

(b)

**Figure 3-8**   Examples of direct-coupled complementary-symmetry stages.

electron flow through $Q1$. Similar circuit action occurs in the arrangement of Fig. 3-8(b), with a different supply-voltage location, and the audio signal voltage developed across the speaker provides negative feedback in the input branch of $Q1$ and $Q2$, thereby producing a high value of input resistance. Transistors $Q3$ and $Q4$ are connected in the CE configuration to match the output resistance of $Q1$ and $Q2$. As in amplifier stages with a single transistor, the CE configuration in the cascaded complementary-symmetry arrangement provides high power gain to a low-impedance load.

**Compound-connected Complementary-symmetry Circuitry**   The current gain, voltage gain, and power gain of a transistor are directly proportional to its short-circuit forward-current amplification factor. This factor is defined as the ratio of the output current to the input current, with the output load equal to zero (short-circuited). To obtain maximum gain in an amplifier stage, it is necessary to use a transistor that has a high value of short-circuit forward-current amplification factor. Most transistors have an $\alpha_{fb}$ value ranging from 0.940 to 0.985, with an average value of 0.960. However, no matter what the value of $\alpha_{fb}$ may be, this amplification factor will decrease as the emitter current increases. Thus, when an amplifier stage utilizes a single transistor, there is always a nonlinear relation of emitter current to collector current. This nonlinearity becomes most prominent at high-current levels (peak power output).

This nonlinear relation results in a reduction of the current amplification factor for a single transistor at high values of emitter current. In power amplifiers that draw heavy emitter current and are operated near the maximum rated output of the transistor, this variation is aggravated. On the other hand, if two transistors are compound-connected, as exemplified in Fig. 3-9, this nonlinearity can be made negligible. The dashed lines in the diagram enclose the pair of compound-connected transistors. Note that the base of $Q1$ is connected to the emitter of $Q2$, and the two collectors are connected together. Both transistors operate in the CB configuration. The current gain for the compound-connected transistors is greater than for a single transistor, in addition to providing much greater linearity of operation. Suppose that each of the transistors has a current-gain value of 0.95; in the compound connection, their combined current-gain value becomes 0.9975. This increase corresponds to an increase in beta value from 19 to 399.

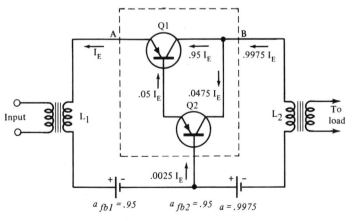

**Figure 3-9**    Flow diagram for compound-connected transistors.

It is not mandatory that the transistors in Fig. 3-9 have equal current-amplification factors. Also, compound-connected transistors are used to advantage in single-ended amplifiers, in conventional push-pull amplifiers, and in complementary-symmetry amplifiers. An example of compound-connected (Darlington) transistors in a complementary-symmetry power-amplifier arrangement is shown in Fig. 3-10. This circuit is basically similar to the complementary-symmetry configuration depicted in Fig. 3-6. However, $Q1$ is replaced by the compound connection of $Q1A$ and $Q1B$ in Fig. 3-10. Similarly, $Q2$ is replaced by the compound connection of $Q2A$ and $Q2B$. Since the pairs of transistors are connected as Darlington pairs, this arrangement is also termed a Darlington-pair complementary-symmetry configuration. Because the transistors operate basically in the CC mode, a large amount of negative feedback takes place, and the percentage of distortion is very low.

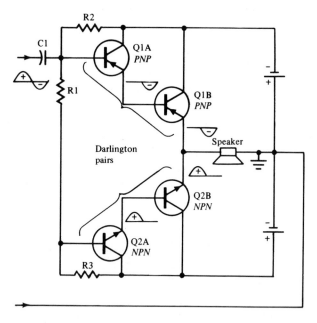

**Figure 3-10**  Complementary-symmetry compound-connected (Darlington) output-amplifier arrangement.

**Complementary-symmetry Bridge Arrangement**  Audio power amplifiers are also designed in the complementary-symmetry bridge configuration, as exemplified in Fig. 3-11. The arms of the bridge, $W, X, Y, Z$, can be arranged for balance, whether the circuit elements are resistors,

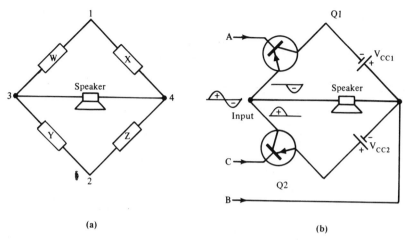

**Figure 3-11** A basic bridge arrangement, and a bridge with two transistors and two batteries: **(a)** basic bridge circuit; **(b)** transistors and batteries operate in bridge arms.

capacitors, transistors, or batteries. Bridge balance occurs when, regardless of the voltage applied at points 1 and 2, the voltage drops across the bridge arms are such that zero voltage is developed across points 3 and 4; that is, no current flows through the speaker. Thus, the resistors in the basic bridge circuit can be replaced by transistors $Q1$ and $Q2$ and batteries $V_{CC1}$ and $V_{CC2}$, as shown in Fig. 3-11(b). If, in turn, the transistors are biased to draw equal emitter currents (or to draw no emitter-collector current) under quiescent conditions (no input signal), the bridge is balanced and zero current flows through the speaker. On the other hand, if an input signal causes either transistor to conduct more current than the other, the bridge becomes unbalanced, and current flows through the speaker. Sine-wave input signals applied to points $A$-$B$ and $C$-$D$ 180 deg out of phase will result in an amplified sine-wave signal across the speaker. If the transistors are operated in class A or in class B, no DC current will flow through the speaker.

It is undesirable to have a DC current flow through a speaker voice coil, because cone offset results, which introduces distortion into the reproduced sound. Observe that if a conventional push-pull power amplifier were employed, the speaker voice coil would have to be center-tapped, and only one-half of the coil would be used for each half-cycle of the input signal. This center-tapped operation entails reduced efficiency in the conversion of electrical energy into sound energy. Observe the bridge configuration depicted in Fig. 3-12. All four arms of

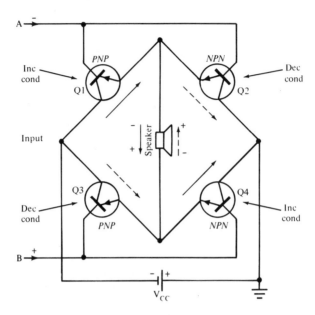

**Figure 3-12**    Complementary-symmetry bridge arrangement.

the bridge consist of transistors. Transistors $Q1$ and $Q3$ are *PNP* types, whereas $Q2$ and $Q4$ are *NPN* types. This configuration has an advantage in that no part of the input circuits or the output circuits need be operated at ground potential. Moreover, a complementary-symmetry bridge amplifier can be energized from a single-ended driver.

Assume that under quiescent conditions all of the transistors in Fig. 3-12 are zero-biased and that they draw no current (class B operation). If the transistors draw no current, there is no completed circuit across $V_{CC}$ and no current flows through the speaker. Next, if an input signal causes point $A$ to become negative with respect to point $B$, $Q1$ and $Q4$ will become forward-biased, and $Q2$ and $Q3$ will become reverse-biased. Thus, $Q1$ and $Q4$ will conduct and electrons will flow from the negative battery terminal through $Q1$ collector-to-emitter, through the speaker, through $Q4$ emitter-to-collector, and back to the positive battery terminal. This path for current flow is indicated by the solid-line arrows, and a voltage of the indicated polarity is developed across the speaker.

Next, if an input signal causes point $A$ to become positive with respect to point $B$, $Q3$ and $Q2$ will conduct, and $Q1$ and $Q4$ will be reverse-biased. In turn, the electron current path is indicated by the dashed-line arrows. A voltage of the indicated polarity is developed across the speaker. Assume that under quiescent conditions that the transistors are biased to draw equal currents in class A operation. (This bias circuit is not shown in the diagram.) Under this condition of operation, electrons emerge from the negative battery terminal. One-half of the electron current flows through $Q1$ collector-to-emitter and through $Q2$ emitter-to-collector, and thence into the positive battery terminal. The other half of the electron current flows through $Q3$ collector-to-emitter and through $Q4$ emitter-to-collector, and thence back into positive battery terminal. Consequently, the bridge is balanced and there is no current flow through the speaker.

Assume next that an input signal causes point $A$ to become more negative with respect to point $B$. Transistors $Q1$ and $Q4$ become less forward-biased and they draw less collector current. Transistors $Q2$ and $Q3$ become less forward-biased and draw less collector current. Accordingly, the bridge becomes unbalanced, and the difference in current between $Q1$ and $Q2$ flows through the speaker in the direction of the solid-line arrow and through $Q4$ into the positive battery terminal. A voltage is accordingly developed across the speaker in the indicated polarity. If the input signal causes point $A$ to become positive with respect to point $B$, $Q2$ and $Q3$ become more forward-biased and draw more collector current. Transistors $Q1$ and $Q4$ become less forward-biased and draw less collector current. The difference between the $Q3$ and $Q4$ currents flows through the speaker in the direction of the dashed-line arrow, and develops a voltage of the indicated polarity.

**Summary of Power-amplifier Characteristics**
1. The noise factor of an amplifier is defined as the quotient of the signal-to-noise ratio at the output of the amplifier and the signal-to-noise ratio at the input of the amplifier.
2. The noise factor of a transistor increases as its collector voltage is increased. The noise factor, or noise figure, is stated for a given bandwidth, and is equal to the ratio of total noise at the output to the noise at the input.
3. A CE amplifier with degeneration develops a comparatively high value of input impedance.
4. Zero-biased class B push-pull amplifiers produce crossover distortion.
5. Crossover distortion can be minimized or eliminated by operating a push-pull amplifier in class AB.
6. Stretching distortion results from application of excessive forward bias in class-AB operation.
7. Complementary-symmetry push-pull amplifiers have numerous advantages over related configurations, and are widely

used. However, transistors must have closely matched characteristics to minimize distortion.

8. Compound-connected or Darlington-connected transistors provide a comparatively high amplification factor.

9. Darlington-connected transistors are frequently used in complementary-symmetry amplifier arrangements to obtain high gain and high power output with minimum circuit complexity.

### 3-3  OTHER CLASSES OF AUDIO POWER AMPLIFIERS

In addition to the classes of amplifier operation discussed above, the class D amplifier is used in special applications. The basic principle of class D amplification is shown in Fig. 3-13. Note that the input waveform is converted into a pulse train that drives the power amplifier.

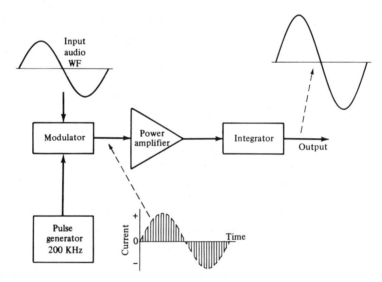

**Figure 3-13**  Principle of a class D amplifier.

After amplification, the pulses are integrated to reconstitute the original input waveform. This mode of operation is used to obtain higher operating efficiency in the power-amplifier section. Instead of the simple amplitude-modulated pulse waveform depicted in Fig. 3-13, a more sophisticated design employs a pulse-width modulation (PWM) waveform, as shown in Fig. 3-14. This mode of operation utilizes pulses of uniform amplitude, wherein a narrow pulse corresponds to a low-amplitude input, and a wide pulse corresponds to a high-amplitude input. (See Fig. 3-15.) After the PWM waveform has been amplified, it is integrated to reconstitute the original input waveform. A class D PWM amplifier operates at high efficiency.

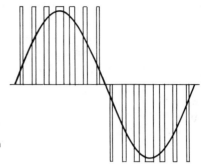

**Figure 3-14** Example of pulse-width modulation (PWM) waveform.

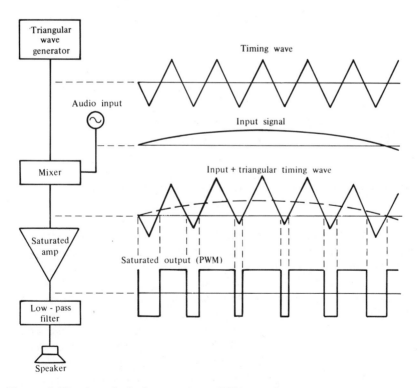

**Figure 3-15** A method of generating a PWM waveform.

### 3-4   TROUBLESHOOTING AUDIO POWER AMPLIFIERS

Harmonic distortion is checked and its percentage is measured as shown in Fig. 3-16. An audio oscillator is used to drive the amplifier. A power resistor with rated load value for the amplifier is connected at its output terminals, and the voltage developed across the load resistor is applied to the input of a harmonic distortion meter. It is helpful, although not essential, to connect an oscilloscope across the output terminals of the harmonic distortion meter. The audio generator should provide a sine-wave output with substantially less distortion than the amplifier rating. In turn, the generator is tuned to 1 kHz, and its output is increased to drive the amplifier to maximum rated power output. Many harmonic-distortion meters contain built-in AC voltmeters for measuring the voltage developed across the load resistor.

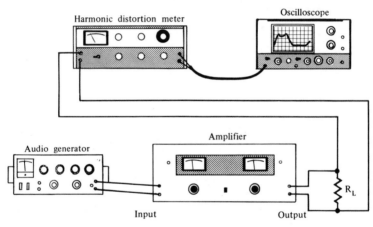

**Figure 3-16**   Measurement of percentage of harmonic distortion.

To measure the percentage of harmonic distortion, the harmonic distortion meter is tuned precisely to 1 kHz (in this example), so that the fundamental test frequency is trapped out. In turn, the scale on the harmonic-distortion meter indicates the percentage of distortion. That is, the second harmonic, third harmonic, and so on are passed by the 1-kHz trap, and are applied to the meter. In turn, the meter indicates the magnitude of these distortion products in percentage units. These distortion products are also applied to the input of the oscilloscope. Thereby, the technician can observe the general nature of the distortion products. As an illustration, the chief component might be a second harmonic, a third harmonic, or a combination of both. Again, the oscilloscope will show if the distortion products include a 60-Hz or 120-Hz hum component. If appreciable noise voltage is present, this fact will also be evident on the oscilloscope screen.

Although an amplifier is usually rated for percentage of harmonic distortion at 1 kHz, the technician may measure the distortion at any frequency within the range of the amplifier. In general, an amplifier "looks best" at approximately 1 kHz. In other words, as the test frequency approaches the low-frequency end or the high-frequency end of its range, the measured percentage of harmonic distortion usually increases. The reason for this increase is that phase shift becomes increasingly great toward the ends of the frequency range, with the result that negative feedback decreases and is replaced by more or less positive feedback. For example, it might be observed that the harmonic distortion at 10 kHz is three times as great as at 1 kHz. If an amplifier is not direct-coupled, it might be observed that the harmonic distortion is twice as great at 50 Hz as at 1 kHz. Any audio amplifier will have a rapidly increasing percentage of harmonic distortion as its maximum power output rating is approached.

A frequency response test setup is shown in Fig. 3-17. The basic check is made at maximum rated power output. When a frequency response curve is plotted, it is essential that the signal level from the generator be maintained precisely constant at all test frequencies. If the generator has a built-in output level meter, the technician can use this meter to check the signal level each time that the generator frequency is changed. Otherwise, an auxiliary AC voltmeter should be connected across the output terminals of the generator. Note that some amplifiers are not designed to operate at sustained maximum rated power output with the test frequency set to the high end of the amplifier's range. Thus, an amplifier may be rated for only 20-min operation

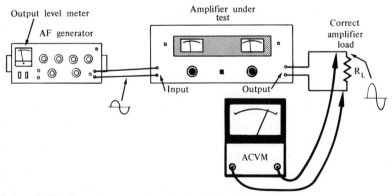

**Figure 3-17**   Frequency response test setup.

at maximum rated power output with a test frequency of 25 kHz. This limitation (when included in amplifier ratings) is based on the maximum permissible temperature of the output transistors.

An intermodulation distortion test setup is depicted in Fig. 3-18. Observe that the IM distortion meter supplies the required two-tone test signal. Typical test frequencies are 60 Hz and 6 kHz. A power resistor with the rated value of load resistance for the amplifier is used, and an AC TVM is connected across the load resistor. This AC voltmeter is used to determine the required signal level for checking the amplifier at maximum rated power output. Measured values of IM percentage of distortion are generally about the same as harmonic distortion percentages. Similarly, lower values of IM percentage of distortion are measured at lower power test levels (unless crossover distortion is the primary source). In other words, crossover distortion results in higher percentages of either harmonic or intermodulation distortion at lower volume levels.

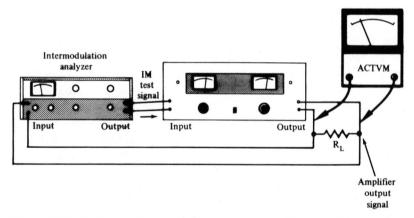

**Figure 3-18**   Test setup for measuring percentage of intermodulation distortion.

When distortion is substantial, it will be clearly apparent in an oscilloscope pattern. A standard test setup is shown in Fig. 3-19. These are basically Lissajous patterns produced by the input and output signal voltages of the amplifier under test. This is often a helpful method of preliminary analysis, because the type of distortion that is occurring may provide clues concerning specific kinds of malfunction. For example, overload distortion throws suspicion on bias voltages. Collector-junction leakage is a common source of overload distortion. Phase shift is always encountered as the frequency limits of an amplifier are ap-

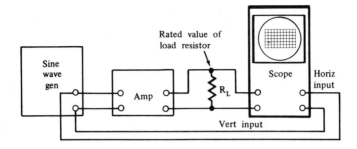

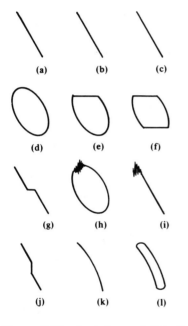

(a) No overload distortion, no phase shift;
(b) Overload distortion, no phase shift;
(c) Driving into saturation and past cutoff no phase shift;
(d) Phase shift;
(e) Overload distortion and phase shift;
(f) Phase shift, driving into cutoff, and into saturation;
(g) Crossover distortion, no phase shift;
(h) Parasitic oscillation and phase shift;
(i) Parasitic oscillation, no phase shift;
(j) Stretching distortion, no phase shift;
(k) Amplitude nonlinearity;
(l) Amplitude nonlinearity, with phase shift.

**Figure 3-19** Basic types of distortion screen patterns.

proached. However, phase shift that occurs at midband frequency points to a defective capacitor somewhere in the signal channel. Parasitic distortion can be caused by a defective transistor, or by a fault in a negative-feedback circuit.

Distortion products can also be viewed directly when a spectrum analyzer is used, as shown in Fig. 3-20. A spectrum analyzer displays each distortion product as a pulse on an oscilloscope-type screen in which vertical deflection represents voltage and horizontal deflection represents frequency. A logarithmic vertical amplifier is used in a

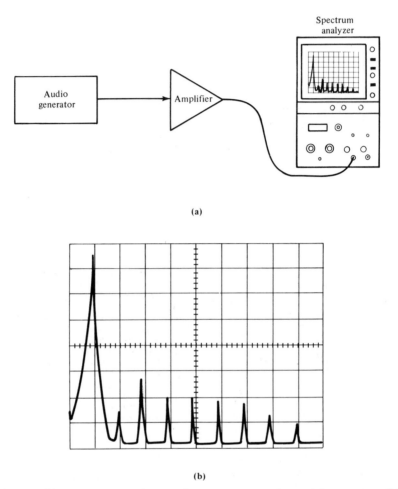

(a)

(b)

**Figure 3-20** Distortion analysis with a spectrum analyzer: **(a)** test setup; **(b)** typical screen pattern.

spectrum analyzer, so that the vertical deflection occurs in decibel units. To avoid overload of the vertical amplifier, a fundamental trap may be included in the input section of the instrument. Thereby, the fundamental output from the amplifier is suppressed, and only the distortion products are displayed on the spectrum-analyzer screen. These distortion products consist of harmonics of the fundamental frequency, and sum-and-difference frequencies corresponding to intermodulation distortion.

It is instructive to note the effects of open- and short-circuited transistor junctions on the audio signal. With reference to Fig. 3-21, an

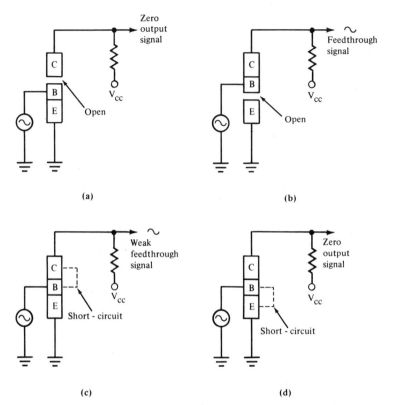

**Figure 3-21** Signal effects of open- and short-circuited junctions: **(a)** open collector junction, no output signal; **(b)** open emitter junction, feedthrough signal; **(c)** short-circuited collector junction, weak feedthrough signal; **(d)** short-circuited emitter junction, no output signal.

open collector junction results in zero output signal. On the other hand, if the collector junction is short-circuited, the signal is weakened owing to the fact that a feedthrough signal is passed. This feedthrough is not inverted in phase; it has the same phase as the input signal. If the base-emitter junction is short-circuited, there is also a weak feedthrough signal that has the same phase as the input signal. However, if the base-emitter junction is short-circuited, there is zero output signal from the collector.

If the source circuit is open, as depicted in Fig. 3-22, there is zero output signal from the drain. This fault can be puzzling while DC voltages are being measured, because the internal resistance of a multimeter can complete the source circuit, and the transistor will then function as long as the test leads are applied. Then, when the test leads are

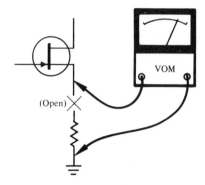

**Figure 3-22**    Internal resistance of the multimeter closes the open circuit.

removed, the transistor ceases operation. With reference to Fig. 3-23, a class AB output stage is checked for current balance with a DC voltmeter connected from emitter to emitter of the output transistors. If the stage is balanced, the meter indicates zero. A small unbalance can be corrected by adjustment of base bias voltages. On the other hand, a large unbalance points to unmatched output transistors.

The transient response of an audio amplifier can be checked to best advantage with a 2-kHz square-wave input voltage, as shown in Fig. 3-24. If good high-fidelity response is obtained, the output square wave will be virtually undistorted. A square-wave test is generally made at about one-half of maximum rated power output. Note that, if an amplifier is driven by a square wave that has the same amplitude as a sine wave that develops maximum rated power output, the square wave will seriously overload the output section. In other words, the rms power value of a square wave is 40 percent greater than the rms power value of a sine wave that has the same amplitude.

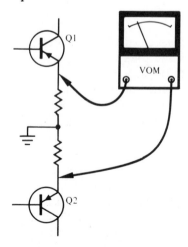

**Figure 3-23**    Typical check of current balance.

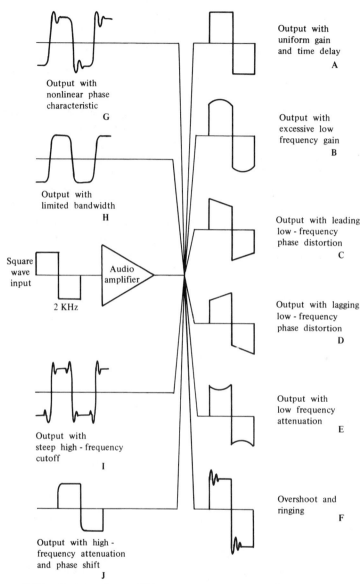

Output with
nonlinear phase
characteristic
G

Output with
limited bandwidth
H

Square
wave
input

Audio
amplifier

2 KHz

Output with
steep high - frequency
cutoff
I

Output with high -
frequency attenuation
and phase shift
J

Output with
uniform gain
and time delay
A

Output with
excessive low
frequency gain
B

Output with leading
low - frequency
phase distortion
C

Output with lagging
low - frequency
phase distortion
D

Output with
low frequency
attenuation
E

Overshoot and
ringing
F

**Figure 3-24**    Basic audio-amplifier square-wave responses.

**Single-pass and Multiple-pass Testing**    Ideally, a technician would be
able to pinpoint a defective component or device with a single-pass
test. In practice, however, multiple-pass testing is usually required to
narrow down the trouble area, and to finally close in on the fault. For

example, a click test must often be followed by DC-voltage measurements. Sometimes these measurements are not completely conclusive, and must be followed by resistance measurements. Multiple-pass testing is generally required in direct-coupled circuitry owing to the extensive circuit interactions that are present.

**Class G Amplification**   A new design of high-efficiency high-fidelity amplifier is termed the class G configuration. A skeleton circuit for this form of amplifier is shown in Fig. 3-25. $V_{in}$ denotes the input audio signal; the output is developed across $R_L$ (usually a speaker load). The input signal voltage is applied to the bases of transistors $Q1$ and $Q2$. Supply voltage $V_1$ is applied through diode $D1$ to the emitter of $Q1$ and to the collector of $Q2$. In turn, the collector of $Q1$ is connected to a higher value of supply voltage, $V_{cc}$. When the input signal voltage $V_{in}$ is less than $V_1$, $Q1$ has a reverse base-emitter bias, and its collector current is cut off. Current flowing through $R_L$ is obtained from $V_1$ via diode $D1$.

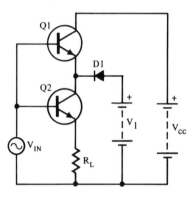

**Figure 3-25**   Skeleton circuit for a class G amplifier.

Next, if the signal voltage increases to a value greater than $V_1$, but less than $V_{cc}$, $Q1$ becomes forward-biased. Its collector current is turned on. Now, current flowing through $R_L$ is obtained from $V_{cc}$ via $Q1$. Diode $D1$ also has the function of preventing current flow from $V_{cc}$ back into source $V_1$. The operating efficiency of the class G configuration is considerably greater than that of a class B arrangement. However, in its most basic form, a class G amplifier develops an objectionable amount of distortion. This distortion is seen in the waveform depicted in Fig. 3-26. This distortion results from the circumstance that

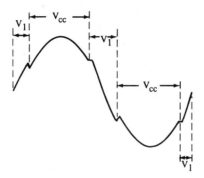

**Figure 3-26**   Distorted output waveform developed by a simplified class G amplifier configuration.

$Q1$ is not turned on until the amplitude of the input signal voltage exceeds the collector voltage of $Q2$ by a value equal to the base-emitter voltage of $Q1$. In turn, $Q2$ starts to saturate before $Q1$ begins conduction, and an irregularity is introduced into the output signal waveform.

This "changeover" distortion can be reduced by adding another diode, $D2$, as shown in Fig. 3-27. In turn, when $V_1$ has a smaller value than the input signal voltage, the potential between the collector and emitter of $Q2$ is lower than the saturation level by an amount equal to the threshold value of $D2$, and $Q2$ remains unsaturated. Diode $D3$ also serves an essential function. Inasmuch as a reverse bias voltage is applied between the base and emitter of $Q1$ when the input signal voltage is lower than $V_1$, the base-emitter junction of $Q1$ must be able to withstand a reverse voltage that is greater than $V_1$.

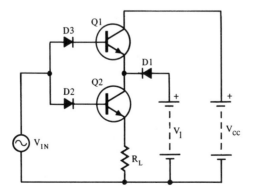

**Figure 3-27**   Distortion is reduced by action of diode $D2$.

Thus, *D3* protects the junction against breakdown. A skeleton class G push-pull amplifier configuration is seen in Fig. 3-28. Diodes have been omitted from the base circuits to avoid unnecessary detail. Note that *Q3* and *Q4* are *PNP* transistors, whereas *Q1* and *Q2* are *NPN* transistors. In other words, this is a complementary configuration. Its efficiency is considerably greater than that of a conventional complementary arrangement.

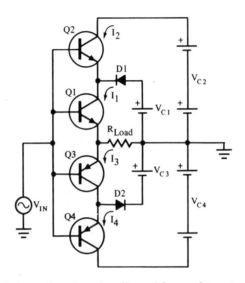

**Figure 3-28**    Skeleton class G push-pull amplifier configuration.

# FM Tuners and
# Stereo Decoders

## 4-1 GENERAL CONSIDERATIONS

As noted previously, most high-fidelity systems include an FM tuner and stereo decoder. The FM tuner is usually combined with an AM tuner, as exemplified in Fig. 4-1. It is evident that high-fidelity reproduction of FM radio transmissions depends considerably upon the operating condition of the tuner and the stereo decoder. In other words, malfunctions in the FM tuner can cause distorted sound output, poor stereo separation, interference, noisy output, or intermittent reception. An FM monophonic receiver is basically the same as an FM stereophonic receiver up to and including the FM detector (this section of any FM receiver is called the FM tuner). The difference between a mono receiver and a stereo receiver consists in the addition of a stereo decoder following the FM detector in a stereo receiver. In normal operation, an FM tuner has no response to AM transmissions.

A block diagram for a typical FM mono receiver is shown in Fig. 4-2. Note that the FM RF amplifier is the only AVC-controlled stage in the receiver. Thus, the IF section operates at maximum gain at all times. The third IF stage functions both as an amplifier and as a partial limiter to clip excessive amplitude variations from the incoming FM signal. Most of the limiting (quieting) action occurs in the ratio detector; this stage has an inherent limiting function. An FM IF amplifier has comparatively wide-band response; thus, each FM channel has a bandwidth of 200 kHz, compared with an AM channel bandwidth of 10 kHz, as depicted in Fig. 4-3. As detailed subsequently, most FM tuners include an automatic frequency control (AFC) arrangement.

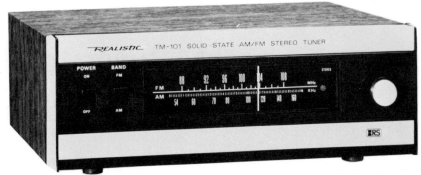

**Figure 4-1** A high-quality FM/AM tuner. (*Courtesy of Radio Shack, a Tandy Corp. company.*)

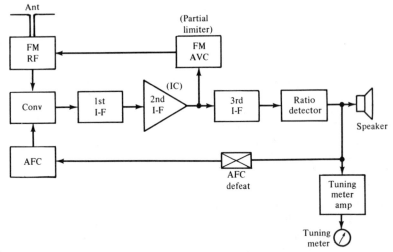

**Figure 4-2** Block diagram for a typical FM mono receiver.

This is a desirable feature, because the FM converter operates at a comparatively high frequency, and may have a tendency to drift. An AFC circuit locks the converter frequency to the incoming signal frequency.

### 4-2 FUNDAMENTALS OF RF CIRCUIT OPERATION

Tuned circuits are utilized throughout the FM tuner network. These RF and IF circuits operate in a series-resonant or in a parallel-resonant

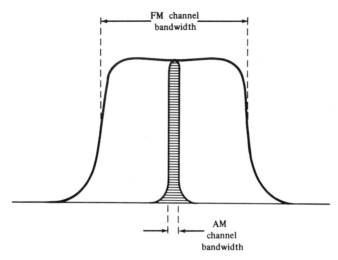

**Figure 4-3**　Comparison of FM and AM channel bandwidths.

mode. Two basic functional advantages are provided by resonant operation. First, tuned circuits provide selectivity and thereby eliminate interference. Second, RF and IF amplifier efficiency is enormously increased by resonant circuit operation. This enhanced efficiency results from the facts that any active device has junction capacitances, and all physical circuit arrangements have stray capacitance. Although these incidental capacitances can be ignored in audio-frequency operation, they become a serious handicap at radio frequencies; capacitive reactance is inversely proportional to the operating frequency.

In addition to overcoming the handicaps of junction capacitance and stray capacitance, resonant-circuit operation also provides effective amplification from a practical viewpoint. In other words, a series-resonant circuit has a signal-voltage magnification equal to its $Q$ value, and a parallel-resonant circuit has a signal-current magnification equal to its $Q$ value. Efficiency is also increased by the circumstance that tapped resonant circuits can be used to match the output impedance of one device to the input impedance of a following device. That is, maximum power is transferred from a source to a sink under matched impedance conditions. Although this is not a highly critical requirement, a serious mismatch can account for a large amount of wasted signal power.

Resonant circuits prevent the bypassing action of stray capacitance and junction capacitance by including these capacitances with the tuning capacitor or with the trimmer capacitor that is provided for resonating an RF inductor to the incoming signal frequency. Since all components and devices have tolerances, it is helpful to consider their effect on source impedances and load impedance in regard to maximum signal power transfer. Suppose, for example, that a load impedance is too low, and is 80 percent from its optimum value. In such a case, 40 percent of the available signal power is lost. Next, consider the four forms of resonant circuits depicted in Fig. 4-4. From a practical viewpoint, each of these circuits resonates at a frequency given by the equation

$$f_r = \frac{1}{2\pi\sqrt{LC}}$$

Consider the effect of component tolerances on the resonant-frequency value of an $LC$ circuit. If the tolerance on $L$ is $\pm20$ percent, and the tolerance on $C$ is $\pm20$ percent, the worst-case condition will occur when both of these tolerances have their lower limiting values. In turn, the resonant frequency of the $LC$ circuit will shift 25 percent above its nominal value, as depicted in Fig. 4-5. Note that the quality factor $Q$ of a parallel-resonant circuit is equal to the ratio of tank current $I_L$ or $I_C$ to the line current $I$, at the frequency of resonance, as shown in Fig. 4-4. This $Q$-value relation is not true for circuit operation off-resonance.

If the $Q$ value of a parallel-resonant circuit is high, the line current will be small at resonance, whereas the capacitor current $I_C$ and the inductor current $I_L$ will be large. In turn, the inductor must be capable of handling adequate RF current without objectionable loss. Also, the leads between the capacitor and the inductor must have suitably low RF resistance. In general, the $Q$ value of a resonant circuit is essentially the same as the $Q$ value of the inductor; most tuning capacitors and trimmer capacitors have very high $Q$ values. Note that the $Q$ value of either an inductor or a capacitor is equal to its reactance divided by its RF resistance. It is often preferred to specify a capacitor in terms of its dissipation $(D)$ factor; this is the reciprocal of the capacitor's $Q$ value.

To measure the RF resistance of an inductor at a specified operating frequency, a $Q$ meter is generally used. With the $Q$ value known, and the tuning-capacitance known, the inductance of the coil can be calculated from a frequency measurement (as with an electronic frequency counter), and the $Q$ value is then calculated from the relation

$$Q = \frac{X_L}{R}$$

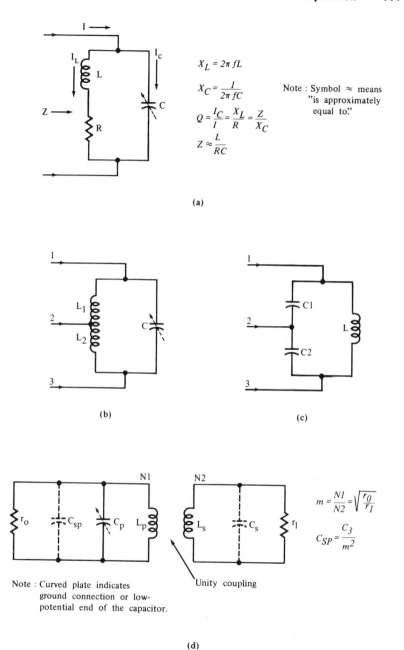

$$X_L = 2\pi fL$$

$$X_C = \frac{1}{2\pi fC}$$

$$Q = \frac{I_C}{I} = \frac{X_L}{R} = \frac{Z}{X_C}$$

$$Z \approx \frac{L}{RC}$$

Note : Symbol $\approx$ means "is approximately equal to."

(a)

(b)

(c)

$$m = \frac{N1}{N2} = \sqrt{\frac{r_0}{r_1}}$$

$$C_{SP} = \frac{C_3}{m^2}$$

Note : Curved plate indicates ground connection or low-potential end of the capacitor.

Unity coupling

(d)

**Figure 4-4**  Basic relations in typical parallel-resonant circuits: **(a)** basic circuit; **(b)** tapped inductor; **(c)** split capacitor; **(d)** tuned primary, untuned secondary.

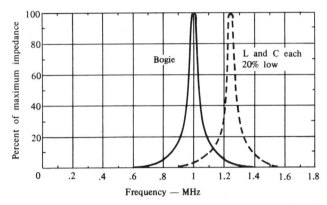

**Figure 4-5** Error incurred in resonant frequency, owing to 20 percent tolerances on *L* and *C* values.

A typical digital frequency counter is illustrated in Fig. 4-6. The RF resistance of a coil is always greater than its DC resistance, and will be very much higher at high frequencies. Skin effect, proximity effect, possible eddy currents, dielectric losses, and radiation loss all contribute to the measured RF resistance value. The *Q* value of a parallel-resonant circuit is inversely proportional to its bandwidth, or, in other words, its *Q* value is directly proportional to its selectivity. A resonant circuit has a bandpass value equal to the number of hertz between the half-power points on its resonance curve. These half-power points are −3 dB down from the peak of the curve, or the half-power points are at the 70.7-percent-of-maximum level along the curve. The bandwidth and *Q* values are related by the approximate equation

$$BW \approx \frac{f_r}{Q}$$

where *BW* denotes the resonant-circuit bandwidth in hertz.

$f_r$ is the resonant frequency of the circuit.

*Q* is the quality factor of the inductor.

Tolerances in the bandwidths of parallel-resonant circuits result from tolerances on the RF resistance of inductors. The worst-case condition occurs when the RF resistance value is at its lower tolerance limit. As an illustration, if the RF resistance is 20 percent below the design-center value, the *Q* value of the coil will be 25 percent above its design-center value. Accordingly, the bandwidth will be 20 percent less than intended. These considerations are of basic importance, both to the

**Figure 4-6**   A digital frequency counter. (*Courtesy of Heath Co.*)

designer of RF circuitry, and to the troubleshooter, who must select suitable replacement coils upon occasion.

Tapped inductors are widely used in RF circuitry. Refer to Fig. 4-4(b). In this example, the resonant frequency and the unloaded $Q$ value of the parallel-resonant circuit remain the same whether the signal is injected across terminals 1 and 3, or across terminals 2 and 3. However, the input impedance between terminals 1 and 3 is much less than the impedance between terminals 2 and 3; this difference is a function of the square of the turns ratio between terminals 1 and 3, and between terminals 2 and 3. As an illustration, if terminal 2 is a center-tap, the input impedance between terminals 1 and 3 is four times the input impedance between terminals 2 and 3. As another example, if terminal 2 were taken ⅓ of the way up from terminal 3, the input impedance between terminals 1 and 3 would be nine times the input impedance between terminals 2 and 3. To continue the foregoing example, the input impedance between terminals 1 and 3 would be 2¼ times the input impedance between terminals 2 and 3. Thus, an error of 20 percent in center-tap location on a coil results in a 56 percent worst-case error in the impedance relation.

With reference to Fig. 4-4(c), the resonant frequency and the unloaded $Q$ value remain the same, whether the signal voltage is injected across terminals 1 and 3, or across terminals 2 and 3. However, the input impedance between terminals 2 and 3 is smaller than the input impedance between terminals 1 and 3. As an illustration, if $C1$

and $C2$ have equal values, the input impedance between terminals 1 and 3 is four times as great as the input impedance between terminals 2 and 3. This fact is apparent when it is recognized that if terminal 2 were connected to a center tap on $L$, the circuit action would remain unchanged, inasmuch as a balanced-bridge configuration is then utilized. In general, the relation between capacitance values and input-impedance values is given by the equation noted in Fig. 4-7.

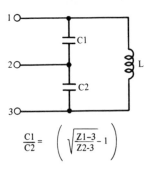

$$\frac{C1}{C2} = \left( \sqrt{\frac{Z1\text{-}3}{Z2\text{-}3}} - 1 \right)$$

**Figure 4-7** Relations of capacitance ratio and impedance ratio in a split-capacitor parallel-resonant circuit.

In many tuners, a tuned resonant circuit (capacitor $C_p$ and inductor $L_p$) in the primary circuit of a transformer is coupled to the nonresonant secondary of the transformer, as exemplified in Fig. 4-4(d). In this arrangement, if $N1$ represents the number of primary turns, and $N2$ represents the number of secondary turns, then the turns ratio $m$ of the primary to the secondary under matched impedance conditions is given by the equation

$$m = \frac{N1}{N2} = \sqrt{\frac{r_o}{r_i}}$$

where $r_o$ and $r_i$ denote the impedance values that are to be matched.

Note that if the secondary winding is connected to a capacitive load, this capacitance $C_S$ will be reflected (referred back) to the primary circuit by transformer action, and will appear as a capacitance $C_{SP}$ in the primary circuit, with a value given by the equation

$$C_{SP} = \frac{C_S}{m^2}$$

It is apparent that the worst-case condition for the value of $m$ is encountered when $N1$ has its high-tolerance limit value and $N2$ has its low-tolerance limit value. As an illustration, a 10 percent winding tolerance under the foregoing relations results in a 22 percent error on the value of $m$.

## 4-3  TRANSISTOR AND COUPLING NETWORK IMPEDANCES

Radio frequency circuit operation has a basic relation to the input and output impedances of transistors that are included in the circuit. In the first analysis, a transistor works into or out of the generalized three-terminal coupling configuration depicted in Fig. 4-8(a). In many circuit designs, the three-terminal network is elaborated into a four-terminal network. One basic advantage of a four-terminal coupling network is DC isolation between one transistor and the next. The output impedance of a transistor can be regarded as a resistance $r_o$ connected in parallel with a capacitance $C_o$, as shown in Fig. 4-8(b). In the same manner, the input impedance of a transistor can be regarded as a resistance $r_i$ connected in parallel with a capacitance $C_i$, as depicted in the diagram.

In the first analysis, the output capacitance $C_o$ and the input capacitance $C_i$ of the transistors are considered to be a part of the coupling network, as indicated in Fig. 4-8(c). There is an appreciable tolerance on junction capacitances of transistors, which cannot be disregarded either in the design or in the maintenance of RF circuitry. For example, assume that the required capacitance between terminals 1 and 2 of the coupling network is 500 pF. A particular transistor may have a value of 10 pF for $C_o$. In turn, a capacitor with a value of 490 pF will be required across terminals 1 and 2 so that the total capacitance will be 500 pF, and the coupling network will be resonated to the correct frequency. In the same manner, the required tuning capacitance required across terminals 3 and 4 is determined.

Because of production tolerances on input and output capacitance values of transistors, the circuit designer generally provides a trimmer capacitor or a tuning slug in the coupling network, so that tolerances on junction capacitance can be compensated. Thus, if there is a production tolerance of $\pm 20$ percent on the value of $C_o$, a fixed capacitor with a value of 488 pF, paralleled by a trimmer capacitor with a maximum value of 4 pF, will suffice to compensate for junction capacitance tolerance. To obtain maximum signal power transfer from $Q1$ to $Q2$, the input impedance between terminals 1 and 2 of the coupling network must equal $r_o$; the output impedance of the coupling network, looking back into terminals 3 and 4, must equal $r_i$. Input and output impedance values are generally controlled by means of tapped inductors, or tapped capacitor arrangements, as noted previously.

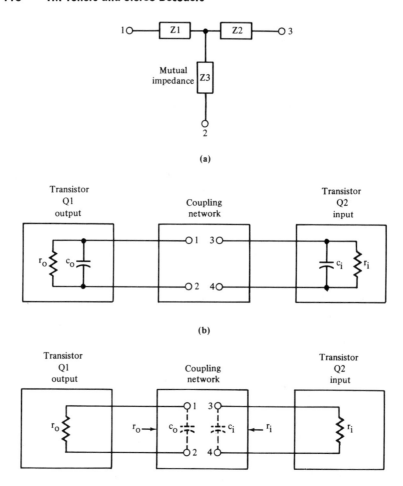

**Figure 4-8** Equivalent input and output circuits for transistors with a coupling network: **(a)** generalized three-terminal coupling arrangement; **(b)** representation of transistor input and output impedances; **(c)** input and output capacitances referred to coupling network parameters.

## 4-4   BASIC TRANSFORMER COUPLING WITH TUNED PRIMARY

Transistor interstage coupling networks may utilize the bifilar type of transformer that provides practically unity coupling. The construction of a bifilar transformer is depicted in Fig. 4-9(a). Next, the basic coupling arrangement is shown in (b). This is an inductively coupled configuration in which the primary winding is resonated at the operating frequency of the stage. Capacitance $C_T$ denotes the output capacitance of $Q1$ plus the input capacitance of $Q2$ referred to the primary of $T1$. To match the output impedance of $Q1$ to the input impedance of $Q2$, a corresponding turns ratio is used between the primary and secondary windings. With reference to Fig. 4-9(c), if $L_P$ denotes the inductive reactance between terminals 1 and 2 of the primary, then the resonant frequency $f_r$ for the coupling transformer is given by the equation

$$f_r = \frac{1}{2\pi\sqrt{L_P C_T}}$$

Consider a concrete example using the configuration depicted in Fig. 4-9(b) for an IF stage with two transistors operating in the CE mode. In turn, the circuit parameters will be

Resonant frequency $f_r$ = 500 kHz.
Frequency bandwidth $\Delta f$ = 10 kHz.
$Q1$ output resistance $r_o$ = 12,000 $\Omega$.
$Q1$ output capacitance $C_o$ = 10pF.
$Q2$ input resistance $r_i$ = 700 $\Omega$.
$Q2$ input capacitance $C_i$ = 170 pF.
Insertion loss of coupling network = 3 dB.
Signal power response for frequencies at extremes of bandwidth
($f_r \pm \Delta f/2$) = ¼ of response at $f_r$.

It follows from these data that the unloaded $Q$ value of the tuned circuit (before it is connected into the amplifier configuration) must be 288. Also, the primary inductance $L_P$ must be 7.7 $\mu$H, the secondary inductance $L_s$ must be 0.45 $\mu$H, capacitor $C_T$ must have a value of 13,100 pF (including $C_o$ = 10 pF and $C_i$ = 10 pF referred to the primary). However, to construct a transformer with this high $Q$ value of 288 and with the low inductance value of 7.7 $\mu$H is very difficult. Consequently, a tapped primary winding is employed, as shown in Fig. 4-9(c). In turn, the primary inductance can be made many times the value calculated above. For example, the inductance value $L_{1-3}$ between terminals 1 and 3 can then be made 100 times the previously calculated value for $L_P$ between terminals 1 and 2. In other words, $L_{1-3}$ may now have a value of 770 $\mu$H, and construction of a transformer with an adequate value becomes feasible.

To maintain the same resonant frequency as before the primary winding was tapped, the capacitance value across terminals 1 and 3 ($C_{1-3}$) must be reduced to 0.01 of the previously calculated value. Accordingly, a capacitance of 131 pF is connected across terminals 1 and

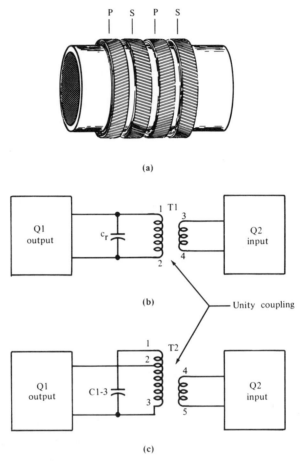

**Figure 4-9** An interstage coupling network with a tuned-primary transformer: **(a)** construction of bifilar coils; **(b)** basic coupling arrangement; **(c)** tapped primary for impedance matching.

3. Then, to maintain a matched impedance relation for maximum signal power transfer, the inductance value between terminals 2 and 3 of $T2$ must be equal to the previously calculated value of $L_P$ between terminals 1 and 2 of $T1$; that is, an inductance value of 7.7 $\mu$H is utilized. Because of production tolerances on components and devices, an alignment slug is customarily provided. In addition to compensating for tolerances, a suitable slug will increase the $Q$ value of the transformer.

**Autotransformer with Tuned Primary** Some RF coupling arrangements utilize tuned autotransformer coupling between transistors, as

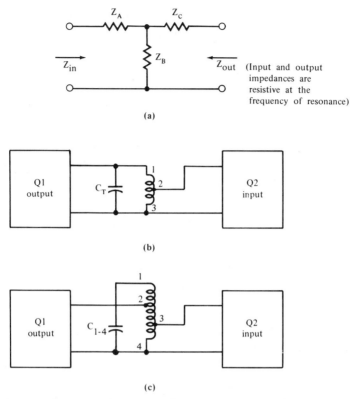

**Figure 4-10**  Tuned autotransformer coupling arrangements: **(a)** generalized coupling configuration; **(b)** basic tuned autotransformer network; **(c)** tapped autotransformer circuit for impedance matching.

shown in Fig. 4-10. The basic impedance relations are the same as explained above; however, DC isolation is not provided between $Q1$ and $Q2$. Capacitance $C_T$ in (b) includes the output capacitance of $Q1$ and the input capacitance of $Q2$ referred to the primary branch. If $L_{1-3}$ denotes the inductance between terminals 1 and 3 of the autotransformer, the resonant frequency is given by the equation

$$f_r = \frac{1}{2\pi\sqrt{L_{1-3}C_T}}$$

To match the impedances of $Q1$ and $Q2$, a tap at terminal 2 is selected on the autotransformer winding. If the $Q$ value between terminals 1 and 3 is low, selectivity will be poor. This condition is corrected by employing the arrangement shown in Fig. 4-10(c). In turn, the value of $C_{1-4}$ is reduced so that the product of $L_{1-3}$ and $C_T$ in (b) is equal to the product of $L_{1-4}$ and $C_{1-4}$ in (c). Impedance matching is maintained if $L_{2-4}$ and $L_{3-4}$ of $T2$ equal the inductances $L_{1-3}$ and $L_{2-3}$, respectively, of $T1$.

**Capacitance Coupling Relations**    In high-frequency RF amplifiers, inductors may be limited to a small number of turns. Consequently, it may be impractical to obtain unity coupling, or even tight coupling with inductive coupling. In this situation, capacitive-divider coupling may be utilized, as shown in Fig. 4-11. When a suitable ratio of $C2/C1$ is used, the output impedance of $Q1$ will be matched to the input impedance of $Q2$. In most situations, $C2$ will be considerably greater than $C1$. Note that the input junction capacitance of $C2$ may suffice, and $C2$ may be omitted. In this case, $T1$ employs simple capacitance coupling to $Q2$. In the event that greater selectivity is required than is provided by the basic arrangement, the inductor may be tapped as depicted in Fig. 4-11(c). In turn, a larger value of inductance is employed, with a smaller value of total capacitance.

### 4-5  DOUBLE-TUNED INTERSTAGE COUPLING NETWORKS

Operating advantages are provided by elaborated interstage coupling networks comprising double-tuned transformers, as exemplified in Fig. 4-12. When suitable parameters are employed, a more uniform frequency response within the pass band is obtained; also, the response curve has steeper "skirts." A sharper dropoff (rolloff) past the cutoff frequencies of the network provides comparatively high attenuation of signal frequencies near the pass band. That is, greater selectivity is provided. Note the frequency response curves depicted in Fig. 4-13 for a double-tuned transformer with three different coefficients of coupling. Radio frequency amplifier circuits often employ such transformers with a coefficient of coupling on the order of 1 percent. Tuned inductively coupled coils have a coupling coefficient $k$ given by the equation

$$k = \frac{L_m}{\sqrt{L_1 L_2}}$$

where $k$ = coefficient of coupling.
   $L_m$ = mutual inductance.
$L_1$ and $L_2$ = coil inductance values.

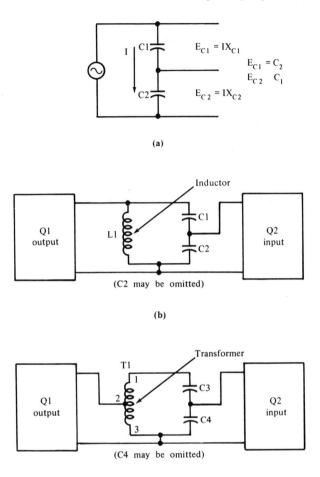

$$E_{C1} = IX_{C1}$$

$$\frac{E_{C1}}{E_{C2}} = \frac{C_2}{C_1}$$

$$E_{C2} = IX_{C2}$$

(a)

(C2 may be omitted)

(b)

(C4 may be omitted)

(c)

**Figure 4-11** Amplifier interstage coupling with a capacitor divider: **(a)** basic capacitor-divider principle; **(b)** coupling circuit with a split capacitor; **(c)** split capacitor supplemented by tapped inductor.

A signal-voltage magnification (gain) of 94 times is provided by the tuned transformer exemplified in Fig. 4-13 at a frequency of 1 MHz when critical coupling is utilized. Although the $Q$ value of each coil is 100, the network $Q$ magnification is 94 times, owing to incidental circuit losses. Observe that a $k$ value of 1 percent provides a secondary bandwidth of 25 kHz. The bandwidth is increased, at the expense of gain, by resistive loading of either the primary or of the secondary.

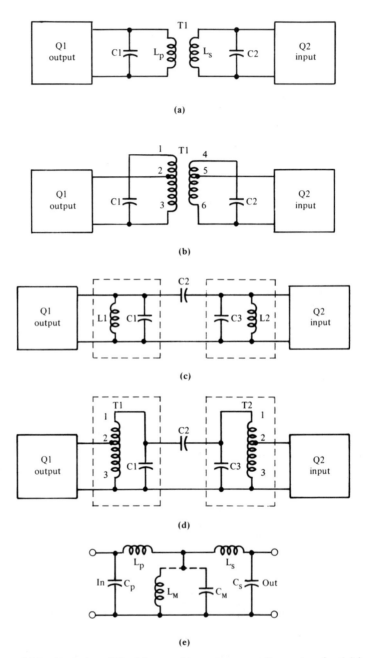

**Figure 4-12** Varieties of double-tuned interstage coupling networks: **(a)** basic double-tuned transformer; **(b)** tapped double-tuned transformer; **(c)** basic double-tuned transformer, capacitance-coupled; **(d)** tapped double-tuned transformer, capacitance-coupled; **(e)** equivalent circuit for the foregoing coupling networks.

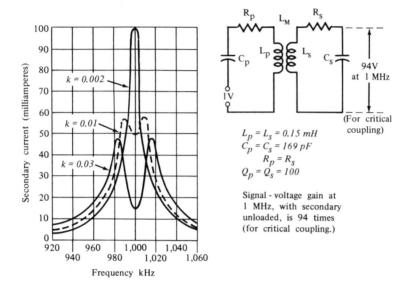

Signal - voltage gain at
1 MHz, with secondary
unloaded, is 94 times
(for critical coupling.)

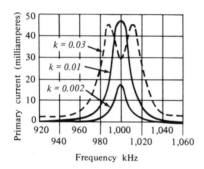

**Figure 4-13**   Primary and secondary characteristics for a typical double-tuned transformer, for three coefficients of coupling.

When considerable bandwidth is needed, it is better practice to use resistive loading with a comparatively small value of $k$, than to use no loading with a large value of $k$. In other words, large values of $k$ result in excessive midband sag of the frequency response curve, and this disadvantage is avoided by resistive loading.

Maximum secondary current flow occurs at critical coupling ($k = 0.002$). Refer to Fig. 4-14. Greater bandwidth can be obtained from a double-tuned transformer with comparatively high secondary current if coils with higher $Q$ values are employed. However, excessive

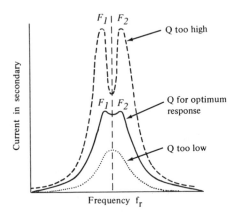

Note : Both coils are tuned to $f_r$

**Figure 4-14**  Response curves for a double-tuned transformer with three different Q values.

sag occurs at midband in the frequency response curve. Conversely, if the coils have excessively low $Q$ values, the secondary current is greatly reduced. In other words, at any chosen bandwidth, there is an optimum $Q$ value for the coils that will develop maximum secondary current with a comparatively flat-topped frequency response curve. Another technique that is used to obtain a desirable wide-band response is to stagger-tune the primary and secondary coils. That is, a reasonable amount of stagger tuning will increase the pass band without introducing excessive sag. Stagger tuning, like resistive loading, reduces the secondary current flow.

Note the response-curve contours depicted in Fig. 4-15. A single tuned parallel-resonant circuit has comparatively poor selectivity and little approximation to a flat-topped peak response. However, a double-tuned coupling transformer that has a $kQ$ product of 2 will provide a reasonable approximation to a flat-topped peak response. It also has a relatively rapid rolloff past the cutoff frequencies. Observe that $kQ$ products less than 2 result in less selectivity and poorer approach to flat-topped response. With reference to Fig. 4-12(a), and its variation depicted in (b), $C1$ and $L_P$ form a tuned circuit. Also, $C_2$ and $L_S$ form a tuned circuit. Each circuit is tuned to the center of the pass band; double-humped responses, as shown in Fig. 4-13, are the result of overcoupling—not of stagger tuning.

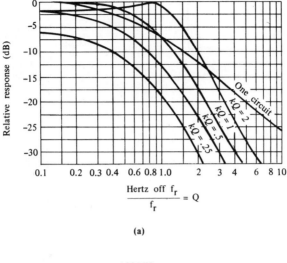

(a)

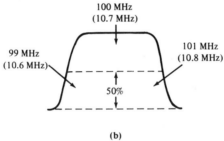

(b)

**Figure 4-15** Response-curve skirt contours for double-tuned coupling arrangements: (a) rolloff profiles for various $kQ$ products; (b) RF and IF response-curve specification for an FM tuner.

## 4-6 STEREOPHONIC DECODERS

A composite stereo signal at the output of the ratio detector in an FM tuner has the development shown in Fig. 4-16. In this example, a square wave has been chosen for the $L$ signal, and a triangular wave has been chosen for the $R$ signal. A $-R$ signal is obtained by polarity inversion of a $+R$ signal. Similarly, a $-L$ signal is obtained by polarity inversion of a $+L$ signal. An $L + R$ signal is obtained by mixing an $L$ signal with an $R$ signal. An $L - R$ signal is obtained by mixing an $L$ signal with a $-R$ signal. At the stereo FM transmitter, the $L - R$ signal is amplitude-modulated on the subcarrier, and mixed with the

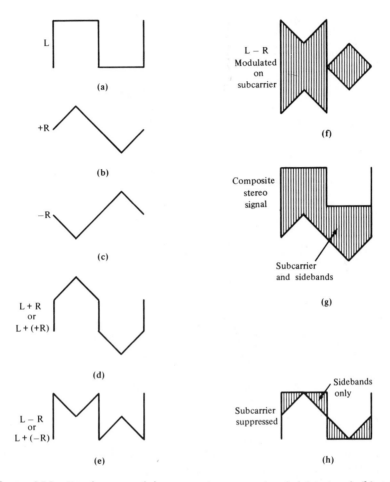

**Figure 4-16** Development of the composite stereo signal: (a) $L$ signal; (b) $+R$ signal; (c) $-R$ signal; (d) $L + R$ signal; (e) $L - R$ signal; (f) $L - R$ signal modulated on subcarrier; (g) composite stereo signal—mixture of the $L + R$ signal and the $L - R$ signal modulated on the subcarrier; (h) composite stereo signal with suppressed subcarrier.

$L + R$ signal to form the composite stereo signal. However, to obtain optimum signal-to-noise ratio in transmission, the 38-kHz subcarrier frequency is suppressed from the modulated waveform, leaving the composite stereo signal with suppressed subcarrier, as depicted in Fig. 4-16(h). This is the signal that is fed to the decoder. In the decoder, the subcarrier is reinserted to form the composite stereo signal as in Fig. 4-16(g). Note also that the signal is demodulated, and the $L$ signal is fed to one audio amplifier, while the $R$ signal is fed to another audio amplifier.

The most common stereo decoder configuration is the switching-bridge arrangement shown in Fig. 4-17. Note that the 19-kHz pilot subcarrier is developed across the 19-kHz tuned circuit in the emitter branch of $Q1$. Thence, the pilot subcarrier proceeds to synchronize the 38-kHz oscillator $Q4$. Meanwhile, the stereo signal develops in the collector branch of $Q1$, and after passing through the 67-kHz trap, is applied to the buffer amplifier $Q2$. In turn, the amplified stereo signal is mixed with the reconstituted subcarrier in $T4$, and fed to the switching bridge comprising diodes $X1$ through $X4$. The diodes are oppositely polarized in pairs and conduct in alternate pairs according to the prevailing phase of the subcarrier voltage. In turn, the left $(L)$ stereo component is demodulated and fed to the $L$ output terminal, as the right $(R)$ stereo is demodulated and fed to the $R$ output terminal.

## 4-7 TROUBLESHOOTING FM TUNERS AND STEREO DECODERS

Preliminary troubleshooting of an FM tuner is often done by signal substitution, as shown in Fig. 4-18. A signal generator is a preferred signal source, and a TVM serves as an adequate indicator. When there is no output from a tuner, the first task is to determine where the signal is being stopped. In others words, any stage in Fig. 4-18 could be at fault. Therefore, the TVM may be connected at $A$, and a 10.7-MHz signal may be injected at 1, to determine whether the second IF stage is operating. The TVM is operated on its AC-voltage function, or is used with an RF probe, as required. Next, if the second IF stage is not at fault, the TVM test lead is moved to $B$, and then to $C$, to check whether the third IF stage is working, and whether the FM detector is working. If the technician must proceed with further tests, the generator signal is then injected successively at 2, 3, and 4.

In the event that the converter responds to a 10.7-MHz signal but is "dead" when a 100-MHz signal (for example) is injected, suspicion falls on the FM oscillator. That is, the oscillator may be inoperative, or it may be operating far off-frequency because of a component defect. To check for FM-oscillator malfunction, another signal generator is used to loosely couple an oscillator-frequency signal voltage into the converter stage. In most receivers, this oscillator frequency signal will be 10.7-MHz above the frequency to which the first generator is set. In a few receivers, however, the second generator will need to be set 10.7-MHz below the frequency to which the first generator is set.

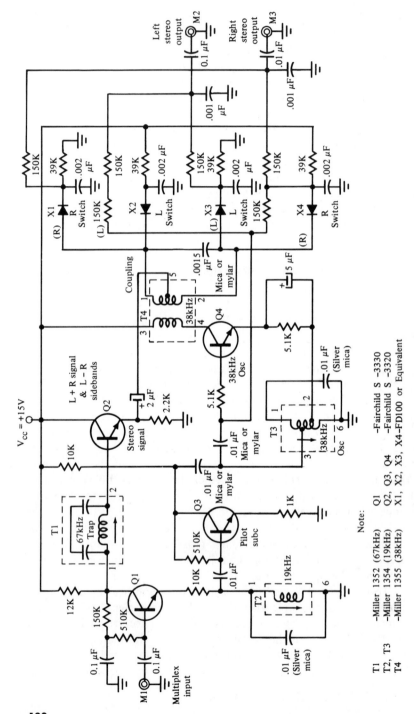

**Figure 4-17** Configuration of a switching-bridge stereo decoder.

Note:

| | | |
|---|---|---|
| T1 | —Miller 1352 (67kHz) | Q1 |
| T2, T3 | —Miller 1354 (19kHz) | Q2, Q3, Q4 |
| T4 | —Miller 1355 (38kHz) | X1, X2, X3, X4-FD100 or Equivalent |

Q1 —Fairchild S –3330
Q2, Q3, Q4 —Fairchild S –3320

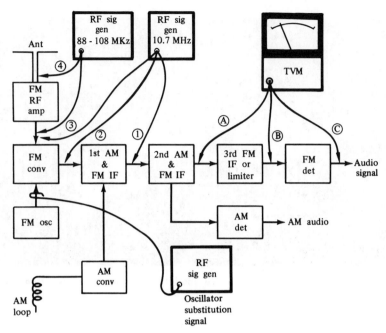

**Figure 4-18**   Signal injection procedure for an AM/FM receiver with common IF stages.

If the system is workable from the FM detector through to the speaker(s), the technician may prefer to use the speaker sound output as an indicator, instead of a TVM. In such a case, the generator used to inject test signals should be operated with amplitude modulation. Although a normally operating FM receiver does not respond to amplitude modulation, service-type AM signal generators have appreciable incidental frequency modulation that accompanies the amplitude modulation (see Fig. 4-19). This incidental FM component is passed by the FM detector, and produces a sound output with a pitch equal to the modulating frequency. Note that economy-type FM tuners occasionally use some form of slope detection. The slope detection process is depicted in Fig. 4-20. A limiter is always used with a slope detector, so that the input waveform has a uniform amplitude.

Trouble symptoms in FM tuners can be caused by misalignment; in most cases, misalignment results from a component defect, such as an open capacitor. With reference to Fig. 4-21, if $C1$ becomes "open," $T1$ will operate off-frequency. Moreover, the stage becomes regenerative, which causes the pass band to be subnormal. In case positive feedback is substantial, the stage will break into uncontrolled self-

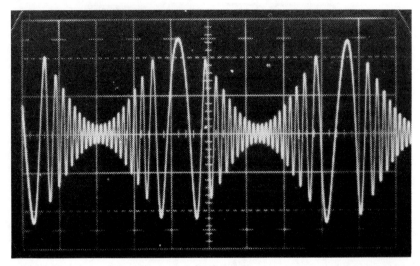

**Figure 4-19** Example of amplitude modulation with incidental frequency modulation.

oscillation, and signal passage will be blocked. If $C2$ becomes "open," $T1$ will resonate at an abnormally high frequency. Again, if $C3$ becomes "open," the stage gain will be greatly subnormal owing to emitter degeneration. Note that when an IF stage is oscillating violently, the transistor terminal voltages are changed. The forward bias decreases, and sometimes the transistor will be reverse-biased. This reverse bias results from class C operation, wherein the base conducts forward current in narrow high-amplitude pulses.

An ideal stereo-multiplex composite-audio test signal is depicted in Fig. 4-22(a). This waveform will be identified as either a left ($L$) signal, or as a right ($R$) signal, depending on the phase of its 38-kHz subcarrier component. Reproduction of this test signal at the output of the FM detector can be checked initially with an oscilloscope. One type of distortion that can occur is baseline curvature, as illustrated in Fig. 4-22(b). This sinusoidal curvature is caused by IF phase shift, owing to misalignment. Therefore, if this form of distortion is observed, the technician should troubleshoot and realign the FM IF section before proceeding to other tests. Alignment instructions and procedure are provided in the FM tuner service data. As noted previously, many FM stereo-multiplex signal generators include a 10.7-MHz sweep generator; a 100-MHz sweep facility is often provided, also.

A stereo decoder may be checked individually, or in combination with the FM tuner. When an overall response test is made, it is

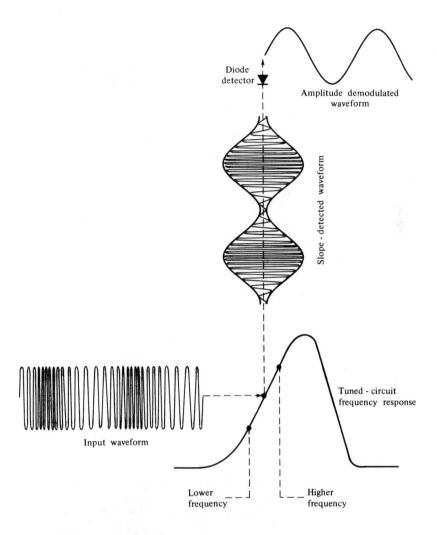

**Figure 4-20**   Slope detection process.

necessary first to verify that the tuner is operating normally. Note that a decoder (Fig. 4-17) includes several tuned circuits that are resonated at 19-kHz, 38-kHz, and 67-kHz. If a decoder is found to be out of alignment, it is most probable that a component or device defect has occurred. Accordingly, all troubleshooting requirements should be completed before realignment is started. Decoder alignment instructions and procedure are provided in the FM tuner service data. Suitable test signals are provided in all standard FM stereo-multiplex generators.

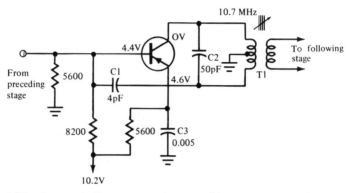

**Figure 4-21** Stage misalignment can be caused by an open capacitor.

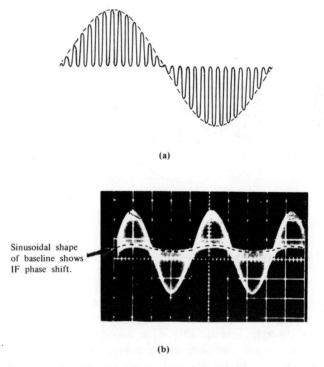

(a)

Sinusoidal shape
of baseline shows
IF phase shift.

(b)

**Figure 4-22** IF misalignment evidenced in reproduction of stereo-multiplex test signal: **(a)** ideal stereo-multiplex composite-audio test signal; **(b)** example of distorted test-signal waveform owing to IF misalignment. (*Courtesy of Sencore, Inc.*)

Measurement of the number of decibels of separation between the $L$ and $R$ signals (channels) is the most fundamental test of decoder operation. This test is made with a stereo signal generator and an oscilloscope or TVM, as shown in Fig. 4-23. If the tuner and decoder are to be checked as a unit, RF output from the generator is applied to the antenna-input terminals of the tuner. On the other hand, if the decoder is to be tested individually, composite audio output from the generator is applied to the input of the decoder. Both tests are desirable in case of a poor-separation complaint, in order to determine whether the malfunction is in the tuner circuits or in the decoder circuits. In either case, to measure the amount of separation, an $R$ test signal is applied, and the output voltages from the left and right channels are measured. In theory, the output from the left channel would be zero, with an $R$ signal applied. Actually, separation is incomplete in practice, and 30-dB separation is considered normal. Similarly, when an $L$ test signal is applied, there will normally be 30-dB separation between the $L$ and $R$ outputs from the decoder.

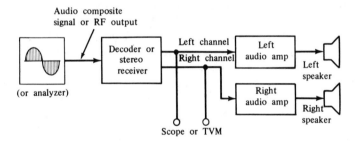

Note : FM-stereo analyzers include
dB meters for indication of
separation values.

**Figure 4-23** Separation test of an FM tuner-decoder combination, or of the decoder individually.

**Audio Channel Crosschecks** When there is a malfunction in the $L$ audio channel, for example, the $R$ audio channel can be used for cross checks in preliminary troubleshooting procedure. For example, a basic audio stereo system is depicted in Fig. 4-24. In case the output from the $L$ channel is absent, or badly distorted, the question arises whether the fault may be in an $L$ transducer, or in the $L$ amplifier. Thus, if the signal source is a phono cartridge, the leads from the $L$ and $R$ sections of the cartridge can be temporarily interchanged, to determine whether the $L$ section is operating normally or abnormally. If

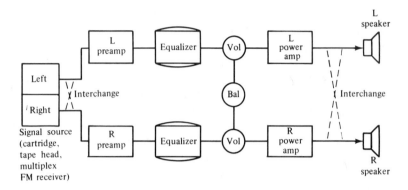

**Figure 4-24**    Interchange of input and/or output connections provides a comparison test.

the cartridge does not need to be replaced, the speaker leads can next be interchanged, as indicated. This quick check will show whether a speaker malfunction is causing the trouble symptom.

In the event that transducer trouble is ruled out by the foregoing quick checks, it follows that the fault will be found in the L amplifier. In turn, it becomes necessary to localize the malfunction to a particular stage. This can be easily accomplished by using the good audio channel to check out the faulty channel step by step, as shown in Fig. 4-25. A 0.5-$\mu$F test capacitor is used, with test leads to temporarily connect the output from one stage in the L amplifier to the input of the corresponding following stage in the R amplifier. At some point in the test procedure, sound output will be obtained from the L speaker. Suppose, for example, that sound output is first obtained in step 4 of the procedure. This result indicates that the L volume control is defective. It is good practice to turn the amplifiers off each time before test leads are connected or disconnected and to discharge the test capacitor. This precaution ensures that semiconductor devices will not be damaged by surges from the test capacitor.

**Single and Multiple Faults**    As a general rule, the technician expects to find only one fault when a trouble symptom develops. Thus, a power transistor may have become defective, a capacitor may have become leaky, a diode may have a poor front-to-back ratio, a solder connection may be defective, a module may be making poor contact in its receptacle, the lead to a voice coil may be broken, and so on. In most cases, after the defective device or component is replaced, or the abnormal condition is corrected, the audio system resumes normal operation.

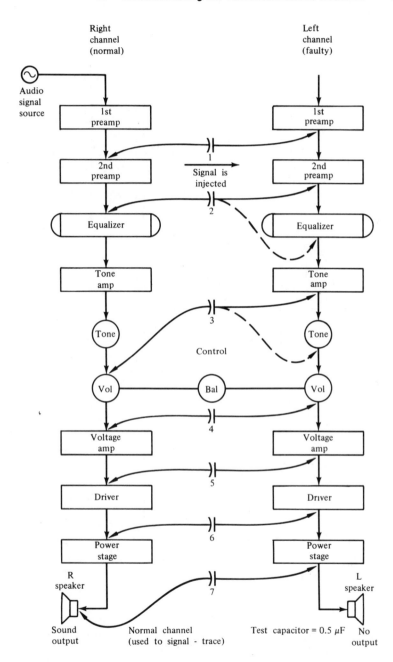

**Figure 4-25** A good stereo channel can be used to check out the faulty channel.

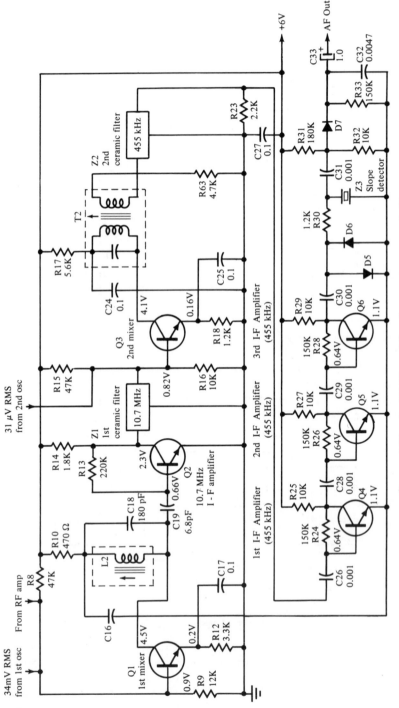

**Figure 4-26** An FM IF amplifier that employs ceramic filters.

However, this is not always the outcome. For example, if a resistor drifts off-value in a power-output stage, and an output transistor draws excessive current, the sound output will become distorted. After the off-value resistor is replaced, the sound output may still be distorted, and may be subnormal in volume also. This continuing trouble symptom results from thermal damage to the power transistor, which must also be replaced to restore normal operation.

**Basic Definitions** A *phase-locked loop* in a communication circuit denotes a local oscillator that is synchronized in phase and frequency with a received signal. As an illustration, the 38-kHz oscillator ($Q4$) in Fig. 4-17 operates in a phase-locked loop. This oscillator is synchronized by the incoming 19-kHz pilot subcarrier. Steep-sided IF response curves may be obtained by means of *ceramic filters*. These are bandpass filter configurations that employ barium titanate crystals. A typical schematic is shown in Fig. 4-26. In this example, *double conversion* is utilized. In other words, the incoming RF signal is first converted to a 10.7-MHz IF frequency, and is then converted to a 455-kHz IF frequency. This mode of operation provides optimum discrimination against interference. A typical ceramic-filter arrangement is depicted in Fig. 4-27. Observe that *slope detection* is utilized in the example of Fig. 4-26. Slope detection is defined as a discriminator operation on one of the slopes of the response curve for a tuned circuit, as was shown in Fig. 4-20.

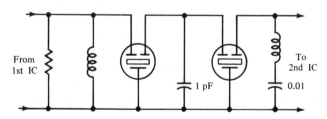

**Figure 4-27** Representative ceramic filter arrangement.

# 5

## Electrophonic Music Systems

Electrophonic music systems represent a growing area of audio technology. The electrophonic method utilizes electronic oscillators, electric generators, wave filters, gating and switching devices, modulators, mixers, wave shapers, amplifiers, and speakers. An electrophonic system can be compared in some aspects with electronic organ technology, although its basic plan is unique. For example, an electronic organ is designed to produce traditional musical forms, whereas an electrophonic music system is designed to produce novel musical forms with tones that are not necessarily related in a harmonious manner, and which do not necessarily follow any established rules of musical composition. Tones are often employed that are unconventional and undefined in traditional musical terminology. An electrophonic instrument may be controlled by a performer, or it may be partially or entirely programmed. Again, the output from the instrument may be completely unpredictable, with operation determined by a random-number or random-noise source.

Electrophonic instruments can be grouped into melodic and polyphonic types. A melodic instrument provides sequences of individual tones or sounds, whereas a polyphonic instrument develops chords of various kinds. Musical tones occupy a wide sonic range that grades imperceptibly from harmonized structures, such as melodies, to percussive sounds, such as drum beats. Traditional musical tones are characterized by pitch (frequency), loudness (amplitude), timbre (harmonic or overtone content), attack (rise time), and decay (fall time). These are the basic steady-state and transient parameters that characterize a note that is produced by pressing a key on an electronic organ, for example. Following the rise mode or growth of a tonal waveform, a greater or lesser duration (sustain time) ensues, terminated by the fall mode. In addition, a tonal waveform may be characterized by a tremolo (amplitude-modulated form), by a vibrato (frequency-modulated form), by a combination of tremolo and vibrato, or by a portamento (frequency glide form).

## 5-2   TONE WAVEFORM CHARACTERISTICS

A pure pitch has a sinusoidal waveform of a given frequency; the tone becomes louder as its amplitude is increased, as depicted in Fig. 5-1.

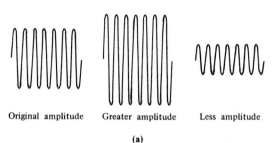

Original amplitude     Greater amplitude     Less amplitude

**(a)**

**(b)**

**Figure 5-1**   A fixed pitch at three different amplitudes: **(a)** waveforms as displayed on oscilloscope screen; **(b)** a function generator that provides sine, square, and triangular waveforms. (*Courtesy of Heath Co.*)

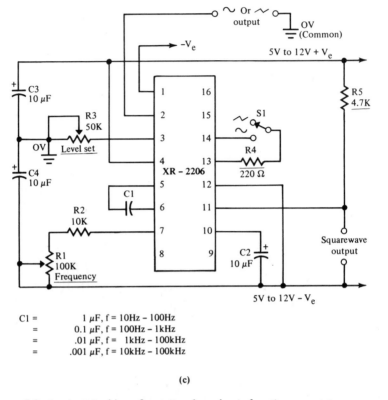

C1 =      1 μF, f = 10Hz – 100Hz
  =      0.1 μF, f = 100Hz – 1kHz
  =      .01 μF, f = 1kHz – 100kHz
  =      .001 μF, f = 10kHz – 100kHz

(c)

**Figure 5-1** *Continued*   **(c)** configuration for a basic function generator.

In these examples, the attack and decay are instantaneous. The sustain time is comparatively short, and is constant. This type of pitch waveform is often called a *tone burst*. Tone bursts do not necessarily have a fixed pitch, or frequency. For example, a tone-burst sequence that includes three different pitches is exemplified in Fig. 5-2. Each burst has the same amplitude and the same duration (sustain time); each burst follows its predecessor by the same time interval; attack and decay are instantaneous for each burst. However, the second burst has a lower pitch than the first; the third burst has a higher pitch than either the first or the second; the fourth burst has the same pitch as the first. For this reason, this type of electrophonic music waveform is termed a tone-burst frequency-shift waveform.

By way of comparison, traditional musical tones generally have relatively gradual attack and decay intervals, as shown in Fig. 5-3. A sudden attack is characterized by a percussive quality, whereas a gradual attack provides an unelaborated tonal onset. Examples of vibrato

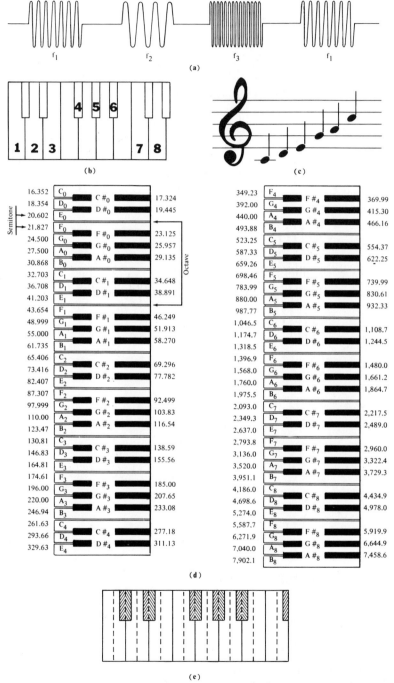

**Figure 5-2** Tone-burst frequency-shift waveform: **(a)** successive bursts of different pitches; **(b)** the "open scale" may be utilized; **(c)** pentatonic scale is also employed; **(d)** semitone sequence; **(e)** an octave of half semitones.

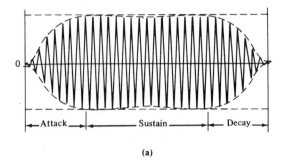

(a)

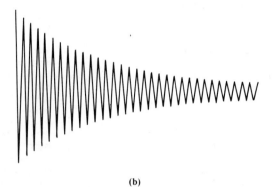

(b)

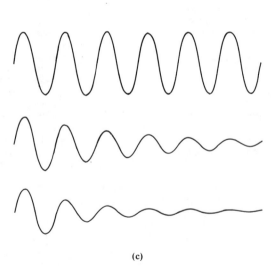

(c)

**Figure 5-3**   Illustrations of attack, sustain, and decay intervals: **(a)** gradual attack and gradual decay; **(b)** rapid attack and exponential decay; **(c)** three progressive rates of decay.

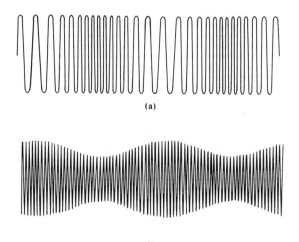

(a)

(b)

**Figure 5-4**   Examples of vibrato and tremolo modulation: **(a)** vibrato modulation of sustained tone; **(b)** tremolo modulation of sustained tone.

and tremolo modulation of fixed pitches are seen in Fig. 5-4. The modulation rate is typically about 7 Hz, although any modulation rate less than the pitch value can be employed for special effects. Again, the degree of modulation may be small or large. As noted previously, some electrophonic instruments utilize a combination of vibrato and tremolo modulation. Any modulation process introduces new frequencies that are not present in the unmodulated waveform. For example, if a 1-kHz sinusoidal wave is tremolo-modulated by a 7-Hz sinusoidal wave, the modulated waveform contains a 993-Hz frequency and a 1003-Hz frequency, in addition to the original 1000-Hz frequency. Again, if a 1-kHz sinusoidal wave is vibrato-modulated to a substantial degree, an extensive spectrum of new frequencies is introduced.

There is a basic distinction between the mixing of one waveform with another, and the modulation of one waveform by another. With reference to Fig. 5-5, the mixing process results in a complex waveform in which both of the frequency components retain their original amplitudes. On the other hand, the modulation process results in a complex waveform in which the higher-frequency component does not retain its original amplitude. To the ear, a mixed waveform presents a blended tone in which each of the component pitches is audible. However, a tremolo-modulated waveform presents a single (high-frequency component) tone that rises and falls in loudness. Waveform mixing is termed a *linear process,* whereas waveform modulation is termed a *nonlinear process.*

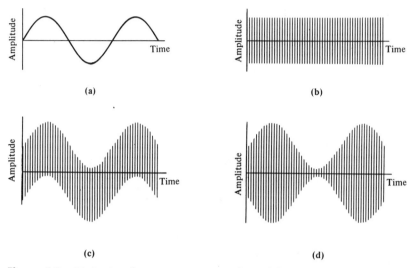

**Figure 5-5**   Distinction between mixing and modulation processes: **(a)** Sine wave; **(b)** higher-frequency sine wave; **(c)** mixing of (a) and (b); **(d)** modulation of (b) by (a).

Pure (single-frequency) tones are utilized to some extent in electrophonic music. A single frequency has a "thin" sound, as exemplified by a tuning fork. Most musical tones have comparatively elaborate overtone (harmonic) spectra, as shown in Fig. 5-6 for several traditional tones. Most tonal spectra are dominated by the fundamental pitch; however, there are exceptions, as indicated for a soprano voice and for a guitar string in the diagrams. Tonal timbres are determined primarily by overtone structure, and secondarily by the loudness of a tone. In other words, the ear is a nonlinear organ, particularly at low volume levels, and this factor tends to cause a change in timbre with a substantial change in volume level. Overtones are integral multiples of the fundamental waveform frequency, by definition.

Note in passing that complex waveforms may have subharmonics, in addition to harmonics. For example, synthetic bass is produced by generating a harmonic spectrum from which the fundamental is absent. If the lower harmonics are exalted (artificially increased in amplitude), the ear is deceived into believing that the fundamental frequency of the tone is actually present. This illusion results from the nonlinear characteristic of the hearing process, whereby pairs of harmonic frequencies beat together in the ear and generate their difference frequency. Thus, synthetic bass is an aspect of tonal timbre. A wave with half the frequency of the fundamental of another wave is called the

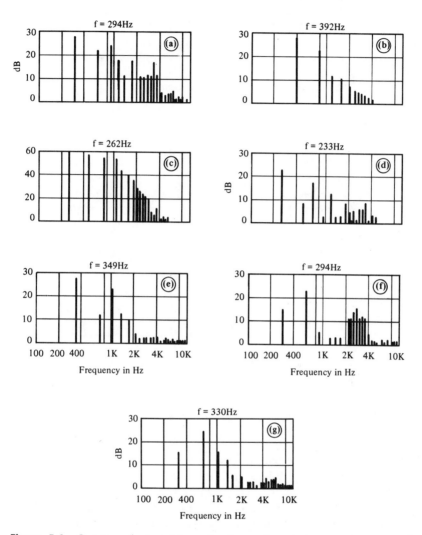

**Figure 5-6** Overtone (harmonic) spectra for various instrumental tones and organ voices: **(a)** open violin string; **(b)** flute; **(c)** reed organ pipe; **(d)** clarinet; **(e)** trumpet; **(f)** soprano voice; **(g)** guitar string.

second subharmonic of that wave; one with a third of the fundamental frequency of another wave is called a third subharmonic, and so on.

Phase relations of harmonics in complex waveforms have a marked effect on waveshape, as exemplified in Fig. 5-7. In turn, it might be supposed that the timbre of a tone would depend considerably upon harmonic phase relationships. However, this is actually a very

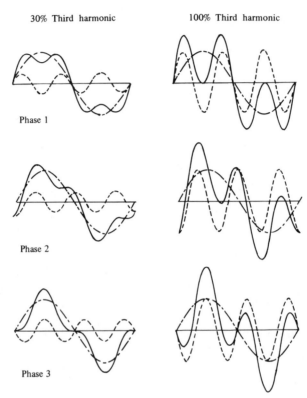

**Figure 5-7** A fundamental with a 30 percent and a 100 percent third harmonic in various phase relations.

minor factor in timbre parameters. In other words, it is difficult for a listener to detect any difference in a tone as its harmonic content is shifted in phase. There are some situations in which phase relations do play a noticeable role in timbre. For example, if the harmonics in a square wave are shifted considerably, the listener can perceive a change in tonal quality. As shown in Fig. 5-8, the effect of progressive harmonic phase shift is to tilt the top and bottom excursions of a square wave.

A rapid frequency glide is depicted in Fig. 5-9, as it would be displayed on the screen of an oscilloscope. This is an example of portamento, or the continuous change of a tone from one pitch to another, or it is an example of glissando. A portamento waveform may proceed from a lower pitch to a higher pitch, or vice versa. When one procession is followed by a reversed procession, as exemplified in Fig. 5-4(a), a portamento modulation is termed a *vibrato modulation*. From the viewpoint of electronic technology, a frequency glide is a form of chirp

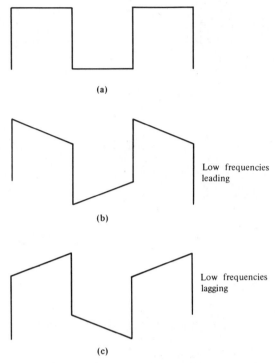

(a)

(b)

Low frequencies
leading

(c)

Low frequencies
lagging

**Figure 5-8**   Square wave becomes tilted by progressive harmonic phase shift:
**(a)** Original square wave; **(b)** result of harmonic phase shift; **(c)** another example of harmonic phase shift.

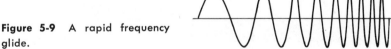

**Figure 5-9**   A rapid frequency
glide.

modulation, whereas a vibrato is a form of frequency modulation. Electrophonic music may employ tone bursts that include vibrato or glide modulation, as depicted in Fig. 5-10. The tone bursts may differ in duration, amplitude, and pitch.

As shown in Fig. 5-11, some complex waveforms have odd harmonics only; other waveforms have even harmonics only; still others have both even and odd harmonics. This is a point of some importance to designers of electrophonic music systems, because these parameters determine whether linear or nonlinear waveshaping circuitry is required in formant filters. A formant filter functions to alter the sound quality of

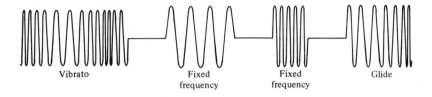

Vibrato          Fixed          Fixed          Glide
                 frequency      frequency

Repetitive frequency shift

**Figure 5-10**   Burst tones comprising fixed pitches and frequency glides.

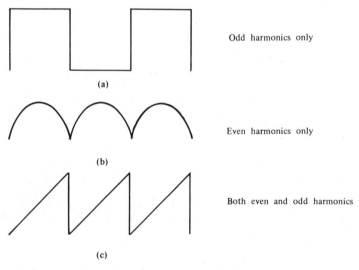

Odd harmonics only

(a)

Even harmonics only

(b)

Both even and odd harmonics

(c)

**Figure 5-11**   Examples of basic harmonic parameters: **(a)** square wave; **(b)** full-rectified sine wave; **(c)** sawtooth wave.

a tonal waveform that passes through the filter. This alteration is accomplished by a change in waveshape. A basic law of electricity states that no new frequencies can be introduced into a complex waveform by any linear operation. In other words, since a square wave contains odd harmonics only, it cannot be changed into a sawtooth wave by passage through any type of linear formant filter. On the other hand, since a sawtooth wave contains both even and odd harmonics, it can be changed into a square wave by passage through suitable linear formant filters. Although very elaborate filter circuitry would be required in this example, this waveshaping operation is technically possible.

Similarly, since a fully rectified sine wave contains even harmonics only, it is impossible to change this waveform into a square waveform by means of linear formant filters. Again, it is impossible to change a fully rectified sine wave into a sawtooth wave with linear formant filters. On the other hand, since the sawtooth waveform contains both even and odd harmonics, it can be changed into a fully rectified sine waveform by passage through suitable linear formant filters. As before, although very elaborate filter circuitry would be required for this waveshaping operation, this linear transformation is technically possible. Because both even and odd harmonics are included in traditional tone spectra, as exemplified in Fig. 5-6, designers often employ a sawtooth waveform source, so that linear formant filters can be utilized to develop waveshapes that simulate desired tonal timbres.

Of course, nonlinear formant circuitry is also exploited in electrophonic system design. Thus, peak clippers, slicers, modulators, and heterodyne configurations are used separately or in combination with linear wave filters. The basic types of wave filters are the low-pass, high-pass, bandpass, and band-reject filters. In addition, a comb filter is a type of filter network that is effectively a multiple-bandpass design that passes only frequencies within a number of narrow bands, or provides outputs corresponding to each of its passbands. Thus, a comb filter could be utilized to change a sawtooth waveform into a square waveform. A trap is a type of band-reject or notch filter that has a very narrow bandwidth. Filters can be broadly classified into active and passive types. An active filter provides incidental amplification, whereas a passive filter imposes an insertion loss. Active filters often use operational amplifiers. Apart from its amplification, an active filter has an advantage in that comparatively extensive waveshaping operations are feasible.

A simple passive trap configuration is shown in Fig. 5-12. This is an LCR bridged-T configuration. Since its bandwidth is very narrow, it can be used to filter out a chosen component frequency from a complex waveform. Thus, the inductive, capacitive, and resistive values may be chosen to filter out the fundamental frequency from a given square wave. In turn, the timbre of the output waveform is quite different from the timbre of the input waveform. Note in passing that the fundamental frequency in a square wave has a greater amplitude than that of the square wave itself. In other words, if the amplitude of a square wave

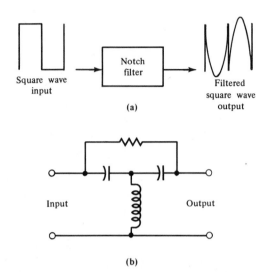

**Figure 5-12** Timbre of tone is changed by filtering the fundamental frequency from a waveform: **(a)** Input and output waveshapes; **(b)** notch filter configuration.

is assigned a value of unity, then the amplitude of its fundamental frequency component is equal to $4/\pi$, or 1.273. This amplitude difference is not intuitively apparent, and results from the fact that some of the harmonics have phases that tend to cancel part of the peak excursion of the fundamental in the complete waveform,

Other examples of simple formant filters are RC differentiating and integrating circuits. A differentiating circuit is a simple type of high-pass filter; an integrating circuit is a simple type of low-pass filter. If a differentiating circuit is connected in series with an integrating circuit, an elementary form of bandpass filter is obtained. Slightly elaborated differentiating and integrating circuitry is utilized in twin-T (parallel-T) RC filters that operate as traps or notch filters. However, the bandwidth of an RC twin-T filter is considerably greater than that of an LCR bridged-T filter, such as that shown in Fig. 5-12(b).

Frequency spectra for square, sawtooth (ramp), and triangular waveforms are shown in Fig. 5-13. A square wave has extremely rapid attack and decay, whereas a triangular wave has very gradual attack and very gradual decay. Again, a sawtooth wave has very gradual attack and very rapid decay. A sawtooth wave has a fuller timbre than a square wave, owing to its even-harmonic content. In other words, a sawtooth waveform does not have as harsh a timbre as a square wave.

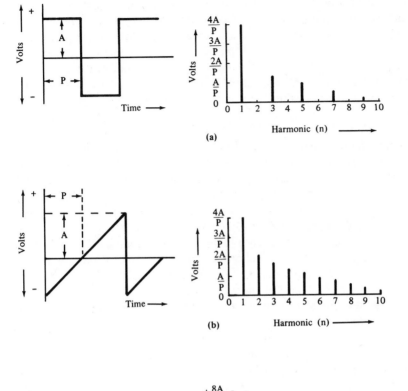

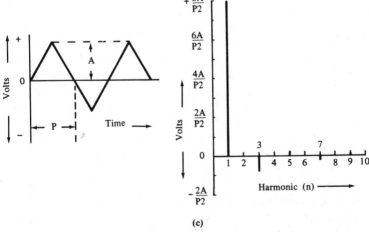

**Figure 5-13** Frequency spectra for three basic waveforms: **(a)** square wave; **(b)** sawtooth wave; **(c)** triangular wave.

As noted previously, a sine wave has a pure and thin timbre by way of comparison. A triangular wave, which has odd harmonics only, is comparable in the first analysis to a square wave. However, a triangular wave has comparatively low-amplitude harmonics. In turn, the timbre of a triangular wave is intermediate to that of a square wave and a sine wave. If the higher harmonics of a triangular wave are removed by means of a low-pass filter, the output waveform approximates a sine wave.

The relation of a sawtooth waveform frequency spectrum to the standard musical pitches is shown in Fig. 5-14. It is evident that this frequency spectrum is not identifiable with any traditional musical chord. However, if desired, the electrophonic system designer could operate on sawtooth waves with linear formant filters to obtain any traditional chord that might be chosen. In general, electrophonic music seeks to be different from conventional music, and harmony is not one of its cornerstones. *Harmony* is defined as the combination of simultaneous musical notes into a chord, or the structure of a piece of music according to the composition and progression of its chords. A harmonic series is a series of partial tones consisting of a fundamental or first harmonic and all of the overtones whose frequency ratio to it can be expressed in whole numbers.

A *melody* is defined as a rhythmically organized and meaningful succession of single musical notes or tones having a definite relationship one with the other and forming an esthetic whole. Thus, melody is distinguished from harmony. Rhythm is an aspect of all music that comprises the totality of elements (as accent, meter, time, and tempo) that relate to forward movement as contrasted with pitch sequence or tone combination. It is a symmetrical and regularly recurrent grouping of tones according to accent and time value, or of a particular accent pattern that groups the beats of a composition or movement into measures. Both traditional and electrophonic musical concepts are highly subjective. As a supplementary example, the pentatonic scale is a musical scale of five tones in which the octave is reached at the sixth tone. It is similar to a major scale with its fourth and seventh tones omitted. Whether the pentatonic scale is a better keystone for musical structures than the major scale is essentially a subjective judgment.

Electrophonic tones are not necessarily symmetrical. For example, the fully rectified sine waveform depicted in Fig. 5-11(b) may be utilized. The sawtooth waveform shown in Fig. 5-11(c) has mirror-image symmetry. The dual-tremolo waveform seen in Fig. 5-15 is unique to electrophonic music. The higher-frequency tremolo component is modulated by the lower-frequency tremolo component. In other words, the higher-frequency tremolo effect rises and falls in its

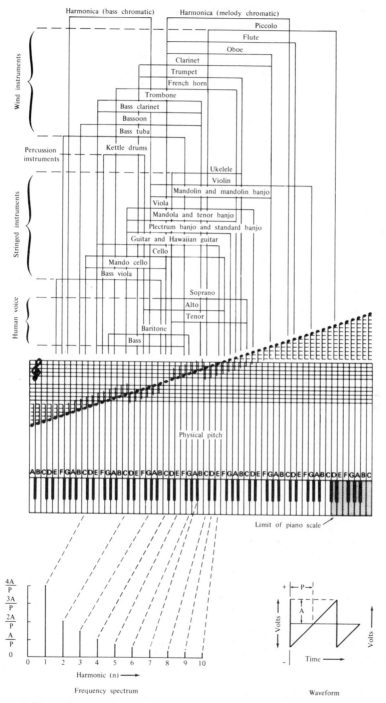

**Figure 5-14** Relation of sawtooth wave harmonic frequencies to standard musical pitches.

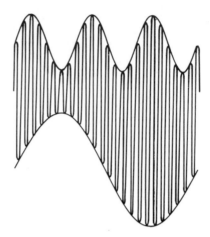

**Figure 5-15**    Asymmetrically modulated AM waveform.

degree according to the changing amplitude of the lower-frequency tremolo component. Although echo effects are not unique to electrophonic music, they are more widely utilized than in traditional musical passages. An example of a tone waveform with rapid attack and comparatively slow exponential decay was shown in Fig. 5-3(b). When two such tones with somewhat different pitches are mixed, as depicted in Fig. 5-16, the resultant beating waveform alternately rises to maximum and then decays to zero as its amplitude diminishes. In turn, a multiple echo effect is produced.

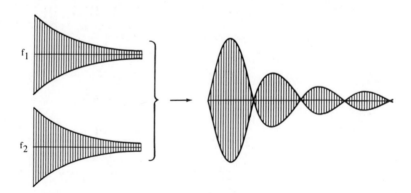

**Figure 5-16**    Resultant beat of two exponential waveforms.

## 5-3   ORGANIZATION OF ELECTROPHONIC MUSIC SYSTEMS

A simple electrophonic music system is depicted in Fig. 5-17. Its output is completely predictable, because the tonal sequence is controlled by perforations in a prepared paper tape. In this example, three tracks or channels are utilized. Typical electrophonic music systems employ from eight to twelve channels. Light beams and photoelectric devices are often used to sense the passage of a perforation. In turn, the electric pulses that are produced activate electronic switches; each switch turns a tone generator off or on, in the example of Fig. 5-17. Accordingly, the sine-wave, square-wave, or sawtooth generator can be switched on individually, or at the same time as the others. Tone-generator outputs are fed into an equalizer unit, and thence into a mixer, where they are linearly combined. Finally, the sequence of tone waveforms is applied to a speaker.

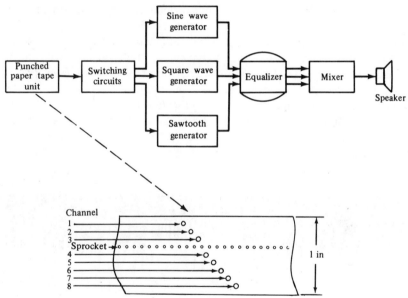

**Figure 5-17**   Example of a simple electrophonic music system.

An example of a pulse sequence from a punched paper tape is shown in Fig. 5-18. Sustained tones are obtained by means of slots cut into the tape, instead of holes. Electrophonic music systems are often constructed in module form, with interconnecting patch cords. This design permits quick interchange of modules and maximum flexibility of

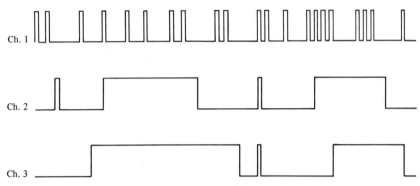

**Figure 5-18**   Example of a pulse sequence from a digital-computer punched paper tape.

interconnection. Many systems include a random noise generator; it may be utilized as a sound source, or it may be used as an unpredictable switching-voltage source. A high-gain audio amplifier has a comparatively high-level noise output. A typical random noise waveform is illustrated in Fig. 5-19. The noise waveform consists of series of pulses that have no orderly sequence and nonuniform amplitudes. If the amplifier has a wide bandpass, noise pulses are produced rapidly (many pulses per second), or, if the amplifier has a narrow bandpass, noise pulses are produced slowly (few pulses per second). Thus, a random-noise switch has an average switching rate that is proportional to the bandwidth of the noise source.

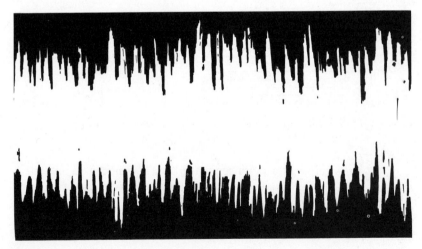

**Figure 5-19**   Random noise waveform.

The frequency spectrum of random noise has an envelope that depends upon the frequency response of the noise source. With reference to Fig. 5-20, *white noise* has a frequency spectrum that is flat on the average; it corresponds to the noise output from an amplifier that has uniform frequency response. If the amplifier has greater gain at low frequencies than at high frequencies, its noise output has comparatively prominent low-frequency components. This type of noise spectrum is called *red noise.* Conversely, if the amplifier has greater gain at high frequencies than at low frequencies, its noise output has comparatively prominent high-frequency components. This type of noise spectrum is called *blue noise. Pink noise* is similar to red noise, except that the former has less prominent low-frequency components. When used as electrophonic sound sources, these various types of noise have different timbres. White noise has a characteristic hissing sound. Although red noise does not have an identifiable pitch, it has a lower-frequency hiss than white noise. Conversely, blue noise has a higher-frequency hiss than white noise. If an audio amplifier is used as a noise source, its output can be changed from white to red or blue by adjustment of the tone controls.

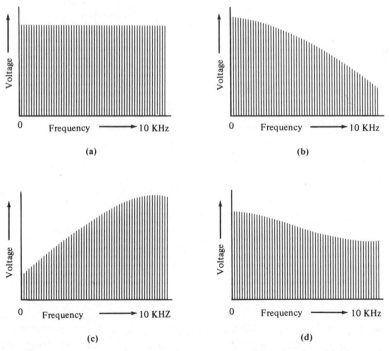

**Figure 5-20** Basic noise spectra: **(a)** white noise; **(b)** red noise; **(c)** blue noise; **(d)** pink noise.

Noise pulses will operate switching circuits in an electrophonic music system, in the same basic manner as pulses from photoelectric devices, provided that the noise pulses have adequate amplitude. As noted previously, random noise pulses have random amplitudes, as well as random occurrence in time. In turn, not all of the pulses from a random noise source will have sufficient amplitude to operate a given switching circuit. A switching circuit is often provided with an adjustable bias threshold, so that one switch is actuated by low-amplitude pulses, whereas another switch is actuated only by high-amplitude pulses.

Both predictable and unpredictable operating factors are incorporated in the electrophonic music system exemplified in Fig. 5-21.

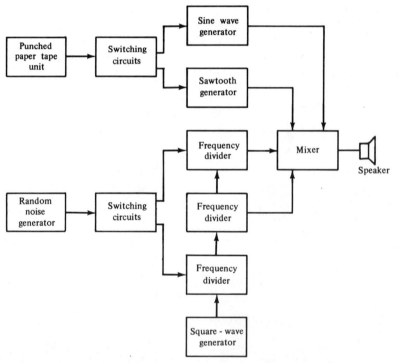

**Figure 5-21** An electrophonic music system that incorporates both predictable and unpredictable operating factors.

The sine-wave generator and the sawtooth generator are controlled by the punched paper tape unit. On the other hand, the three frequency dividers are controlled by the random noise generator. Each frequency divider reduces the repetition rate of the input square-wave voltage, and applies the resultant square wave(s) to the mixer unit. Here, both the predictable and unpredictable waveform voltages are combined and applied to the speaker. Most frequency-divider units are designed as bistable multivibrators for division by two. An elaboration of this arrangement includes Schmitt trigger circuits that produce rectangular-wave outputs, instead of square-wave outputs. Another elaboration employs another random-noise source to operate a gain-control circuit and thereby to vary the loudness of a tone unpredictably.

A basic Schmitt trigger configuration is shown in Fig. 5-22. This is a bistable multivibrator arrangement that changes state at a predetermined negative-voltage level, and then returns to its original state at some predetermined positive-voltage level. The output from the trigger circuit is always a rectangular waveform, regardless of the

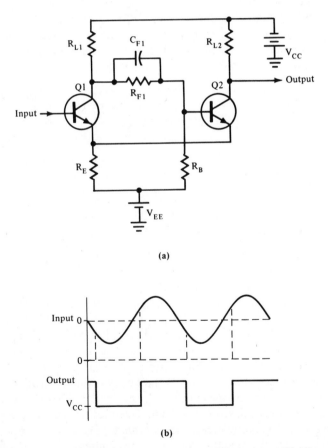

(a)

(b)

**Figure 5-22** Basic Schmitt trigger circuit: **(a)** configuration; **(b)** triggering sequence.

input trigger waveform. Although a sine-wave trigger is depicted in Fig. 5-22, a pulse-voltage input such as that shown in Fig. 5-18 could be used instead. Even random noise pulses may be utilized to trigger a Schmitt configuration. The output from a Schmitt trigger is sometimes used to actuate diode or triode-transistor switches, which in turn may turn modulators or formant filters on and off.

A representative diode keying circuit is shown in Fig. 5-23. In this example, the keying arrangement controls the flow of audio signal from the tone generator to the formant section. Observe that a pair of diodes is connected back to back, and is connected in series with the lead from the tone generator to the formant section. If the key is open, both diodes are cut off, or reverse-biased, from the −7-V source. Accordingly, the output from the tone generator is blocked. However, when the key is closed, the +20-V source overrides the −7-V source, and both of the diodes conduct, because of forward bias. Consequently, the output signal from the tone generator is applied to the formant section. In this configuration, the 40-μF capacitor operates in combination with the associated resistors as a formant filter.

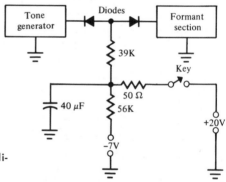

**Figure 5-23**   Representative diode keying circuit.

Next, a typical transistor switching or keying circuit is shown in Fig. 5-24. Its circuit action is similar to that of the diode arrangement explained above. The output from the tone generator is applied at the emitter of the transistor, and the output load circuit is connected to the collector. Suitable bias voltages are applied at the base of the transistor to control switching action. If the key is open, a negative voltage is applied to the base of the transistor through the 2.2-MΩ resistor. In turn, the transistor is biased beyond cutoff. However, if the key is closed, a positive bias voltage overrides the negative bias voltage through the 68-kΩ resistor. Consequently, the transistor conducts and functions as a common-base amplifier.

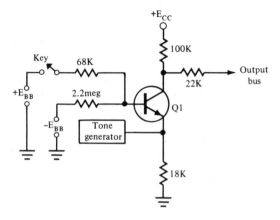

**Figure 5-24**  Typical transistor keying circuit.

More sophisticated types of switching arrangements in electro-phonic music systems employ digital-computer switching circuitry, as exemplified in Fig. 5-25. These are examples of logic gates. An AND gate produces an output only if both of its inputs are logic-high at the same time. In other words, if two positive pulse voltages are applied simultaneously to $A$ and $B$ in Fig. 5-25(a), diodes $D1$ and $D2$ will be cut off for the duration of the pulses. In turn, output $F$ is no longer effectively at ground potential, but is connected to the $+10$-V source through resistor $R$. In turn, the output bus $f$ goes logic-high. (In this example, a $+10$-V output pulse is produced.) Observe that no output pulse will be formed if only $D1$ is cut off by an input positive pulse. In this case, $D2$ remains at ground potential (through the pulse source), with the result that $D2$ is still conducting although $D1$ is cut off. There-fore, output bus $f$ is effectively tied to ground.

Consider next the OR gate depicted in Fig. 5-25(b). The output bus will go logic-high if either input $A$ or input $B$ is raised logic-high. Actually, a positive pulse applied to either one of the input terminals is merely conducted through its associated diode to the load resistor $R$. If both inputs are pulsed logic-high, the same output pulse results as if only one input is pulsed logic-high. The input-output relations for a logic gate are summarized in truth tables, as shown with the diagrams. Although only two inputs are indicated in the examples of Fig. 5-25, a logic gate may have a number of inputs. For example, the configuration for a four-input AND gate is shown in Fig. 5-26. The gate is followed by a transistor amplifier to obtain a higher amplitude output. The first transistor also provides a NAND output (NOT AND). The NAND

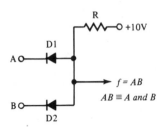

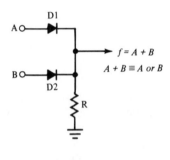

(a)

(b)

**Figure 5-25**    Diode logic gates: **(a)** AND gate; **(b)** OR gate.

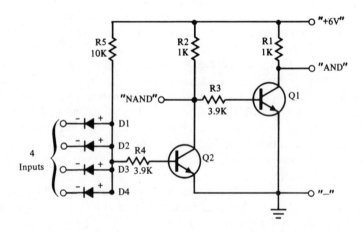

**Figure 5-26**    Configuration of a four-input AND gate.

output has the opposite polarity from the AND output. It will be observed that $Q2$ will remain cut off until all four inputs are pulsed posi-
tively at the same time. Then the transistor becomes forward-biased
and develops a logic-low output that drives $Q1$. In turn, $Q1$ develops a
logic-high output.

A typical configuration for a four-input OR gate is depicted in
Fig. 5-27. Transistors $Q1$ and $Q2$ provide an amplified output, and $Q2$
also supplies a NOR output while $Q1$ supplies an OR output. The OR
gates are operated by positive pulses. Actually, the input pulses are
simply passed by the diodes to the base of $Q2$, thereby forward-biasing
the transistor and causing the collector of $Q2$ to go logic-low. This
logic-low output drives the base of $Q1$, which responds by developing a
logic-high output. OR gates and AND gates are often designed with
transistors instead of diodes, as seen in Fig. 5-28. The chief advantage
of a transistor gate is its transfer gain, whereas a diode gate imposes an
insertion loss. The gate depicted in Fig. 5-27 is an example of diode-
transistor logic (DTL). On the other hand, the gates depicted in Fig.
5-28 are examples of resistor-transistor logic (RTL).

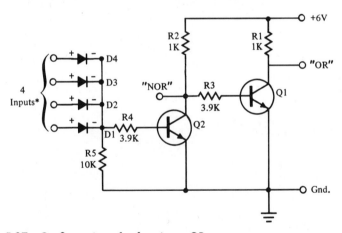

**Figure 5-27** Configuration of a four-input OR gate.

**Audio Delay** Electrophonic music systems may include an audio delay
arrangement, as exemplified in Fig. 5-29. It employs a specialized type
of tape recorder that operates with a simple magnetic-tape belt. The
output from a tone generator or other audio source is applied to a
recording head. After a short time delay, determined by the distance
between the recording head and the playback head, the recorded sound

is played back. Then the recorded information is erased, and the process is repeated. In most systems, one speaker is energized directly from the tone generator, and the second speaker is energized from the playback head. Amplifiers (not shown in the diagram) are utilized to develop the required signal levels.

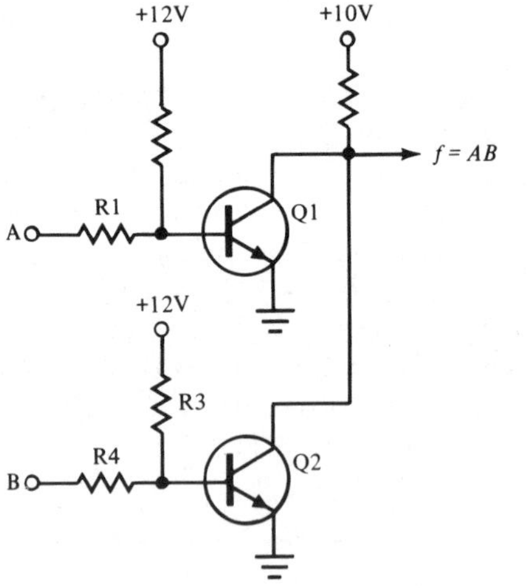


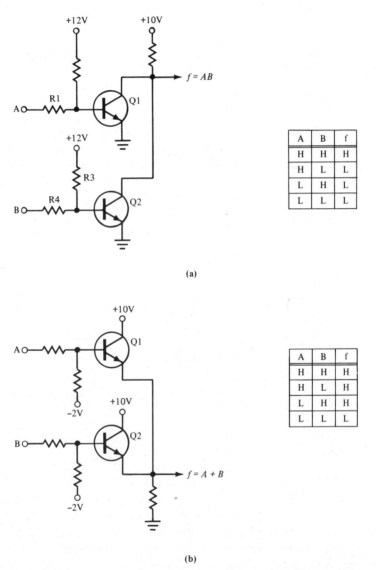

| A | B | f |
|---|---|---|
| H | H | H |
| H | L | L |
| L | H | L |
| L | L | L |

(a)

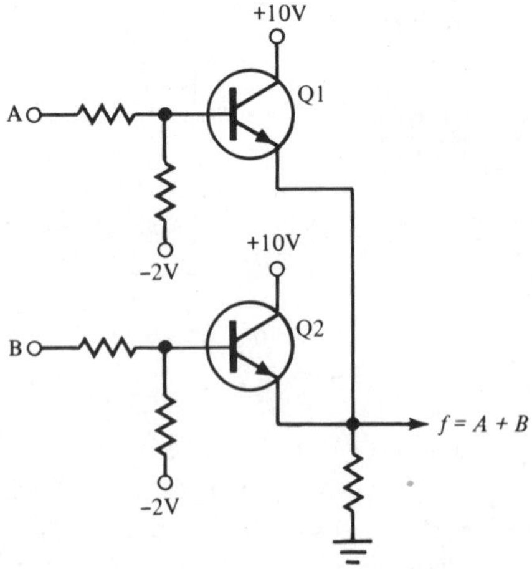


| A | B | f |
|---|---|---|
| H | H | H |
| H | L | H |
| L | H | H |
| L | L | L |

(b)

**Figure 5-28** Examples of direct-coupled transistor logic: **(a)** AND gate; **(b)** OR gate.

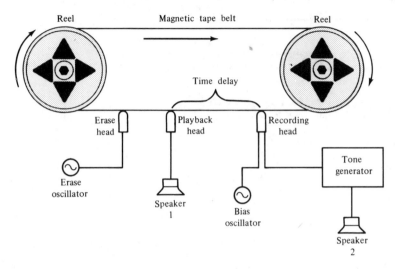

**Figure 5-29**   Audio delay arrangement.

# 6

# Quadraphonic Sound Systems

## 6-1   GENERAL CONSIDERATIONS

In the strict technical sense of the term, quadraphonic sound denotes a sound system wherein sound energy is picked up by four separate microphones and is recorded on four separate channels. For example, four channels may be utilized on a magnetic tape. In turn, these separate channels are played back and drive their own speakers. However, in the relaxed sense of the term, quadraphonic sound also denotes a sound system wherein two additional channels are synthesized from a stereo source. When four separate sound channels are employed, the arrangement is called a discrete or true four-channel system. On the other hand, when two additional channels are synthesized from a stereo source, the residual quadraphonic information that is mixed with the main stereo signal is processed by a synthesizer network. This involves various patterns of frequency discrimination, plus particular phase shifts versus frequency. Gain-riding circuitry may also be included to enhance the front-rear separation effect.

As shown in Fig. 6-1, quadraphonic speakers may be placed in various positions to accommodate the acoustics of a particular room (see Table 6-1). Rear speakers have the purpose of reproducing the reflected sound that is audible to an audience in a concert hall. Quadraphonic reproduction can give these reflected sound sources approximately correct directions and locations for the listener. In the case of a discrete four-channel system, the four sound signals are ordinarily obtained from quadraphonic recordings on eight-channel cartridge tape. Quadraphonic synthesizers are available separately, but are ordinarily built into stereo amplifiers, as exemplified in Fig. 6-2. Any stereo

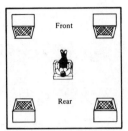

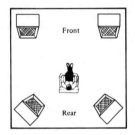

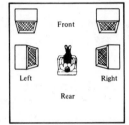

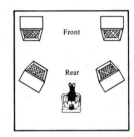

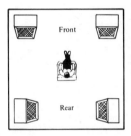

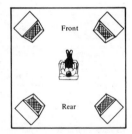

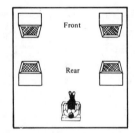

**Figure 6-1** Quadraphonic speakers may be placed in various positions to accommodate room acoustics.

TABLE 6-1
Acoustic Absorption Coefficients

| Material | Coefficient |
|---|---|
| Open window | 1.00 |
| Special acoustic materials | 0.30 to 0.9 |
| Hair felt | 0.58 |
| Carpets | 0.15 to 0.2 |
| Smooth wood | 0.04 |
| Plaster | 0.033 |
| Glass | 0.027 |
| Brick | 0.025 |

**Figure 6-2** A stereo receiver with a built-in four-channel synthesizer. (*Courtesy of Radio Shack, a Tandy Corp. company.*)

source may be used to drive the amplifier, which will also process the two-channel audio signal to simulate a four-channel audio signal. Discrete four-channel sound is recorded on eight-track cartridge tape, as shown in Fig. 6-3.

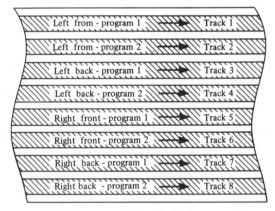

**Figure 6-3** Two quadraphonic programs are recorded on eight-track cartridge tape.

### 6-2 SYNTHESIZED QUADRIPHONIC SOUND

Synthesized quadraphonic sound, although less favored than discrete quadraphonic sound, is in rather wide use. A quadraphonic synthesizer operates from any source of stereophonic sound, and processes (enhances) the stereo signal for utilization as left-rear (LR) and right-rear (RR) quadraphonic signals. This is essentially a simulation process, in which the resulting LR and RR signals do not have the same wave-

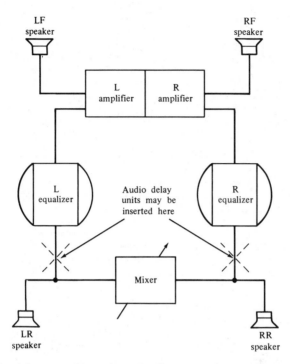

**Figure 6-4**  A basic synthesized quadraphonic sound arrangement.

forms as employed in a discrete system. A basic synthesized quada-
phonic sound arrangement is depicted in Fig. 6-4. The L and R signals
that are applied to the left-front (LF) and right-front (RF) speakers
are also passed through individual equalizers. In turn, the outputs from
the equalizers are partially blended in a mixer and applied to the LR
and RR speakers. Equalizer and mixer controls are adjusted to provide
optimum simulation action. Interconnections for a typical enhanced
stereo system are shown in Fig. 6-5.

In addition to magnetic tapes, disc recordings that provide
stereo signals with encoded quadraphonic signals are available. A widely
used technique employs a frequency-modulated supersonic carrier added
to each channel of the stereo recording. Conventional L and R stereo
channels in turn provide the sum of the front and rear sound sources.
Thus, they reproduce conventional stereo sound output when played on
conventional stereo turntables. The supersonic carriers that are included
in each channel are modulated by the difference of the front and rear
sound sources. In turn, after the carriers are demodulated and then
mixed with the R and L channel signals, four separate (discrete) audio
channels are provided.

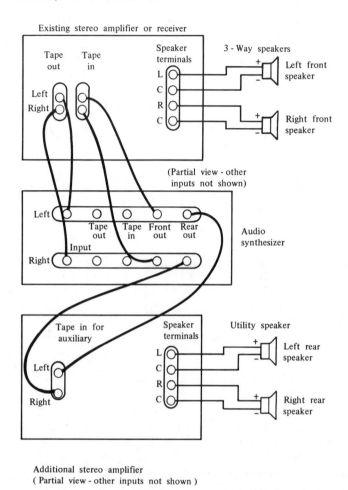

**Figure 6-5** Typical interconnections for an enhanced stereophonic system.

## 6-3  PRINCIPLES OF QS OPERATION

Analysis of the quad-stereo (QS) system is facilitated by first consider-ing discrete quadraphonic recording and playback arrangements. A basic diagram of the system used in recording and playing back four-channel tapes is shown in Fig. 6-6. A pair of microphones is placed at the front of the audience, facing the performers; these microphones are located at the left-hand end and at the right-hand end of the performing group. Thereby, maximum separation of the left and right audio signals is achieved. Another pair of microphones is placed at the rear of the audience, facing the performers. These microphones are located at the

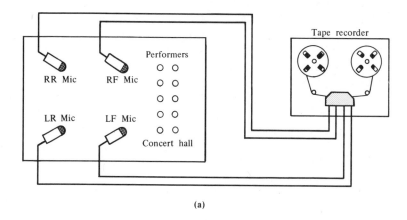

(a)

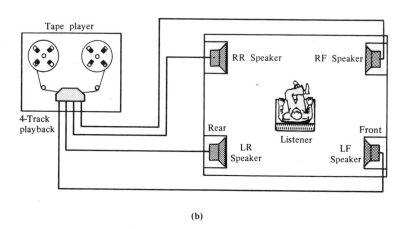

(b)

**Figure 6-6**    Discrete quadraphonic recording and playback arrangements: **(a)** recording setup; **(b)** playback setup.

left-hand end and at the right-hand end of the audience. Thereby, maximum separation of the left and right audio signals is accomplished. It is evident that the RR and LR microphones cannot provide as much separation as the RF and LF microphones. The four audio signals are recorded on individual tape tracks.

In reproduction of discrete four-channel sound, the basic arrangement employs four speakers that are placed in approximately the same relative locations as the four microphones utilized in the recording process. When the relative sound levels of the front and rear speakers are suitably adjusted, a realistic reproduction of concert-hall sound is obtained. It is evident that the RR and LR signals are slightly delayed with respect to the RF and LF signals. In addition, there is a more prominent reverberation component in the rear audio information than in the front audio information. Both L microphones pick up more sound energy from the left end of the group than do the R microphones. Conversely, both R microphones pick up more sound energy from the right end of the group than do the L microphones. Thus, each quadraphonic channel contains somewhat different audio information than the other three channels.

Next, a block diagram of the arrangement that is employed in playing back four-channel discrete quadraphonic records is depicted in Fig. 6-7. Observe that the 30-kHz carrier is frequency-modulated by the stereo-difference signal during the recording process. Then, in the playback process, the audio signals from the two conventional channels are mixed with the signals from the demodulated carriers. This mixing action reconstitutes the original four discrete audio signals, which are then amplified and fed to the four speakers. Another approach to four-channel discrete reproduction utilizes encoders during the recording process, and complementary decoders during playback, as depicted in Fig. 6-8. Various types of encoder/decoder methods are employed. One widely used method encodes audio signals by means of 180-deg phase shifts, as pictured in Fig. 6-9. However, this method has a disadvantage of cancellation of some audio frequencies in localized listening areas.

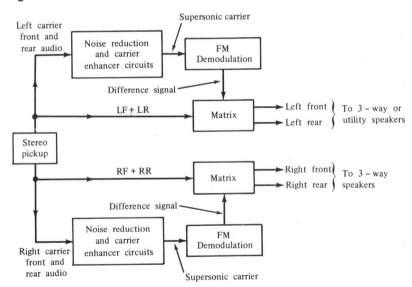

**Figure 6-7** Playback arrangement for four-channel discrete quadraphonic records.

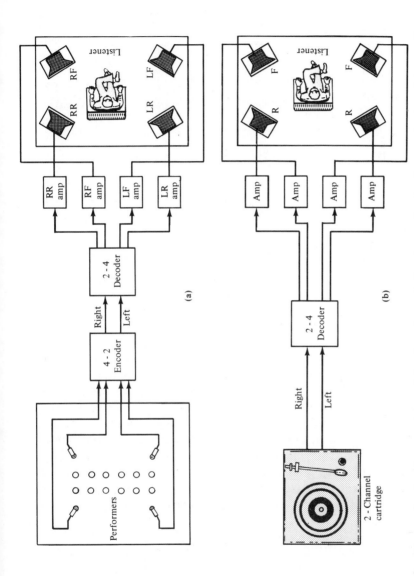

**Figure 6-8** An encoder-decoder arrangement for four-channel discrete quadraphonic reproduction: **(a)** recording setup; **(b)** playback setup.

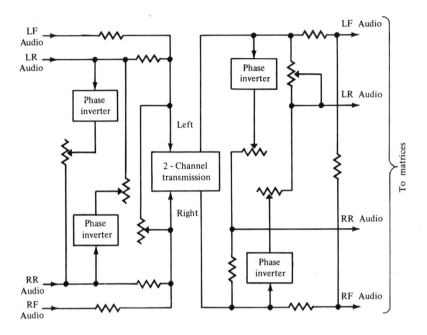

**Figure 6-9** A 180-deg phase-shift encoder-decoder system.

To avoid the foregoing disadvantage, a related design employs 90-deg phase shifts of encoded signals, as depicted in Fig. 6-10. However, this arrangement also has a disadvantage; in this design, there is incomplete separation of front and rear audio signals. Improved separation can be obtained by elaborating the basic configuration and including gain-riding circuitry. A gain-riding circuit automatically exaggerates the separation between the front and rear channels, whenever a separation is sensed. Quad-stereo systems are compatible with conventional stereo equipment. This compatibility is incomplete, to the extent that when a stereo record is played through a four-channel QS system, a synthetic diffused-stereo reproduction occurs. Some listeners approve of diffused-stereo reproduction; others assert that this type of sound is unnatural.

The LF, LR, RR, and RF audio outputs indicated in Fig. 6-9 and 6-10 are fed to final matrices. In other words, these audio outputs are mixed in resistive networks to recover the left, right, front, and rear audio information from the encoded input signal. Thus, LF + LR = 2L; RR + RF = 2R; LR + RR = 2R (rear); LF + RF = 2F (front). Although the audio signals may be applied to identical speakers, many quadraphonic installations utilize high-fidelity speakers for L and R reproduction only; utility-type speakers are often used for RR

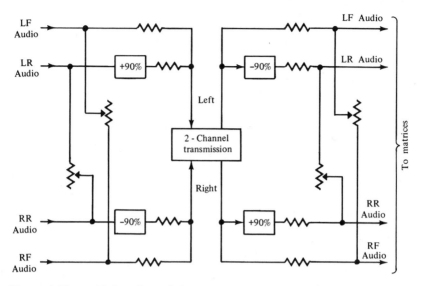

**Figure 6-10**    A 90-deg phase-shift encoder-decoder system.

and LR reproduction. Utility-type speakers are less costly, and many audio buffs feel that the rear speakers in a quadraphonic system contribute chiefly to sound reinforcement, whereas the front speakers develop the basic fidelity of reproduction.

## 6-4  PRINCIPLES OF SQ OPERATION

Although the stereo-quad (SQ) quadriphonic system is similar in many respects to the QS system, its signal-processing action includes gain-riding circuitry for enhancement of front-rear separation. A circuit diagram for an SQ quadraphonic decoder that employs three integrated circuits is shown in Fig. 6-11. The SQ system is a Columbia Broadcasting System development. *IC*1 is the SQ matrix decoder. The *IC* operates in combination with RC phase-shifting networks to provide decoding action. *IC*2 is a four-channel voltage-controlled amplifier that accepts the prevailing digital-logic commands and translates them into enhanced front-rear separation. *IC*3 develops the logic voltages that control the amplifiers in *IC*2. *IC*1 comprises two preamplifiers that are fed with LT (left total) and RT (right total) signals, respectively. Each preamplifier, in turn, drives an all-pass network that generates two LT signals in quadrature and two RT signals in quadrature. Final matrixing action then develops the four separate audio signals that drive the speakers.

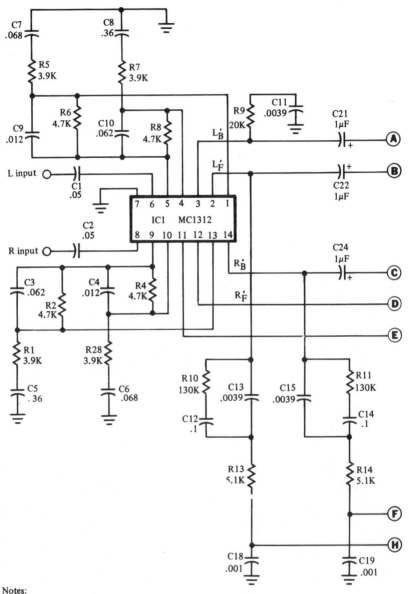

Notes:
Power supply +20V DC @ 75mA
C33, C34, C35, C36 values depend on
load of following stage. Use 0.3μF
for input impedance of 100000 ohms;
0.5μF for input impedance of 50000 ohms.
All resistors 1/4 watt 5% .
All electrolytics 25V or higher.

**Figure 6-11** Schematic diagram for an SQ quadraphonic decoder.

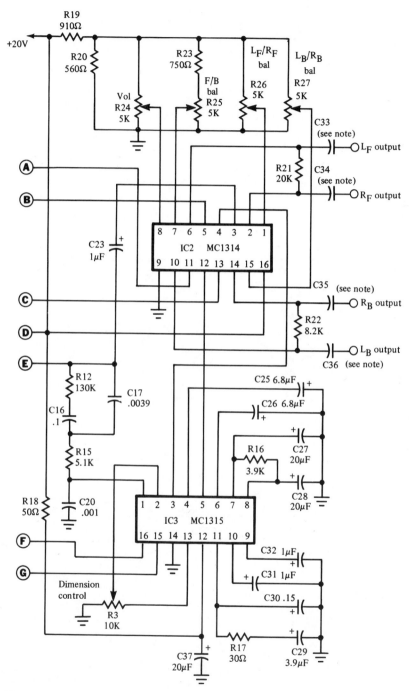

**Figure 6-11** Continued

177

With reference to Fig. 6-11, *IC2*, which provides four voltage-controlled attenuators for varying the amplifier gains, can be set for relative gain between channels by means of three external DC voltages. *IC2* also operates with a master volume control and with the front/rear balance controls. *IC3* provides gain-riding action for optimization of front-rear separation. This IC also provides variable DC logic enhancement (dimension control) for greater flexibility of the basic SQ decoder performance. This decoder is utilized only to play back quadraphonic records. The circuit board for the SQ decoder appears as seen in Fig. 6-12. A separate power supply is used with the decoder; it provides 20 V at 75 mA. The five maintenance controls are not mounted on the circuit board, but are connected to the printed circuitry via cable leads.

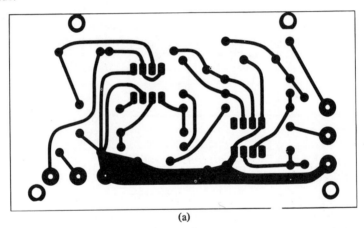

(a)

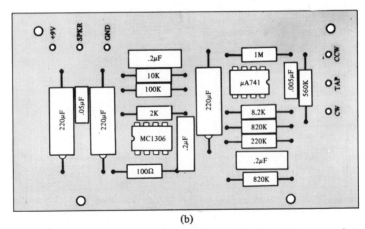

(b)

**Figure 6-12** Layout of the SQ quadraphonic decoder diagrammed in Fig. 7-11: (a) circuit board; (b) parts placement.

## 6-5    AUDIOSCOPE MONITOR OPERATION

Elaborate stereophonic-quadraphonic systems may include a built-in audioscope to monitor system operation. This is essentially a specialized design of oscilloscope with convenient controls for displaying individual left-front, right-front, left-rear, and right-rear signals. These waveforms are displayed on a linear time base (see Fig. 6-13), with a triggered-sweep function. Channel separation can be checked either on a conventional time base, or by means of Lissajous patterns. When the first method is used, an R signal is applied to the stereo section of the system, for example. In turn, the output from the R channel is displayed on the screen and its amplitude is noted. Then, the output from the L channel is displayed; in theory, its amplitude would be zero, but in practice there will be some residual output from the L channel. As an illustration, if the separation is 30 dB, the L-channel output will be approximately 3 percent of the R-channel output. Similarly, the separation of the LF and LR channels can be checked.

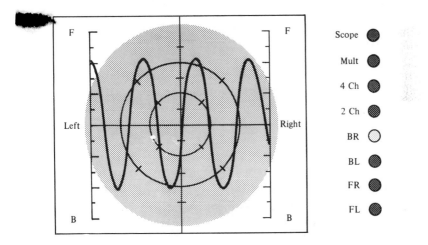

**Figure 6-13**    Typical screen display on built-in hi-fi audioscope.

When the second method is used, an R signal, for example, is applied to the stereo section of the receiver. The output from the R channel is applied to the vertical amplifier of the audioscope, and the output from the L channel is applied to the horizontal amplifier. In turn, a Lissajous pattern is displayed, as exemplified in Fig. 6-14. If separation were perfect, a precisely vertical trace would be displayed on the screen. However, because there is inevitably some residual output from

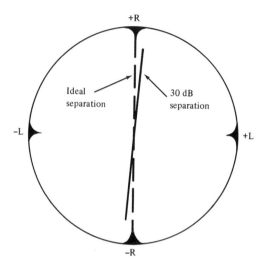

**Figure 6-14**    Lissajous patterns show channel separation.

the L channel, the trace will be more or less inclined on the screen, an example for 30 dB separation is shown. If the separation were zero, the trace would be inclined at an angle of 45 deg. Similarly, the separation of the LF and LR channels, or of the RF and RR channels can be checked, provided that suitable quadraphonic test signals are available. For example, demonstration tapes or records are a convenient source of individual test signals.

An audioscope often includes a built-in audio oscillator with a frequency range from 20 Hz to 20 kHz. However, supplementary stereo or quad signal generators must be employed for specialized test techniques. The built-in audio oscillator is useful for frequency-response checks of the preamplifiers and the power amplifiers in the system. It is also utilized for checking distortion. A distortion test is made by applying the audio-oscillator output to the amplifier under test, and feeding this input signal to the vertical amplifier of the audioscope. Also, the output signal from the amplifier under test is fed to the horizontal amplifier of the audioscope. In turn, a Lissajous pattern is displayed. If the amplifier were distortionless, a precisely straight trace would be displayed on the screen, inclined at a 45-deg angle. In practice, there is at least a slight amount of residual distortion, although it might be very small in normal operation. Distortion has the effect of introducing curvature into the trace (see Fig. 6-15). The acceptable limit for hi-fi reproduction is 2 percent distortion. This amount of curvature is evident when the trace is observed with a critical eye.

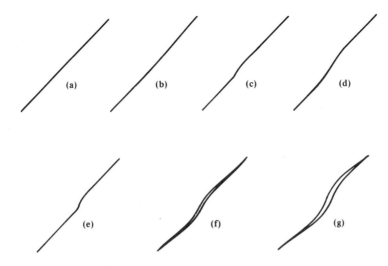

**Figure 6-15**   Lissajous figures with various percentages of distortion: **(a)** negligible; **(b)** 1 percent harmonic distortion; **(c)** 1.5 percent distortion; **(d)** 2 percent distortion; **(e)** 3 percent distortion; **(f)** 5 percent distortion; **(g)** 10 percent distortion; with noticeable phase shift.

It is evident that the vertical and horizontal amplifiers in an audioscope must have less distortion than the amplifier or system under test. A typical audioscope has amplifiers rated for less than 1 percent distortion. With reference to Fig. 6-15(g), a Lissajous pattern will disclose the presence of phase shift between the input and output signals of an amplifier. It is advisable to check for phase shift at a frequency such as 1 kHz, instead of very low or very high frequencies. In other words, any amplifier will develop phase shift when it is operated at a frequency near its cutoff limit. On the other hand, if an amplifier develops phase shift at a test frequency of 1 kHz, this response would be regarded as a trouble symptom. Phase shift can be caused by either component or device faults, and a systematic analysis of circuit operation would be required to pinpoint the defect.

An audioscope is also used to indicate relative signal strength, and can be connected as an FM tuning indicator. If the associated tuner or receiver has a multipath scope output terminal, the audioscope can be switched to check for FM multipath reception. As a general-purpose instrument, an audioscope will usually serve as a high-performance conventional oscilloscope, with a frequency response up to 200 kHz, for example. The time-base range is typically from 10 Hz to 100 kHz. Thus, an audioscope can be used for general troubleshooting procedures in monophonic, stereophonic, and quadraphonic audio equipment. Some audioscopes are designed to match particular cases or cabinets, so that the instrument blends with its associated audio system. Most audioscopes utilize 3-in. cathode ray tubes.

## 6-6 DIMENSIONED STEREO REPRODUCTION

Stereophonic sound increases the realism of reproduction, because it provides a distinction between sounds originating from the left and from the right of the listener. Quadraphonic sound further increases the realism of reproduction by adding a distinction between sounds originating from the front and from the rear of the listener. Despite these directional sound vectors, little information is provided by either system concerning the distance of the sound source from the listener. In other words, neither stereo reproduction nor quadraphonic reproduction can provide precise spatial localization of a sound source. In other words, an additional factor is required in sound reproduction to provide dimension, so that the sound source can be identified by distance units as well as by angle units from the listener. This additional factor is called *biphonic sound reproduction.*

Biphonic sound reproduction is readily accomplished, if the listener utilizes earphones. This entails a certain modification of the conventional stereo technique regarding L and R microphone placement. For biphonic reproduction, the L and R microphones are mounted on a plastic dummy head, so that the sound intensity and phase is processed as in actual hearing on its course to the L and R microphones. In addition, the microphone on each side of the plastic dummy head is mounted in a housing that provides approximately the same frequency characteristics as the human ear. When these specialized microphones are used to make a stereo recording, and the recording is played back into earphones, three-dimensional sound reproduction is obtained. A sense of distance and precise localization of the sound source is thereby provided in the biphonic technique.

Most audio enthusiasts prefer speakers to earphones. In order to obtain effective biphonic sound reproduction with speakers, the system must be elaborated to some extent. This elaboration consists in the addition of a special cross-coupling network between the L and R speakers. In other words, some of the output from the L channel is fed through an equalizer and a short time-delay unit into the right channel. Similarly, some of the output from the R channel is fed through another equalizer and another short time-delay unit into the L channel, as shown in Fig. 6-16. When the equalizers and the time-delay units are

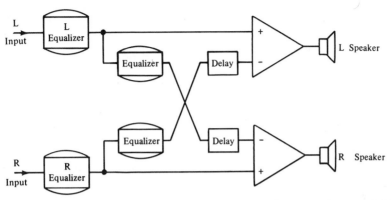

**Figure 6-16**  Cross-channel coupling utilized in speaker reproduction of bi-phonic sound.

precisely adjusted, and the listener positions himself in a restricted part of the area in front of the speakers, biphonic sound reproduction is experienced. The listener is then aware of the location of the original sound source, whether it is in front, behind, to the left, or to the right, and he is also aware of the distance of the original sound source from the recording microphones.

## 6-7  SPEAKER ARRANGEMENTS

A typical small speaker is depicted in Fig. 6-17. An isolated speaker has poor efficiency, and it cannot reproduce low frequencies. In other words, the sound energy from the rear of the cone tends to cancel out the sound energy from the front of the cone, and this cancellation becomes more nearly complete as the operating frequency is decreased. Therefore, a practical speaker arrangement employs some means for prevention of this cancellation. The most basic means is a baffle board.

**Figure 6-17**  Typical small speaker. (*Courtesy of Radio Shack, a Tandy Corp. company.*)

This is a shielding structure or partition that serves to increase the effective length of the external transmission path between the front and the back of the cone. A baffle also increases the efficiency of a speaker by increasing its acoustic loading. *Acoustics* is defined as the science of production, transmission, reception, and effects of sound. This term also denotes the characteristics of a room, or other location, which control reflections of sound waves and the reception in the room.

A speaker is usually mounted in a cabinet. This cabinet may be constructed so that it absorbs the sound energy from the rear of the cone. Again, the cabinet may be designed with a suitable acoustic structure that recovers the sound from the rear of the cone and radiates it in phase with the sound from the front of the cone. Low audio frequencies are reproduced to best advantage by a speaker with a large-diameter cone. This type of speaker is called a *woofer*. Cone diameters up to 15 inches are utilized. On the other hand, a woofer does not reproduce high audio frequencies efficiently. Accordingly, a speaker system customarily includes a speaker with a small-diameter cone for radiation of the higher audio frequencies. This kind of speaker is called a *tweeter*. Many tweeters are designed with small horns to increase their acoustical efficiency. A speaker system may also include a midrange speaker, often termed a *squawker*. A midrange speaker has a cone diameter of 5 or 6 inches.

An example of a small speaker cabinet is shown in Fig. 6-18. The baffle board is cut for installation of a 12-in. woofer, a 6-in. squawker, and a 3½-in. tweeter. Some baffles are designed with a small cutout (port) to feed some of the sound energy from the rear of the speaker cones out of the cabinet to combine with the sound energy from the front of the cones. This type of speaker cabinet is called a bass-reflex speaker system. The port has somewhat critical dimensions and must be properly located. In many designs, the port has the form of an elongated slot along the lower portion of the baffle board. A ported cabinet is sometimes supplemented by an interior labyrinth construction. This is an air channel structure that increases the distance that the sound energy from the rear of the cones must travel before it emerges from the front of the baffle board. Sometimes a tuned port is employed; acoustic tuning is provided by a short tube extending into the cabinet from the rear of the port. Length of the tuning tube is critical, and is determined by experiment.

**Speaker Interconnections**    Speakers may be interconnected in various ways. For example, two or more speakers may be connected in parallel, as depicted in Fig. 6-19. In this example, each speaker has a rated impedance of 8 Ω. It is evident that the input impedance of two 8-Ω

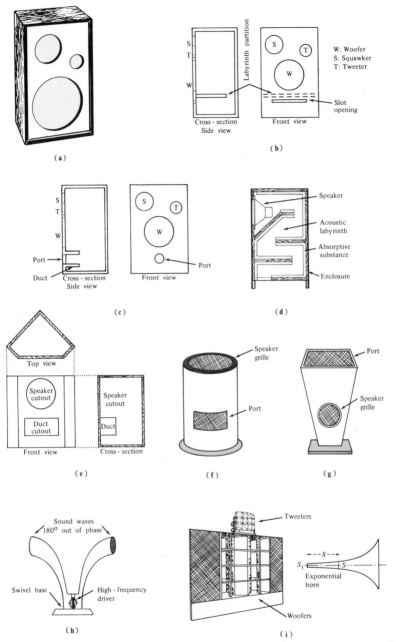

**Figure 6-18** Examples of small speaker cabinets: **(a)** basic arrangement; **(b)** labyrinth construction; **(c)** ducted port design; **(d)** elaborated labyrinth design; **(e)** corner enclosure; **(f)** tuned-column speaker enclosure; **(g)** basic baffle-horn enclosure; **(h)** tweeter dipole horn arrangement; **(i)** typical theater woofer-tweeter installation.

185

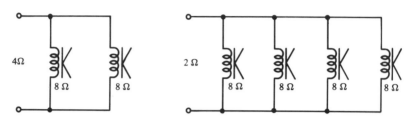

**Figure 6-19**    Examples of parallel-connected speakers.

speakers connected in parallel will be 4 Ω. Similarly, the input impedance of four 8-Ω speakers connected in parallel will be 2 Ω. Next, consider the input impedance to a pair of speakers connected in parallel, one of which has a rated impedance of 8 Ω, and the other of which has a rated impedance of 4 Ω, as seen in Fig. 6-20. These impedance values have a combined value of 2.67 Ω. The essential consideration is that the 4-Ω speaker will draw twice as much audio current as the 8-Ω speaker. Therefore, if both speakers have the same cone diameters and efficiency, the 4-Ω speaker will radiate much more sound energy than the 8-Ω speaker. In most situations, this would be an undesirable condition.

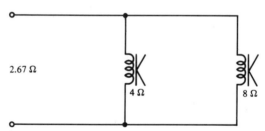

**Figure 6-20**    An 8-Ω speaker connected in parallel with a 4-Ω speaker.

With reference to Fig. 6-21, the other basic method of speaker interconnection is the series arrangement. This mode of operation results in an input impedance to the system that is greater than the impedance of an individual speaker. In other words, the system input impedance is equal to the sum of the impedances of the individual speakers. If a low-impedance speaker is connected in series with a high-impedance speaker, the audio voltage drop will be greater across the latter than across the former. Accordingly, if both speakers have the same cone diameters and the same efficiency, the high-impedance speaker will radiate more sound energy than the low-impedance speaker. As before, this would be an undesirable condition in most situations.

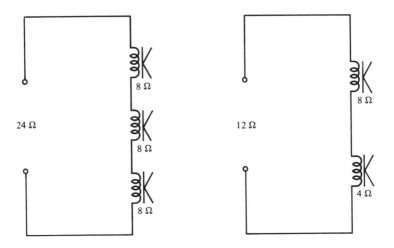

**Figure 6-21** Examples of series interconnection.

A speaker system may also be operated in a series-parallel interconnection arrangement, as exemplified in Fig. 6-22. Each of the speakers in this configuration has a rated impedance value of 8 Ω. Therefore, each series string has an input impedance of 24 Ω, and the two parallel-connected series strings have an input impedance of 12 Ω. If identical speakers are employed, each speaker will consume the same amount of audio power. On the other hand, if the speakers have different impedances, they will draw different amounts of audio power. The principles outlined previously can be applied to calculate the relative power values drawn by each speaker.

**Crossover Circuitry** When a tweeter is used with a woofer in a speaker system, neither a simple series connection nor a simple parallel connection is suitable. In other words, a tweeter cannot withstand high power at low frequencies; a woofer is very inefficient at high frequencies, and largely wastes any high-frequency audio power that is applied. Therefore, a crossover network is utilized. A crossover network is an electrical filter that separates the amplifier output signal into two or more separate frequency bands for a multispeaker system. The crossover frequency is the frequency at which equal power is delivered to each of the adjacent frequency channels when all channels are terminated in the specified load.

A simple crossover arrangement (which is sometimes adequate) is depicted in Fig. 6-23. The tweeter is connected in parallel with the woofer, with a series capacitor between the two speakers. It follows

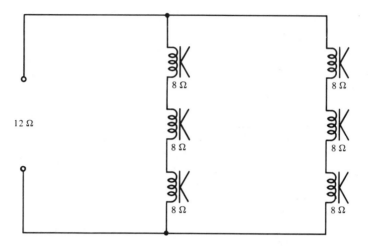

**Figure 6-22** Series-parallel interconnection arrangement.

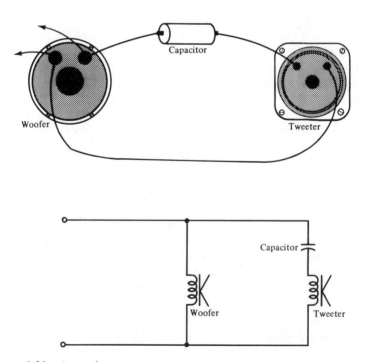

**Figure 6-23** A simple crossover arrangement.

that at some frequency, the reactance (impedance) of the capacitor will be equal to the impedance of the tweeter. This is the crossover frequency. The value of the crossover frequency is determined by the value of the capacitor. For example, suppose that a 4-$\mu$F capacitor is connected in series with an 8-$\Omega$ tweeter. In this case, the crossover frequency will be approximately 5 kHz. Again, if an 8-$\mu$F capacitor is employed, the crossover frequency will be approximately 2.5 kHz. Paper capacitors are utilized in the better-quality crossover networks. Electrolytic capacitors may be used, if they are of the nonpolarized type.

At the crossover frequency, the power delivered to the tweeter is one-half of the audio power applied to the capacitor-speaker combination. In other words, the power demand of the tweeter decreases by 3 dB from its high-frequency value to its crossover-frequency value. Thus, the series capacitor prevents low audio frequencies from flowing into the tweeter. Note that high audio frequencies are not prevented from flowing into the woofer by this simple arrangement. In turn, if the woofer happens to be of a type that can reproduce frequencies above the crossover value appreciably, both of the speakers will reproduce midrange sound energy, with the result that the midrange audio frequencies may be overemphasized. Therefore, many crossover networks include an inductor connected in series with the woofer, as shown in Fig. 6-24.

An inductor has the opposite reactance with respect to a capacitor. In other words, as the frequency increases, the reactance (impedance) of an inductor increases. If an inductor has a value of approximately 0.25 mH, it will have an impedance of 8 $\Omega$ at 5 kHz. If the inductance value is increased to 0.5 mH, the crossover frequency will be approximately 2.5 kHz. Consider the total impedance that a speaker system with a crossover network presents to the amplifier that energizes it. If 8-$\Omega$ speakers are employed in the arrangement of Fig. 6-24, it might seem that the net impedance of the system would be 4 $\Omega$. However, this would be an incorrect conclusion, because the capacitor and the inductor have different impedances at different frequencies. It can be shown that this crossover network will hold the system input impedance practically constant at 8 $\Omega$ when proper $L$ and $C$ values are chosen.

Refer to Fig. 6-25. As shown in the examples, the system input impedance remains virtually 8 $\Omega$ at 10 times and at $1/10$ of the crossover frequency. Note that speakers have some inductance, in addition to resistance. This causes the speaker impedance to rise somewhat as the frequency increases. Consequently, the impedance values could be somewhat different from those indicated in Fig. 6-25. However, this is not necessarily the case, because an efficient tweeter can be selected

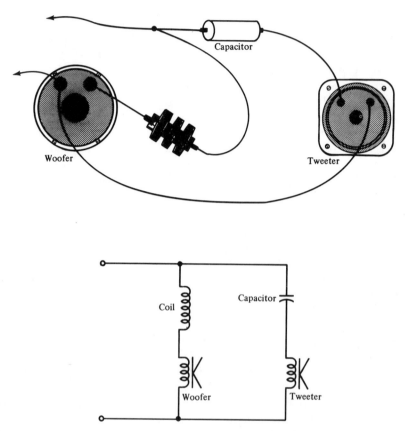

**Figure 6-24**    Example of an *LC* crossover network.

for use with a woofer, and the increase of the woofer impedance at high frequencies can be offset by the changing input impedance to the tweeter. If a simple crossover network is used, as depicted in Fig. 6-24, the rising impedance of the woofer at higher frequencies operates to prevent the system impedance from falling below 8 Ω at the high end of the audio band. Note that the DC resistance of an inductor in a crossover network should be comparatively small. For this reason, the coil is typically wound with no. 18 copper wire. A plastic core with a diameter of 1 in. may be used; the coil may be random-wound on the core. A typical "spool" has a winding cross section of 1 in.² Professional crossover inductors may utilize universal or progressive type windings, with more than one section, connected in series-aiding.

As noted previously, room acoustics can vary considerably from one location to another. Also, some tweeters are more efficient than

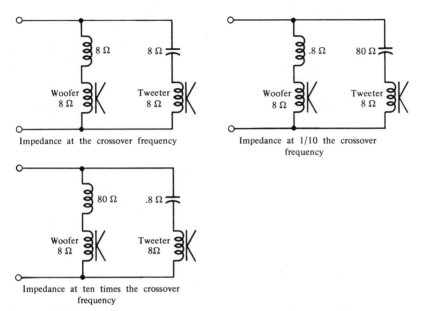

Impedance at the crossover frequency

Impedance at 1/10 the crossover frequency

Impedance at ten times the crossover frequency

**Figure 6-25**   Examples of system input impedances at three different audio frequencies.

others. Therefore, to achieve optimum tonal balance, it is general practice to include a level control in the tweeter branch, as exemplified in Fig. 6-26. Note that tweeters are usually more efficient than woofers, so that the audio current flow to the tweeter must usually be attenuated to some extent. A wirewound rheostat or potentiometer rated for at least 2 W of power dissipation should be utilized. A total resistance of 50 Ω is suitable, unless a horn-type tweeter (previously noted) is employed that requires a resistance range up to 150 Ω.

**Speaker Phasing**   It is essential that a pair of speakers in a system be connected in phase with each other. If the speakers are connected out of phase, the radiation from one speaker will tend to cancel the radiation from the other. This cancellation becomes most apparent for bass tones. To operate in-phase, the speaker cones must move in the same direction at the same time when a voltage is applied at the input of the speaker circuit. With reference to Fig. 6-27, most speakers have a red dot for checking phase in the wiring circuit. In the case of a parallel connection, the red-dot terminals of the speakers are connected together. In the case of a series connection, the red-dot terminal on one speaker will be connected to the contrary colored terminal on the other speaker (this may be a black dot, for example).

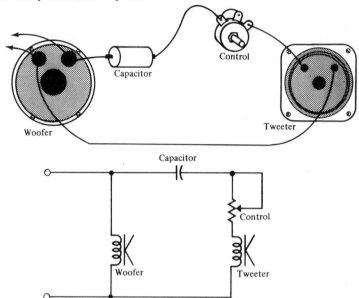

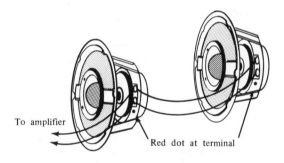

**Figure 6-26**    Level control in a tweeter branch.

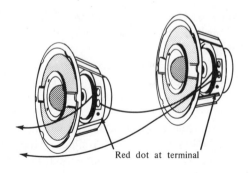

To amplifier

Red dot at terminal

(a) Parallel connection.

Red dot at terminal

**Figure 6-27**    Examples    of
speaker phasing.

(b) Series connection.

**Power Capability** A high-quality super-high-power speaker system is illustrated in Fig. 6-28. Two of these speaker enclosures would be employed in a stereo system, and four of these enclosures would be utilized in a quadriphonic system. A 15-in. woofer is used, with a multicell midrange horn for smooth 800–8000-Hz response and superior sound dispersion. A high-compliance tweeter horn develops clean response from 8000–25,000 Hz. Midrange and tweeter level controls are provided for compatibility to either acoustically "live" or acoustically "dead" rooms. The massive 15-in. acoustic suspension woofer has a brass voice coil that provides full bass response down to 20 Hz. A power capability of 100-W music-power surges is provided.

**Figure 6-28** A high-quality super-high-power speaker system. (*Courtesy of Radio Shack, a Tandy Corp. company.*)

Some audio enthusiasts prefer to build their own speaker enclosures. Speakers are selected first, before any type of enclosure is chosen. After the number and types of speakers have been selected, a suitable enclosure can be designed or chosen. Thus, if a listener is interested chiefly in bass output and dynamic range, he will select a corresponding type of speaker design and a matching enclosure. However, if a listener is interested primarily in high-fidelity output, he will select another type of speaker design and a different kind of matching enclosure. In either case, the question arises concerning how much audio power can be applied without damage to the speaker(s). In any case, a speaker should not be operated at a power level greater than its maximum power rating. In some situations, this maximum power value requires derating. For example, if a speaker is to be driven by an electronic organ, it is good practice to observe a power derating factor of 50 percent.

With reference to Fig. 6-29, a skeleton cross-sectional view of a speaker is shown. Bass tones are produced by large organ pipes, oboes, and so on. In turn, bass radiation would be expected to require large speaker cones. Moreover, loud bass reproduction requires comparatively great displacement (travel) of the cone; this requires deep skiver rolls, or an equivalent cone suspension. Catalog listings often use the term "cloth roll suspension" to indicate this design. Note that although large cones (such as 12-in. to 15-in. types) with "soft" suspensions are well adapted for reproduction of bass tones, these cones are too heavy to vibrate efficiently at high audio frequencies. Consequently, the frequency range of a large cone is somewhat limited.

When operated at high audio frequencies, such as 10 kHz, a speaker cone has a comparatively small displacement. In turn, a lightweight 5-in. cone with a stiff suspension is suitable for reproducing treble tones. As noted previously, a tweeter may employ a small cone, with a supplementary horn for acoustical impedance matching. In various designs, a tweeter is combined in the same frame (basket) with a woofer. This design is termed a *two-way* or *coaxial speaker*. Again, a 12-in. woofer may be combined with a 6-in. midrange cone and a 3-in. tweeter. This design is called a three-way coaxial speaker. Coaxial speakers generally have built-in crossover networks.

When a drumhead is tightened, it becomes "stiffer," and its resonant frequency is increased. In the same manner, a stiffer cone suspension has a higher resonant frequency than a "soft" suspension. This stiffness factor is determined by the design of the skiver rolls and the spider assembly in the speaker. Another major parameter in speaker resonance is the total mass of the cone and voice-coil arrangement. The volume of air behind a speaker in an airtight enclosure provides effective stiffness to the suspension and raises the resonant frequency of the speaker. In practice, a type of enclosure that compensates for the resonant peak of the speaker is commonly used, in order to obtain greater uniformity of output over the low-frequency end of the audio range.

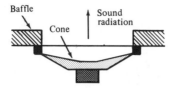

(a) Placement of a speaker against baffle

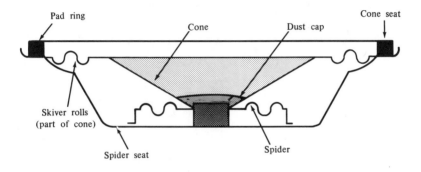

(b) Basic constructional features

**Figure 6-29**   Skeleton cross section of a speaker. (*Courtesy of Radio Shack, a Tandy Corp. company.*)

**Voice Coils and Their Magnetic Circuits**   With reference to Fig. 6-30, the design of typical voice coils and magnets is depicted. The voice coil is firmly secured to the speaker cone. A large voice coil will handle a comparatively large amount of power. However, a large voice coil has lower efficiency and poorer high-frequency response than a small voice coil. A small voice coil has limited power-handling capability; on the other hand, it has comparatively high efficiency and comparatively good high-frequency response. In practice, voice coils have a minimum diameter of approximately ½ in., and a maximum diameter of about 3 in. A commercial sound installation generally employs speakers with 1-in. voice coils; this type of speaker generally uses a 6.8-oz Alnico-V, or a 10-oz barium ferrite magnet. Note that a large voice coil requires a large magnet to realize its potential operating efficiency. Economy-type speakers ordinarily have a minimum magnet weight of ½ oz of Alnico-V, with a ½-in. voice coil. In mass-produced units, magnet

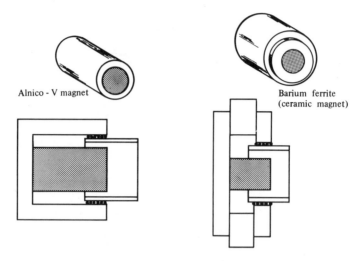

Alnico - V magnet

Barium ferrite
(ceramic magnet)

**Figure 6-30** Typical voice-coil and magnet design. (*Courtesy of Radio Shack, a Tandy Corp. company.*)

weights range up to 3 lb of Alnico-V, operating in combination with 3-in. voice coils.

Power ratings of speakers are dependent upon both electrical and mechanical design factors. A speaker's audio power capability is limited by the amount of heat that the voice coil can dissipate. Its mechanical power capability is determined by the distance that the voice coil can be displaced. In other words, as the power level is increased, the voice coil or spider will reach a maximum travel, beyond which point it strikes a metal part of the speaker. This abnormal condition is called *bottoming*. In turn, the maximum power rating of a speaker may be determined by its audio power capability, or by its mechanical power limit, whichever is less. However, it should not be supposed that a power rating of a speaker represents an absolute maximum rating that must never be exceeded under any operating condition.

For example, if a sealed enclosure is employed, the cone and its voice coil are restricted to less displacement than if the enclosure were unsealed. In turn, a higher audio power level can be utilized, provided only that the heat-dissipation capability of the voice coil is not exceeded. Electrical power ratings are sine-wave (rms) ratings, unless otherwise specified. That is, a speaker can process a recorded-music power value greater than its rms power rating, whether the speaker enclosure is sealed or unsealed. As noted previously, a recorded-music waveform is not sinusoidal; it is characterized by occasional power peaks, with sufficient time between peaks for the voice coil to cool. However, the power input should always be limited to a level that the voice coil does not "bottom" against the speaker frame.

The acoustic-suspension design features a suspension that permits extended voice-coil travel before bottoming occurs. Greater efficiency is thus obtained in low-frequency operation, a lower frequency limit is realized, and the cone's resonant frequency is reduced. Large-cone acoustic-suspension speakers have essentially the same high-frequency limitations as the more conventional large-cone speaker designs. Some speaker manufacturers employ an expedient to obtain improved high-frequency performance at moderate production cost. This expedient consists of a small horn-shaped cone that is mounted coaxially with the large cone. This "whizzer" cone increases high-frequency acoustic radiation because of its comparatively light weight and stiff construction. If maximum high-fidelity response is not required of an installation, this type of speaker will often be a good choice.

Note that if a 12-in. speaker and a 15-in. speaker are both driven to develop the same amount of acoustical power at 50 Hz, the 12-in. cone must move twice the distance that the 15-in. cone moves. If two 12-in. speakers are utilized in a system, each of their voice coils will be displaced only one-half as much as if a single 12-in. speaker were utilized. Audio enthusiasts who prefer to build their own speaker enclosures should keep all of the foregoing design factors in mind. An important consideration in operation of sealed enclosures is to observe sufficiently sturdy construction that cracks and "blowholes" will not develop when the speaker system is radiating maximum acoustical power. Any air leak that develops in a sealed speaker enclosure is likely to result in serious damage to the speaker on peak power intervals.

# 7

---

# Electronic Organs

## 7-1 GENERAL CONSIDERATIONS

Electronic organs can be regarded as high-fidelity systems in some respects. On the other hand, there are basic functional differences to be considered. In the first analysis, an electronic organ is designed to *produce* musical tones, whereas a high-fidelity system is designed to *reproduce* musical tones. This distinction becomes apparent when the functional sections of an organ are compared with those of a hi-fi system. For example, an organ employs tone generators, keying circuits, voicing sections with formant filters, tremolo and percussion circuitry, preamplifiers, power amplifiers, and speakers. A hi-fi system utilizes preamplifiers, equalizers, preamplifiers, power amplifiers, and speakers; audio signal sources include tape decks, turntables, tuners, and microphones. In other words, the elements common to electronic organs and high-fidelity systems are limited to the amplifier and speaker sections. Note in passing that an electronic organ is a distinctive musical instrument, and that various of its voices are unique.

Although the schematic diagram for an electronic organ appears to be highly complex, its fundamental simplicity is seen when the configuration is divided into functional sections. Thus, a filter function may be repeated many times, with progressive minor changes in component values. Again, a keyboard switching circuit is repeated many times. A typical electronic organ contains five main functional sections comprising tone generators (audio generators), keying (switching) networks, voicing (formant filter) sections, audio amplifiers, and tone cabinets (speakers). All modern organs employ solid-state circuitry, and much of the keying arrangement utilizes logic-gate technology that was originally developed for digital-computer systems. Most of the organ networks have direct-coupled circuitry, although RC coupling is also used to some extent. Audio generators (tone generators) develop complex waveforms with both even and odd harmonic content. There is a trend to oscillator circuitry that includes J-K flip-flops that were formerly used only in digital-computer systems.

## 7-2 BASIC ORGANIZATION AND FUNCTIONS

A popular type of electronic organ is illustrated in Fig. 7-1. It provides a 44-note manual and a 13-note pedal board with numerous tab switches. A skeleton block diagram for this instrument is shown in Fig. 7-2; it indicates the main sections, with signal progression from one

**Figure 7-1**  A 44-note manual and 13-note pedal board with 35 controls are provided by this modern electronic organ. (*Courtesy of Heath* Co.)

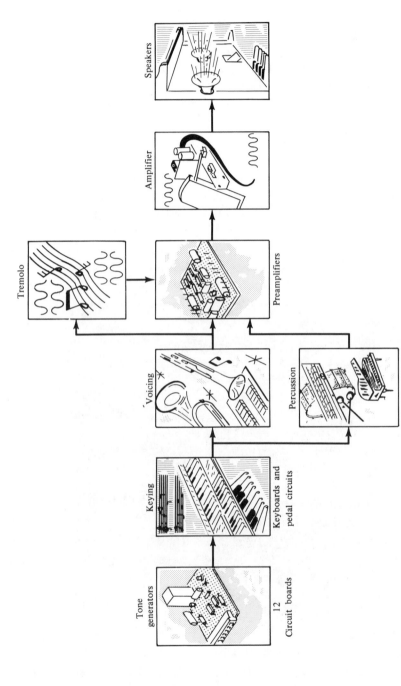

**Figure 7-2** Skeleton block diagram for electronic organ: (a) arrangement; (b) illustration of elaborate electronic organ. (*Courtesy of Baldwin.*)

**Figure 7-2**  *Continued*

section to another. Each tone in the organ is produced by one of the 12 tone generators, which operate continuously. The keying, or "keyswitching" sections that include the keyboards, pedals, and keyer circuits connect the desired tone signals to the voicing and percussion sections. The voicing section consists of various types of filter circuits that are operated by tab switches and which give the tones the desired timbre or quality. The percussion circuits alter the tones to sound as if a percussion instrument is also being played.

Output signals from the voicing and percussion circuits are coupled to the preamplifiers, which amplify the signals and apply them to the power amplifier section. The output from the voicing section can also be applied to the preamplifier through the tremolo circuits in order to phase-modulate the signal at a rate of approximately six times per second. From the preamplifiers, the audio signals are coupled to the output amplifier, which increases the signal power and applies them to the speakers. With reference to Fig. 7-3, 12 tone-generator circuit boards are utilized in this example. One tone generator is provided for each note of the musical scale. All 12 tone generators are identical except for values of tuning capacitors $C1$-TG and $C2$-TG, and the voltage-divider capacitor $C3$-TG in Fig. 7-4. These 12 oscillator frequencies are developed with only three different sets of values for these capacitors. Each set allows the tone generators to be adjusted by inductor $L1$-TG through a range of four different notes.

## 7-3  MASTER OSCILLATOR OPERATION

Each tone-generator circuit board in this example contains a master oscillator and two IC frequency dividers. The master oscillator delivers an output signal to its corresponding key and also provides a signal for the first frequency divider on the tone-generator circuit board. A modified Hartley circuit is used for the master oscillators. When the power switch is turned on, supply voltage is applied to each master oscillator. The collector current in transistor $Q1$-TG (Fig. 7-4) develops a voltage drop across resistor $R3$-TG. This voltage drop causes the collector voltage to decrease (to become less positive).

Observe that the collector end of inductor $L1$-TG also becomes less positive at this time, as a result of collector-voltage decrease. Because of the mutual coupling between the two halves of the inductor, the opposite end, which is connected to the transistor base terminal via resistor $R1$-TG and capacitor $C2$-TG, becomes more positive. This increase in positive potential causes the collector current of $Q1$-TG to increase, and a further drop in collector voltage ensues. This is a regenerative process, and it drives the collector into saturation. When saturation occurs, the field around the opposite end of the inductor collapses, all polarities are reversed, and the collector current starts to decrease. In turn, the base becomes negative, and the collector current is cut off.

After the collector current is cut off, the tuned circuit continues to cause current flow in the same direction until tuning capacitors $C1$-TG and $C3$-TG are fully charged. At this point, the capacitors then start to discharge, thereby building up a field in the inductor again; all polarities reverse, and a new cycle of operation starts. The output waveform from the master oscillator is rich in both the even and odd harmonics that are essential for development of desirable organ tones.

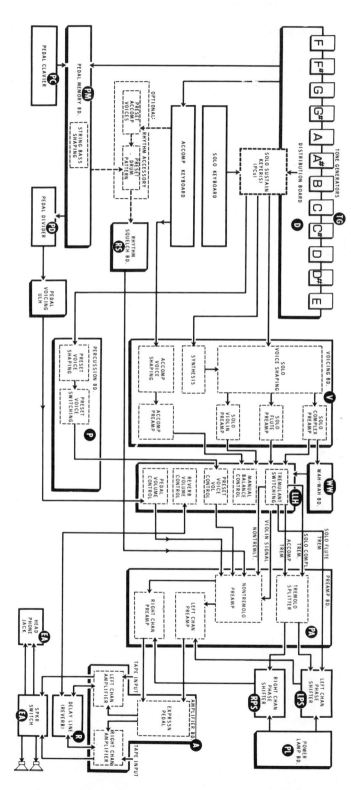

**Figure 7-3** General block diagram. (Courtesy of Heath Co.)

203

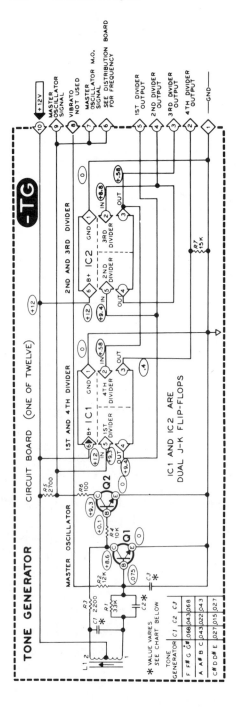

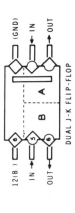

**Figure 7-4**    Tone generator configuration. *(Courtesy of Heath Co.)*

Recall that a square wave has odd harmonics only, that a full-rectified sine waveform has even harmonics only, and that a sawtooth waveform has both even and odd harmonics. The tone-generator output is depicted in Fig. 7-5. In addition to its even- and odd-harmonic content, the steep negative-going excursion indicated by the arrow is amplified by transistor $Q2$-TG and is utilized as a driving pulse for the first frequency divider.

**Figure 7-5** Tone-generator output waveform. (*Redrawn with permission of Heath* Co.)

## 7-4 FREQUENCY DIVIDER OPERATION

Each of the tone generators in this example has five output signals. The highest frequency output is obtained directly from the master oscillator. In turn, this master-oscillator signal is divided by two dual flip-flop circuits (*IC*1-TG and *IC*2-TG in Fig. 7-4) to develop the remaining four output signals. Note that the output signal from a flip-flop is always one-half of the input signal frequency. In other words, two cycles are required at the input to form one cycle at the output. A simplified block diagram of flip-flop interconnections is shown in Fig. 7-6. Frequency-divider relations are indicated by the idealized waveforms. Note that the output from each flip-flop, in addition to being applied to the input of the following flip-flop, also serves as one of the tone-generator outputs.

Thus, the five outputs from the master oscillator and the four frequency dividers permit each tone generator to cover a five-octave range. These 12 tone generators are plugged in 12 sets of pins provided along the edge of a distribution circuit board. Outputs from the tone generators are connected to packaged circuits (PC's) that are installed on the distribution board. These PC's function as signal-mixing networks. A schematic diagram of the resistive mixing circuits and their idealized input waveshapes is shown in Fig. 7-7. Each tone-generator board provides the various octaves of output signals for a particular note. The master oscillator develops an output signal that is rich in even and odd harmonics. However, the output waveforms from the frequency dividers are essentially square waves that contain only odd harmonics. However, the printed circuitry modifies the output waveform from each frequency divider so that it contains both even and odd harmonics before application to the accompaniment keyboard.

For example: C Tone generator

| Output | Frequency | Note |
|---|---|---|
| Master oscillator (M.O. ) | 2093.003 | C6 |
| First divider | 1046.502 | C5 |
| Second divider | 523.251 | C4 |
| Third divider | 261.626 | C3 |
| Fourth divider | 130.813 | C2 |

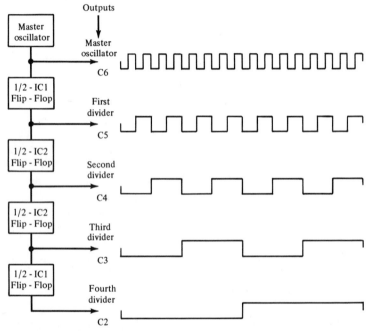

**Figure 7-6**  Elementary block diagram of flip-flop interconnections.

Mixing circuits are not required for the frequency-divider signals employed by the solo keyboard, because these signals are mixed in the solo voicing circuits. Mixing networks utilized in each printed circuit are simple Y arrangements, as depicted in Fig. 7-8. Two tone-generator signal sources are isolated by the 100-kΩ and 220-kΩ resistors, and the output currents from the resistors combine to form a staircase waveform. The junction of the mixer resistors is connected to one of the accompaniment keyswitches. A staircase waveform is a variation on a sawtooth waveshape. In turn, the staircase waveform contains both even and odd harmonics, whereas the square-wave input waveforms contain odd harmonics only.

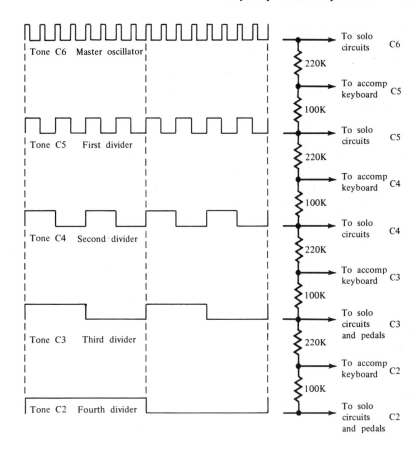

**Figure 7-7** Exemplified resistive mixing circuits and input waveforms.

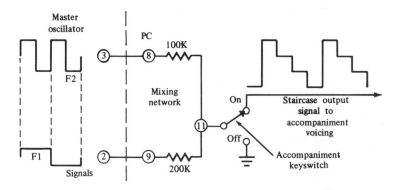

**Figure 7-8** Y mixing circuit for development of staircase waveform.

### 7-5  ACCOMPANIMENT CIRCUITS

Tone generator signals from the distribution circuit in this example are fed to the accompaniment keyboard by a wire harness. Two tones, one octave apart, of the same note are connected through resistors to each key, thereby forming a complex tone (see Fig. 7-3). Whenever a key is depressed, a wire contact and a spring at the rear of each key connect the complex signal to a wire bus and thence to the accompaniment voicing circuits.

**Accompaniment Voicing and Preamplifier**    Signals from the accompaniment keyboard are connected to a terminal on the voicing circuit board (Fig. 7-3). Part of this signal is passed on to the keydown detector for the sustain circuits on the percussion circuit board. There is another direct output at the voicing circuit board, which is used only if the rhythm accessory unit is in operation. The remainder of the incoming signal is applied to the accompaniment voicing networks. When turned off, the tab switches for the five voices indicated in Fig. 7-3 connect the outputs from the voicing networks to ground. When turned on, these switches connect the network outputs through an amplifier to the manual balance control. When turned off, the Accompaniment Bright switch grounds a partial-bypass capacitor to roll off the high frequencies. Conversely, when turned on, this switch restores the high-frequency components in the signal.

### 7-6  SOLO KEYING AND VOICING FUNCTIONS

Tone-generator signals from the distribution circuit in Fig. 7-3 are connected to the solo keyboard by a wire harness. Gold alloy key contacts are employed for signal switching. When a key is depressed, it connects the $+3$-V bus bar to a keyer circuit. The keyer circuits are divided into a row of 4-ft keyers, a row of 8-ft keyers, and a row of 16-ft keyers. This terminology is a carryover from pipe-organ technology. In other words, a 4-ft voice is one octave higher in pitch than an 8-ft voice. When one of the 44 solo keys is depressed, three tones from one of the 12 tone generators are coupled through to the solo voicing circuits. In this example, these three tones are the fundamental (in the row of 16-ft keyers), the second harmonic (in the row of 8-ft keyers), and the third harmonic (in the row of 4-ft keyers). Diode keying is employed to couple the keyer tones to the 4-ft, 8-ft, and 16-ft signal buses.

**Solo Sustain Keyer**  Refer to Fig. 7-9. When a solo key is depressed, +3 V from the percussion keydown detector is applied through $R1$ to the bases of $Q1$, $Q2$, and $Q3$ in $PC3$ through $PC46$; accordingly, these transistors turn on. Their collector voltages decrease, and the keying diodes in $PC1$ and $PC2$ are forward-biased into conduction, and a signal is thereby fed to the 4-ft, 8-ft, and 16-ft buses. Also, the +3-V keying signal causes $SD1$ in $PC3$ through $PC46$ to conduct and to apply voltage to the decay bus and through pin 93 to the auto sostenuto and sustain circuits (pin 25) on the percussion circuit board. The term *auto sostenuto* denotes a tone that is automatically sustained for a very substantial time interval. Two sustain switches are provided on the solo

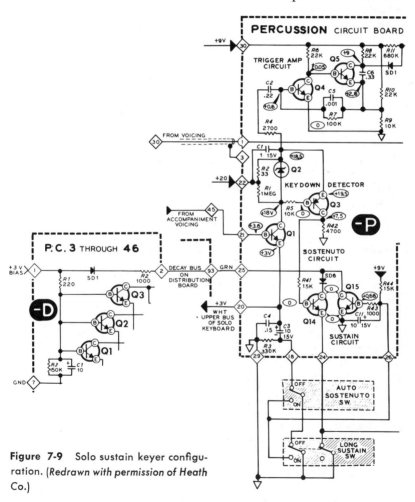

**Figure 7-9**  Solo sustain keyer configuration. (*Redrawn with permission of Heath Co.*)

manual. When the Long Sustain switch is depressed, all notes are played in the sustain mode. However, when the Auto Sostenuto switch is depressed, only the last note will be played in the sustain mode.

When a solo key is depressed in this example, and both the Long Sustain and the Auto Sostenuto switches are turned off, collector voltage is applied to $Q14$ and $Q15$ in Fig. 7-9 through the decay bus. $Q15$ is held on by base current supplied through $R44$ from the $+9$-V supply. Capacitor $C11$ in the base circuit of $Q15$ is charged. When the key is released, $C11$ holds the base of $Q15$ in conduction momentarily and $C1$ (in the $PC3$ through $PC46$) circuit discharges immediately through $SD1$, $R2$, and $Q15$. Therefore, $Q1$, $Q2$, and $Q3$ are turned off, and there is no sustain mode of operation in effect. When the Long Sustain switch is turned on and a key is depressed, $Q14$ cannot conduct, because of its open emitter. $Q15$ is held in a nonconducting state by $R43$ and the Sustain switch. $C1$ (in $PC3$ through $PC46$) now can discharge only through the parallel resistor $R3$. Therefore, $Q1$, $Q2$, and $Q3$ are held on to sustain the note until $C1$ (in $PC3$ through $PC46$) has discharged.

**Auto Sostenuto** When a solo key is depressed and the Auto Sostenuto and the Long Sustain switches are turned off, there is no sustain mode of operation, as was noted above. However, when a solo key is depressed and the Auto Sostenuto switch is turned on (with the Long Sustain switch turned off), $Q15$ is held in a nonconducting state by the ground connection to its base terminal through $R43$ and the Auto Sostenuto switch. $Q14$ is in a conducting state owing to the emitter connection to ground through the Long Sustain switch, the collector voltage from the decay bus, and a positive voltage supplied to its base by the keydown detector circuit as long as a key is depressed. Because $Q14$ is in its conducting state, it provides a discharge path for sustain capacitor $C1$ (in $PC3$ through $PC46$) on the distribution circuit board.

When the depressed solo key is released, $Q14$ no longer conducts, because of the removal of the keydown detector voltage from its base. The discharge path for $C1$ (in $PC3$ through $PC46$) is accordingly closed, and it must discharge through its parallel resistor $R3$, as in the sustain circuit mode. $Q1$, $Q2$, and $Q3$ (in $PC3$ through $PC46$) are held on until $C1$ has discharged and the last note has been played in the sustain mode.

### 7-7 SOLO VOICING OPERATIONS

Voicing filters are used in electronic organs to shape signal waveforms as required to obtain desired timbres. These filters are also called formant filters. As exemplified in Fig. 7-10, they range from simple RC circuits to comparatively elaborate RCL configurations. Signals from the 4-ft, 8-ft, and 16-ft buses on the distribution circuit board are fed to the voicing circuit board. After amplification, the signals are applied to the various voicing filters and to the percussion circuit board. A synthesis filter is a form of trap with RCL circuitry, as exemplified in Fig. 7-10. It suppresses the fundamental frequency of the incoming signal waveform, and passes the second harmonic. The filter output is mixed with the 4-ft voicing filter output.

## 7-8 PERCUSSION FUNCTION

With reference to Fig. 7-11, a percussion keydown detector circuit provides keying pulses to the percussion trigger amplifier and to the auto sostenuto circuit. It is essentially a series voltage-regulator arrangement that supplies regulated keying voltage to the solo manual and detects operation of the solo keys. Base voltage for $Q1$ is set at $+3.6$ V by a divider circuit: $R27$, $R28$, and $R29$ on the voicing circuit board. When solo manual keys are depressed, the current drawn through $Q1$ causes sufficient voltage drop across $R1$, $Q2$, and $R5$ to cause zener breakdown of $Q2$. The voltage across $Q2$ will remain constant until the keys are released. This voltage is applied across the base-emitter junction of $Q3$, causing the transistor to conduct. $Q3$ is the sustain-kill element in the auto sostenuto circuit. When the last note is released, $Q3$ and $Q2$ no longer conduct, thus permitting a sustain mode of operation for the last note played. When auto sostenuto is used, the sensitivity of the keydown detector is reduced by switching $C3$ into the circuit.

When one solo note is depressed, current through $Q1$, $Q2$, and $Q3$ causes the voltage across the parallel combination of $R2$ and $C1$ to decrease. This negative-going voltage is differentiated by $C1$ and is applied to the percussion trigger amplifier $Q4$, shown in Fig. 7-12. Each time that an additional key is depressed, the current through $Q1$ and $Q2$ increases, causing the voltage across $R2$ and $C1$ to drop another step toward ground potential. Each such step produces a negative pulse to the percussion trigger-amplifier circuit. This amplifier steps up the output pulse from the percussion keydown detector and shapes it for reliable percussion multivibrator operation. The incoming signal from the keydown detector circuit is differentiated to negative-going pulses by $C2$. $Q4$ is biased to near saturation by $R7$, $R9$, and $R10$. The input pulses drive the transistor out of conduction, and its collector voltage rises to $+9$ V. $Q5$ is biased just to cutoff by $R9$ and $R10$. The base of $Q5$ is connected to the collector terminal of $Q4$, whose positive-going pulses produce negative-going pulses at the collector of $Q5$.

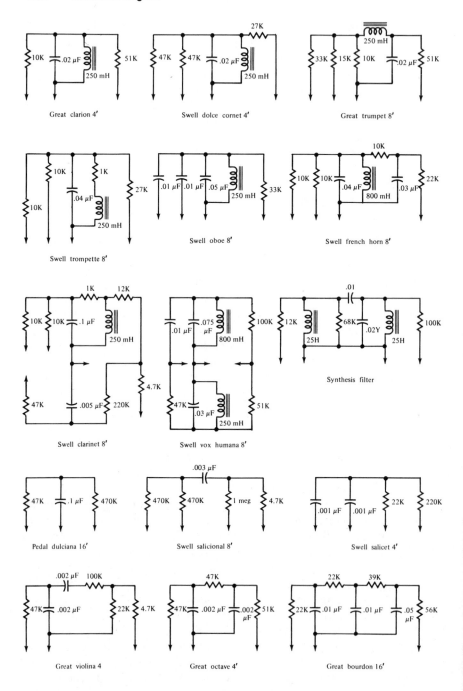

**Figure 7-10** Representative formant filters for various voices.

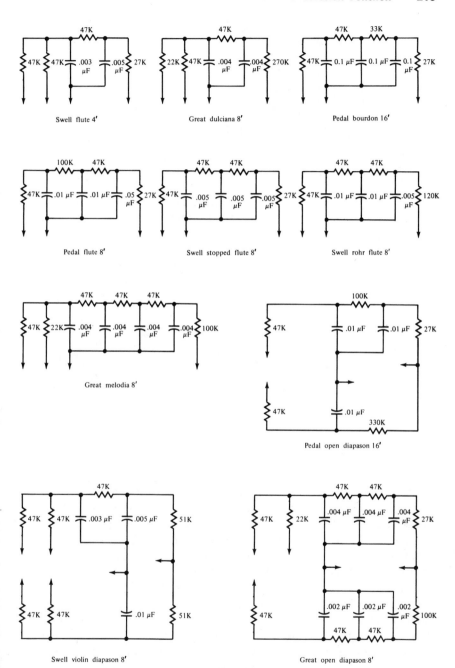

Swell flute 4'

Great dulciana 8'

Pedal bourdon 16'

Pedal flute 8'

Swell stopped flute 8'

Swell rohr flute 8'

Great melodia 8'

Pedal open diapason 16'

Swell violin diapason 8'

Great open diapason 8'

**Figure 7-10** Continued

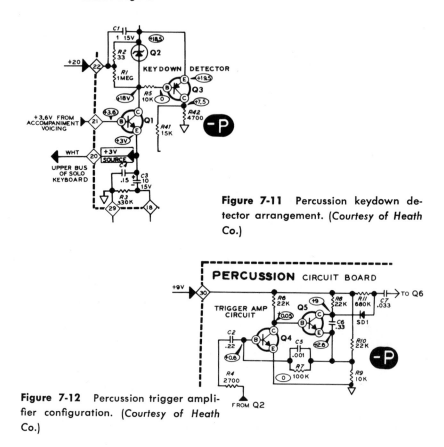

**Figure 7-11** Percussion keydown detector arrangement. (*Courtesy of Heath Co.*)

**Figure 7-12** Percussion trigger amplifier configuration. (*Courtesy of Heath Co.*)

Feedback capacitor C5 serves to stabilize high-frequency response of the amplifier. When a pulse is applied to the base of Q5, the transistor conducts and C6 is quickly discharged. Once discharged, C5 desensitizes the amplifier for a period of time until it is charged again. This desensitization prevents the hazard of double-keying the percussion circuit. The negative pulse output is coupled through SD1 to the percussion multivibrator, depicted in Fig. 7-13. A pulse with a short time duration is required to key the percussion pulse-shaping circuits and the percussion modulator. When the one-shot multivibrator is keyed by the output from Q5, it will either generate a single square wave, or (if repetitively triggered) follow a repetitive pulse "repeat" mode of operation. A conventional multivibrator arrangement is utilized, with either "one-shot" or "astable" modes available. In its astable mode, the multivibrator generates a pulse train that can be restarted at any time by an input trigger pulse.

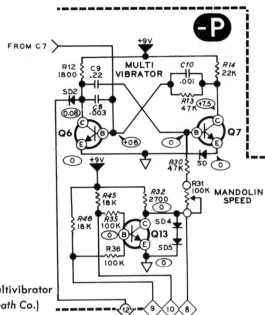

**Figure 7-13** Percussion multivibrator configuration. (*Courtesy of Heath Co.*)

When $Q7$ is biased off by emitter voltage $SD3$, it operates in its one-shot mode; $Q6$ is biased into conduction by $R13$. A negative input pulse to the base of $Q6$ drives the transistor out of conduction. Current then flows through $R12$ and $C9$ to the base of $Q7$, and through $R30$ to ground. $Q7$ will conduct until $C9$ is charged. In turn, $Q7$ cuts off and $Q6$ resumes conduction. In its repetitive or astable mode, $Q6$ is in a conducting state. $C9$ charges via $R30$ until $Q7$ goes into conduction. $Q6$ is then forced out of conduction through $R13$. $C9$ must now discharge in the opposite direction, and $Q7$ is forced out of conduction. As $C9$ recharges in the opposite direction, the cycle is again initiated. At any time, the repeat can be forced to a "restart" condition by a negative trigger induced at the base of $Q6$. This "sync" action makes a single-shot staccato form of the percussive voices available.

When the Mando Preset switch is off, $R3$ is short-circuited to ground, which automatically makes the multivibrator operate in its one-shot mode. The Harpsichord Preset and Piano Preset switches disconnect the base of $Q13$ from ground when either switch is depressed, allowing $Q13$ to conduct. When $Q13$ conducts, the multivibrator operates in its one-shot mode. Thus, if the Mando Preset switch is depressed, there is a repeating voice generated. If the Mando Preset and Piano Preset switches are depressed simultaneously, a one-shot percussion output is generated. Percussive voices require a "strike tone" effect.

Accordingly, the premixed voice is amplitude-modulated by the percussion-modulator section, configured in Fig. 7-14; this arrangement can be regarded as a transformerless balanced-modulator circuit.

Transistors Q8 and Q12 operate in a phase-inverter circuit. If R23, the balance control between the two, is not set correctly, a thumping sound will be audible. This is a feedthrough pulse signal that is normally cancelled out by the balanced-modulator action. The balance control is adjusted so that the currents through Q9 and Q11 are equal during the conduction interval. These transistors are normally cut off until a positive pulse from the multivibrator is applied to their bases, and drives them into conduction. The amplitude of conduction depends on the amplitude of the applied drive voltage. Since the voltage of the driving pulse changes continuously, as seen in the diagram, the amplitude of the tone signal varies accordingly. Modulator action with a continuous tone-signal input is indicated in Fig. 7-14. Waveform A represents the tone input to the phase inverter. Waveform B represents the positive pulse from the multivibrator, and C shows how this waveshape is modified in passage through the circuit. Waveform C is applied to the modulator transistors, and gates them on at a varying rate, which is determined by the instantaneous positive voltage of the waveform. The input audio waveform A thus becomes shaped to an output waveform depicted in D.

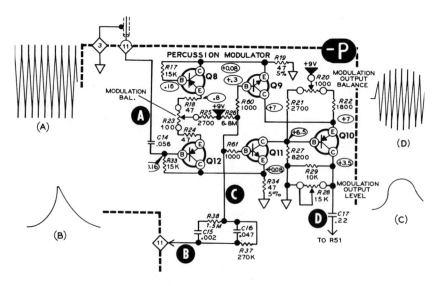

**Figure 7-14**    Percussion modulator configuration. (*Courtesy of Heath Co.*)

The output from the percussion multivibrator is a rectangular pulse. A percussion shaping circuit, shown in Fig. 7-15, tailors the leading and lagging edges of this rectangular pulse. In turn, this shaped output pulse keys the percussion modulator to form the accordion, mandolin, harpsichord, and piano effects. The leading-edge time constant is controlled by capacitors $C22$, $C23$, and $C24$. Its attack characteristics are most rapid in the mandolin, piano, and harpsichord modes of operation. Conversely, the lagging edge, or decay, is shaped by discharge of these capacitors into resistor and diode combinations to obtain the desired effect. In the accordion mode of operation, a slow attack and no decay is provided by the inverting circuit that includes $Q16$.

In the mandolin mode of operation, the positive input pulse is coupled via diode $SD2$ directly to the percussion modulator. $C24$ provides some degree of pulse shaping to prevent objectionable keying transients on attack, and slight extension on decay. From a general viewpoint, a mandolin waveform is a pulse-modulated audio signal that has both a sharp attack and a rapid decay. In the piano mode of operation, the positive input pulse is coupled through $SD2$ in the trigger circuit. $SD2$ provides a low-impedance charge path to capacitors $C22$ and $C23$, and provides sharp attack. After the keying pulse terminates, $SD2$ is nonconducting, so that the discharge path for $C22$ and $C23$ is through $R59$. In turn, a long decay period is provided.

In the harpsichord mode of operation, the same attack format is utilized as in the piano mode. However, the decay interval is about one-half of the piano-mode interval. This is accomplished because $SD7$ is then switched across $C23$. $SD7$ does not conduct during the charge portion of the pulse, and $C23$ is allowed to charge quickly. After the keying pulse capacitor discharges through $SD7$, the only charge left to sustain the note is on $C22$. The accordion mode of operation, unlike the other percussive modes, has a slow attack and no decay. An accordion note will sound until the key is released. This slow attack is provided by $Q16$ and $C12$. With no key depressed, $Q16$ does not conduct, and its collector is at the $+3.7$-V level. This voltage holds the percussion modulator turned on (through the accordion switch), but no sound is produced by the organ, inasmuch as the percussive pre-mix is keyed by the solo sustain keyers.

When a key is depressed, a pulse is generated by the percussion multivibrator. This pulse turns $Q16$ on and quickly discharges $C12$; the collector voltage falls, and the percussion modulator is turned off. Consequently, the note is not sounded initially. After the pulse has passed, $Q16$ turns off, $C12$ charges via $R37$, and the modulator turns on. This action sequence provides slow attack. $C12$ remains charged

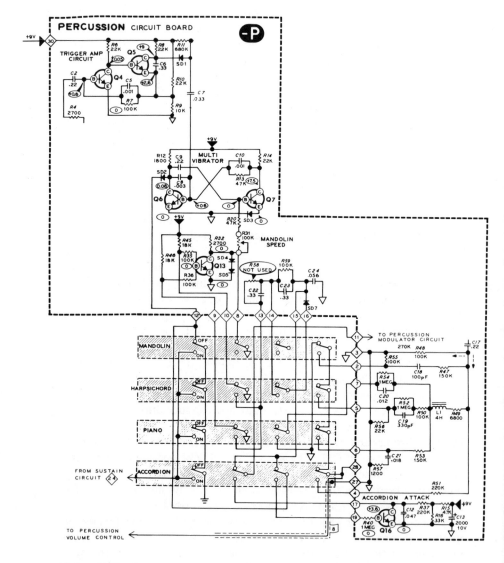

**Figure 7-15** Percussion voicing configuration. *(Courtesy of Heath Co.)*

until the next key is depressed. Consequently, the accordion note has no decay interval, and ceases abruptly. From the Accordion Preset switch, the signal is fed to the level circuit board, and thence to the preset volume control. This control is operated by a slider tab. The controlled signal is then fed to the nontremulant preamplifier.

## 7-9   PEDAL KEYING CIRCUIT FUNCTIONS

With reference to Fig. 7-16, the examples discussed in this topic are based upon depressing the low C (left) pedal of the pedal clavier. This pedal clavier adds an octave at the lower end of the tone range. It comprises 13 pedals, which actuate two-pole double-throw, series-connected switches. Inasmuch as the pedal switch contacts are connected in series, only the lower note can be played if two or more pedals are depressed at the same time. The pedal memory consists of 12 diode keyers with associated resistors and capacitors. A positive voltage is conducted from pin 42P on the pedal memory board through the Preset Drum connector (pins 17 and 18) to the pin at $R2$ on the pedal clavier circuit board. If the left pedal is depressed, this positive voltage will be applied through pin 37 on the pedal memory board and will forward-bias diode $SD2$. The signal from the third divider of the tone generator will then pass through pin 33, $SD2$, $C2$, pin 38, and pin 27 to the pedal divider circuit board.

When the pedal switch closes and applies the positive voltage to pin 37, the circuit is opened to any switches beyond the first one. Therefore, any additional pedals that are depressed will have no effect on the signal output. As a pedal closes the circuit, the signal from the tone generator proceeds through the pulse-amplifier transistors $Q2$ and $Q1$ to the pedal divider. This pulse amplifier is required to boost the signal level so that it will reliably trigger the pedal divider integrated circuit $IC1$. This foregoing process applies to any one of the 13 pedals, except that the right-hand (upper C) pedal cannot, of course, break the series circuit, inasmuch as there are no pedals beyond this point. Resistor $R1$ and its associated switch contacts are utilized only when the Rhythm Accessory is operating.

The pedal signal is conducted through $Q3$ to $Q5$. Both of these transistors are connected as emitter followers. When the Rhythm Accessory is operating, it will supply a pulsed signal to the collector of $Q5$ via pin 17. While this pulse is present, $Q5$ is turned on; a signal from its emitter is applied to $Q4$, where it is amplified and conducted through pin 16 to 6 on the pedal divider circuit board. This is the signal that turns on $SD1$ and $SD2$ on the pedal divider board.

**Pedal Divider**   The pedals provide a one-octave extension at the low-frequency end of the manual ranges. The pedal divider input is taken from the pulse amplifiers $Q1$ and $Q2$ in Fig. 7-16. Operation of this divider is identical to that of the dividers on the tone-generator boards. A mixing network in the pedal divider, resistors $R7$, $R8$, and $R9$, combines portions of the divider signals. This action is similar to that of

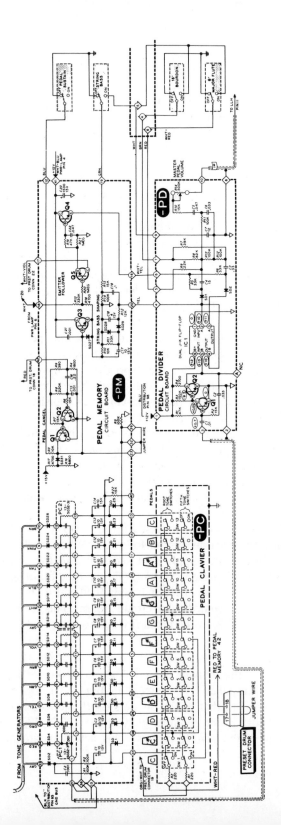

**Figure 7-16** Pedal keying circuitry. (Courtesy of *Heath Co.*)

the mixing networks on the distribution board, thus providing a staircase signal similar to the one available from the keyboards. This signal is applied to the pedal voicing filter and is then delivered to the master pedal volume control $R12$ through $R14$. The output from this control is fed to the nontremolo preamplifier $Q7$.

When the left (low C) pedal is depressed, the tone from pin 27 of the pedal memory board is connected through pin 3 of the pedal divider board to $Q1$, and through $Q2$ to pin 5 of $IC1$, a dual flip-flop. This divided signal is connected: (1) through pin 4 to the string bass shaping circuit on the pedal memory board; (2) through diode $SD1$ and pin 5 to the 8-ft major flute switch; and (3) to flip-flop $A$ (pin 2) $IC1$, which again divides the signal by two. The output from flip-flop $A$ is connected to the 16-ft bourdon switch (through diode $SD2$ and $R7$). When a positive voltage arrives from the pedal memory board through pin 6, diodes $SD1$ and $SD2$ are turned on, which connects the 8-ft major flute and the 16-ft bourdon switches.

The signal from the string-bass shaping section arrives through pin 19, is filtered, and is then routed to the pedal volume control, as are signals from the 8-ft major flute and the 16-ft bourdon when either of these switches is closed to remove its ground connection. Observe that the following pedal voicing circuit components are located on the pedal divider circuit board: $C5$, $C6$, $C7$, $R10$, $R11$, and the level control $R14$ (Fig. 7-16). The string-bass switch, the 8-ft major flute switch, and the 16-ft bourdon switch are all connected to pin 5 on the solo voicing circuit board. This tie point is connected to pin 9 on the pedal divider circuit board and the pedal voicing network. The output from the network is connected through pin 10 to the pedal volume control $R12$.

**String-bass Shaping**  When a pedal and the string-bass switch are depressed, the tone is amplified by $Q3$, an emitter follower, and is applied to the string-bass shaping network. This network both shapes and keys the tone arriving from the pedal divider at pin 20. The tone is then returned to the pedal divider circuit board, the 8-ft major flute, and 16-ft bourdon switches. If the string-bass switch is opened, the output signal from pin 19 is grounded. When the left (low C) pedal is depressed, capacitor $C1$ charges. When the pedal is released, capacitor $C1$ continues to hold the keyer on until the capacitor discharges below the threshold level of diode $SD1$. The discharge path is through the diode, resistor $R3$, and the pedal sustain key. When the pedal sustain key is closed (depressed), the ground connection is removed and the keyer is held on (the note is sustained) for the longer period of time required for $C1$ to discharge through $R5$.

If a memory keyer remains "on" after its pedal is released (because of a charge on its sustain capacitor, $C1$) and a second pedal is depressed, two notes enter the pedal divider at the same time and cause a "burbling" sound. To prevent this effect, a canceling circuit is utilized. When a pedal is depressed, $C1$ starts to charge. While it draws current, $C16$ in the pedal cancel circuit discharges into $C1$ because of the voltage drop across $R9$. A negative bias voltage is developed at the base of $Q2$ (normally saturated) and causes its collector current to decrease as its collector voltage increases. This voltage change causes a positive bias to develop on the base of $Q1$, which effectively shunts any charge on sustain capacitor $C1$ to B-minus via cancellation diode $SD1$ and transistor $Q1$.

Discharge of capacitor $C1$ results in cancellation of the pedal signal for a very brief period. This cancellation occurs so quickly that there is no apparent interruption in sound output. This discharge and subsequent recovery of $C16$ (which occurs as $C1$ becomes charged) causes recycling of reverse bias on $Q2$ and forward bias on $Q1$, and the supply voltage is thereby enabled to again charge $C1$ and to forward-bias $SD1$ for the desired note. Note that the manual balance control is a dual control, $R14$, in Fig. 7-17. One control adjusts the volume between the solo flute preamplifier ($Q5$) and the accompaniment complex preamplifier ($Q8$) outputs. The other control adjusts the relative volume between the complex preamplifier ($Q6$) and the violin preamplifier ($Q7$) outputs.

**Wah-wah Section**     With reference to Fig. 7-17, the wah-wah circuit is an adjustable-frequency bandpass filter. It attenuates frequencies (Solo O voices) other than the band selected by the position of $R17$, which is mechanically linked to the expression pedal. As the pedal is rocked back and forth, it varies the resistance of $R17$, which controls the frequency of the bandpass filter, in addition to the overall volume, and produces a wah-wah sound output. A wah-wah effect is also called a wow-wow modulation. It is basically a very slow vibrato, or frequency modulation of a tone.

**Tremolo Section**     A tremolo effect is an amplitude modulation of a tone at a rate of approximately 6 Hz. In this example, switches are provided to add tremolo effect to all organ voices, except percussion and pedal tones. A complete block diagram of the tremolo circuits is shown in Fig. 7-18. The three tremulant switches serve to introduce the tremolo effect to the solo complex, solo flute, and accompaniment voices or to the nontremulant amplifier (see Fig. 7-19). Organ voices in the non-tremolo mode must be mixed and fed in phase directly to both left and

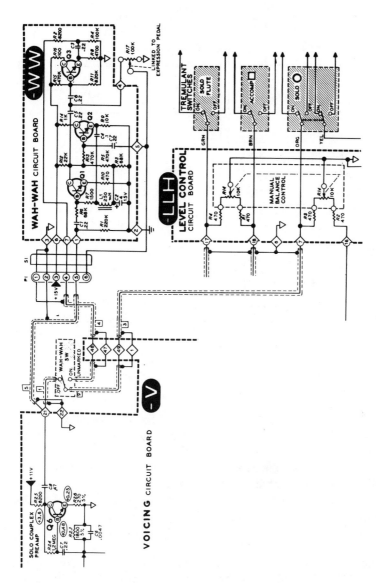

**Figure 7-17**  Voicing circuit board configuration. (*Courtesy of Heath Co.*)

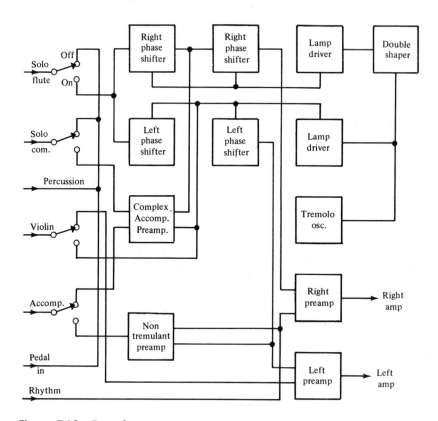

**Figure 7-18** Tremolo system arrangement.

right speaker channels. The outputs from the solo complex, solo flute, and accompaniment complex preamplifiers may be switched to either tremolo or to nontremolo channels.

Signals from the accompaniment and the solo switches are first mixed in a resistive network. Pedal and solo flute voices are also mixed in a like manner, but as a separate group. These two voicing combinations are then mixed in a common emitter-follower load. The output is then buffered by an emitter follower. Output from this mixer preamplifier is fed equally to the left and the right preamplifiers. The signal from the preset volume control $R13$ is amplified by $Q1$. Its output is coupled through $C2$, $C16$, and $R5$ to the input of one mixer stage, $Q6$. The accompaniment manual and solo complex voices are mixed in a resistive network and are fed to $Q6$ via $R40$, $R35$, and $C16$. Emitter load resistor $R44$ is common to both $Q6$ and $Q7$.

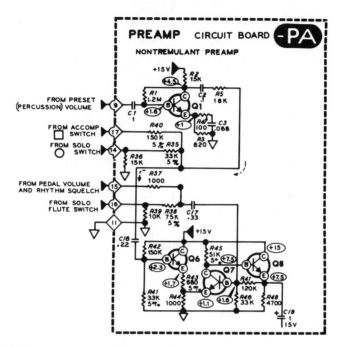

**Figure 7-19**    Preamp circuit-board configuration. (*Courtesy of Heath Co.*)

Pedal and solo flute voices, together with rhythm squelch, are mixed in a resistive network and are then fed through C17 to the base of the second mixer, Q7. Another input is connected to the unbypassed emitter resistor, and their combined output drops across the collector load, R45. Bias for Q7 is provided from the direct-coupled output stage through R46 and R47. The output stage, Q8, is an emitter follower. C18 couples its output to the right and the left preamplifiers, Q5 and Q9, as shown in Fig. 7-20. These outputs are coupled to the right and the left channel amplifiers, respectively.

Prior to being fed to the tremolo phase shifters, the solo and accompaniment voices must be split into two isolated channels, inasmuch as the stereo tremolo effect will be lost if the channels are not isolated from each other. Mixing is accomplished in both emitter-base and in common-emitter configurations. Isolation is provided by a common-base amplifier in the left channel, as depicted in Fig. 7-21. Input from the solo complex preamplifier is split into two channels by Q2. One output, 180 deg out of phase, appears at the collector of Q2. This signal is coupled by R11 and C6 to the right channel phase shifter. The

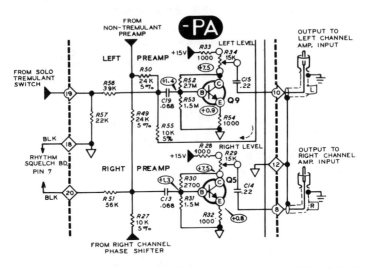

**Figure 7-20** Right and left preamplifier circuitry. (*Courtesy of Heath Co.*)

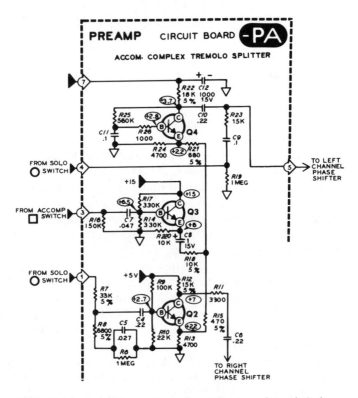

**Figure 7-21** Tremolo splitter configuration. (*Courtesy of Heath Co.*)

in-phase output from the emitter of $Q2$ is coupled to the emitter of $Q4$ and appears at the collector of $Q4$. This signal is coupled to the left channel phase shifter.

The accompaniment manual voices pass through $Q3$. This emitter-follower stage lowers the circuit impedance, to enable driving of the emitter inputs of $Q2$ and $Q4$, the output stages. From Q3, the accompaniment voices are fed into the emitter of $Q2$, where they mix with solo complex voices to provide the correct output phase. The accompaniment voices are also fed to the emitter input of $Q4$ for the left output. The base of $Q4$ is grounded for AC by $C11$, and operates in the common-base mode. This common-base configuration has good output-to-input isolation characteristics and thereby prevents channel crosstalk. Violin voices are preferred only in the left channel; therefore, they are mixed into the output of $Q4$.

To provide the stereo tremolo effect, the electrical phases of the 6 left and right channels must be rotated throughout a programmed 360 deg. Two 180-deg LDR (light-dependent resistor) phase-shifter drivers are used to perform this function. A phase shift of 180 deg is initially provided by a split-load phase-inverter stage. The two outputs from this stage are then combined and scanned in an LR phase-shift circuit. The phase shift across each stage is controlled by a cadmium-sulfide LDR. In turn, the LDR is activated by the varying intensity of a driver lamp; one driver lamp is provided on each phase-shifter circuit board. $Q1$ operates in class A, with input from the solo flute tremulant switch. Its bias point is set by divider $R3$ and $R4$. The load for this stage is equally split in the collector and emitter circuits. Accordingly, two 180-deg out-of-phase outputs are provided. The phase-scanning network is comprised of $L1$ and LDR1.

Rotating phase output (Fig. 7-22) is obtained as follows: When LDR1 has a high resistance (no incident light), $L1$ is unloaded, and little AC current can flow. Thus, the output from the phase shifter is in phase with the collector signal of $Q1$ (180 deg). Next, when the resistance of the LDR equals the inductive reactance of $L1$, the 180-deg output from $Q1$ is lagged 90 deg and provides a 90-deg phase output. At this point, the inductance provides a 90-deg lag, with the output voltage maintained virtually constant. Finally, when the LDR is fully illuminated, it has its minimum resistance value, and it passes zero-deg phase output from the emitter of the transistor. Observe that the first phase shifter is followed by a Darlington phase inverter, $Q2$. This circuit is employed to provide a high input impedance on the first phase shifter (to impose minimum loading), and also a low-impedance split load to drive the second phase shifter.

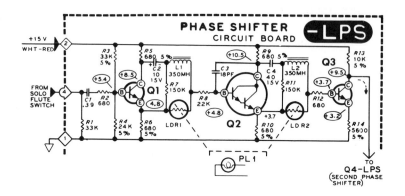

**Figure 7-22**    Phase-shifter circuit-board arrangement. (*Courtesy of Heath Co.*)

Coupling capacitors $C2$ and $C3$ have different values. Their capacitive reactances are chosen to provide optimum phase relations at low frequencies. The second phase shifter, $Q3$, is a common-emitter stage. It is biased directly through $R11$, $L2$, and $R12$ from the emitter potential of the preceding stage, $Q2$. The two phase-shift sections in series ($Q1$ through $Q3$ and $Q4$ through $Q6$) provide nearly 355 deg of electrical rotating phase shift. The output from $Q6$ is fed through $R55$ and $C19$ (Fig. 7-21) to the base of $Q9$ on the preamplifier circuit board (Fig. 7-20). The right channel phase shifter operates in the same manner.

With reference to Fig. 7-23, the tremolo oscillator provides a 6.7-Hz signal to the tremolo modulation system. Two output signals, 180 deg out of phase, energize the lamp driver and the double-shaper circuits. The circuit consists of a relaxation oscillator with an inverted *PNP* transistor $Q10$, as the charging source for $C7$. Positive feedback is provided through two common-emitter direct-coupled stages, $Q11$ and $Q12$. When $Q10$ is conducting, positive charging voltage is supplied through $R27$ to $C7$. As the charge on $C7$ increases, $Q12$ is driven into conduction, and its collector drops to ground potential. As the base voltage on $Q11$ drops, the transistor goes out of conduction, and its collector potential rises. In turn, the base voltage of $Q10$ is caused to rise, and it is forced out of conduction.

$C7$ discharges through $R29$, $R27$, and $R26$ to ground, The reduced base voltage causes $Q12$ to turn off, and its collector voltage rises. In turn, the base voltage of $Q11$ is caused to increase, and the transistor turns on. The collector voltage of $Q11$ falls, and $Q10$ conducts to start the cycle once again. Oscillation frequency is determined

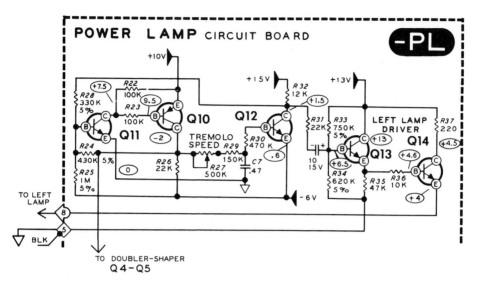

**Figure 7-23**   Tremolo-oscillator power-lamp circuit board. (*Redrawn with permission of Heath Co.*)

by the RC time constant of $C7$, $R29$, and $R27$. The voltage variation at the collector of $Q12$ is capacitively coupled to the base of $Q13$, the left lamp driver. The collector of $Q10$ is capacitively coupled to the doubler-shaper, $Q4$ and $Q5$.

The doubler-shaper circuit depicted in Fig. 7-24 develops a double-frequency pulse to the right lamp driver only. These pulses are used to create the desired Doppler effect when utilized in conjunction with the left channel. Functionally, the circuit may be regarded as a dual switch. One side of this switch acts on the positive-going portion of the input signal, and the other acts on the negative-going portion of the input signal. These outputs are combined to provide a doubled frequency signal. The input is a positive-going rectangular waveform provided by the tremolo oscillator. $C2$ and $C3$ differentiate the rectangular wave to produce positive and negative pulses. The positive pulse turns on $Q5$, which applies a +20-V pulse to the output. As the input pulse through $C3$ goes negative, $Q5$ is cut off. $R10$ is adjusted to set the operating point of $Q5$.

In Fig. 7-24 $Q4$ goes into conduction on the negative pulse from $C2$ and applies a +20-V pulse to the output. $R9'$ is the common load resistor for both $Q4$ and $Q5$. The combined signal to the right lamp driver is developed across $R9$. With reference to Fig. 7-25, the lamp driver circuit provides power to the lamps on the phase-shifter circuit

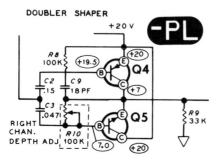

**Figure 7-24** Configuration of the doubler-shaper circuit. (*Courtesy of Heath Co.*)

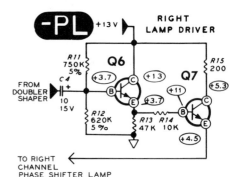

**Figure 7-25** Right lamp-driver circuitry. (*Courtesy of Heath Co.*)

boards. There are two lamp-driver circuits, one for the right tremolo phase and another for the left tremolo phase. These lamps control the signal phases, thereby developing a tremolo effect. The right lamp-driver circuit comprises two emitter followers, $Q6$ and $Q7$, connected in cascade. These transistors develop a pulse current for operation of the lamp on the right phase-shifter circuit board.

A triangular wave is provided from the tremolo oscillator for the left channel, or to the doubler-shaper for the right channel. This signal, coupled through $C4$, has sufficient amplitude that $Q6$ clips the negative peaks of the waveform. $Q6$ is biased through $R11$ and $R12$. $Q7$ is biased through $R14$ from the emitter of $Q6$ and receives its signal from the same source. When $Q7$ conducts, it supplies an increasing amount of current to the lamp on the phase-shifter circuit board until the voltage across the lamp plus the voltage drop across $R15$ is equal to the supply voltage. $Q7$ is then in saturation and limits the lamp current. Tremolo depth is controlled by adjustment of $R18$ on the power-lamp circuit board to vary the supply voltage.

Refer to Fig. 7-20. Two preamplifiers ($Q5$ and $Q9$), one for each channel, are located on the preamplifier circuit board. They are used to amplify the signal input to the amplifier stages. These transistors receive their input from the left and right phase shifters and from the nontremulant preamplifier. Inasmuch as the two amplifiers are identical, only the right preamplifier will be described. Collector-to-base biasing via $R30$ and the unbypassed emitter resistor $R32$ provide degeneration for AC stabilization. The output level is adjustable by control $R29$ in the collector load circuit. Series resistance $R28$ prevents the channel from being unintentionally disabled. Inputs are resistively mixed into their respective channels. The nontremulant preamplifier input feeds each channel through $C18$. The output impedance of the nontremulant amplifier is very low (50 $\Omega$). This low source impedance prevents any significant signal from cross-coupling from one channel to the other via $R49$ and $R50$.

## 7-10 AMPLIFIER CIRCUITS

With reference to Fig. 7-26, the expression pedal controls the volume of sound from the organ. It mechanically actuates a dual control ($R42/R45$), one-half of which controls the input for each channel to the amplifiers. The two sections of the dual control are held above ground by resistors $R43$ and $R46$. Inputs to the right and left channel power amplifiers may come from the organ (controlled by the expression pedal), from right and left channel tape-recorder inputs, and from a left-channel reverberation input. Stereo outputs are provided for console speakers, earphones, and external tone cabinets. A switch selects between the two built-in speakers or the headphone output.

Each channel is described as follows: The expression pedal controls the input to a two-transistor, direct-coupled driver circuit. $Q1$ provides the necessary driving voltage, and $Q2$ is connected as an emitter follower to provide drive at the proper impedance to the primary of the driver transformer. The output amplifier circuit associated with $Q5$ and $Q6$ operates essentially in class B. The power supplies have $+30$- and $-30$-V outputs. Negative feedback is employed around the entire amplifier for AC stabilization and for waveshaping. Input to the amplifier is obtained from one of the preamplifier circuits. The input level is adjusted by control $R42$, which is actuated by the expression pedal. Input coupling to $Q1$ is provided by $C6$ and $R17$.

The base of $Q1$ is biased by a voltage derived from the average DC current flowing in the driver output stage, $Q2$, and this bias voltage

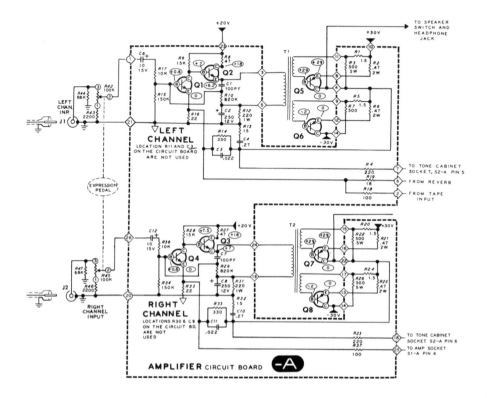

**Figure 7-26** Left and right channel amplifier configuration. (*Courtesy of Heath Co.*)

is supplied by the divider comprising $R10$ and $R15$. $C1$ provides AC feedback for high-frequency stabilization. $R8$ provides some degeneration in the collector circuit of $Q2$ to prevent oscillation. The load for this stage, which is connected as an emitter follower, is the primary of driver transformer $T1$. The secondary windings of the driver transformer provide AC drive, 180 deg out of phase, to the two *PNP* output transistors, which are driven into conduction on the negative portion of the drive cycle. The operating point for $Q5$ is set by $R1/R3$, and for $Q6$ by $R5/R7$. The junctions of the bias dividers are unbypassed, and thereby provide degeneration for each stage.

First, $Q5$ is driven into conduction, which pulls the output up toward the +30-V supply. On the opposite half of the input cycle, $Q5$ is driven into cutoff. Owing to transformer phasing, $Q6$ is now driven into conduction, which pulls the input down toward the −30-V supply.

The output voltage swing is limited to approximately ±28 V. The outputs from the right and left channels are connected to two built-in speakers and to a headphone jack. The switch that selects the output connection is located on the external accessory panel. The outputs are also connected to the tone-cabinet socket on the rear of the amplifier. This socket may be used to drive external speakers. Dual tape inputs are provided on the external accessory panel so that the output from a tape recorder may be played through the left and right channel amplifiers.

**Reverberation Circuit**  With reference to Fig. 7-27, the reverberation circuit in this example takes the output signal from the right channel amplifier, delays the signal, and feeds it back into the left channel preamplifier. This delay causes a small change in phase between the outputs from the two channels, and the organ sounds as if it were being played in a large hall. $R11$ is the reverberation volume control. $Q1$ and $Q2$ amplify the delayed portion of the right-channel output. Refer to Fig. 7-28. The rhythm accessory circuit board generates rhythm accessory tones continuously. In turn, the squelch circuitry is required to short-circuit the rhythm accessory output unless the desired tones are selected by pushbutton switches.

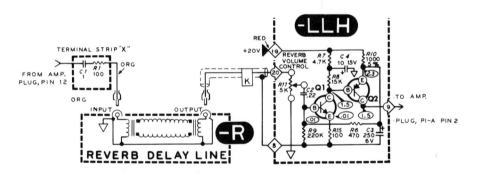

**Figure 7-27**  Reverberation configuration. (*Courtesy of Heath Co.*)

With no voltage present at the gate of $Q1$, the transistor is turned off. The rhythm accessory signal enters pin 4 and exits by pin 2, and band sounds play through the organ. When the rhythm accessory is turned off, a +16-V potential is applied via pin 6 to the gate of $Q1$. In turn, the transistor conducts and short-circuits the band sound signals to ground. When a preset accompaniment voice on the rhythm accessory is turned on, it is necessary to turn off the drum sound so that the

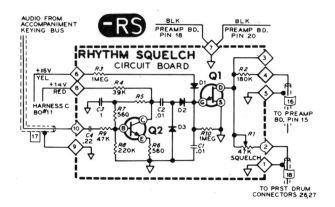

**Figure 7-28**    Rhythm squelch circuitry. *(Courtesy of Heath Co.)*

preset voice can be heard. This is accomplished by feeding a portion of the accompaniment audio signal to pin 10. At the proper rhythm interval, a positive pulse is present at the base of $Q2$. This pulse turns the transistor on. A positive pulse is then coupled via $C2$ to the gate of $Q1$, whereupon it conducts and short-circuits the band sound of the rhythm accessory to ground. The proper sequence of accompaniment audio and band sound is accomplished automatically by the rhythm accessory.

# 8

## Audio System Interference

Audio system interference, also called radio-frequency interference (RFI), is distinguished from noise, in that it consists of RF energy that is picked up by an audio amplifier. When this RF energy becomes noticeable, it has undergone "audio rectification" in a tape recorder, hearing aid, public-address system, hi-fi installation, or electronic organ. In many situations, RF energy is picked up by an audio amplifier, but goes unnoticed, because its voltage is too low to produce audible interference. However, when an audio amplifier is operated in a high-intensity RF field, such as in proximity to a radio transmitter, sufficient RF energy may be picked up to overdrive an audio transistor, integrated circuit, or electron tube; in turn, substantial "audio rectification" results, and objectionable interference occurs in the sound output from the amplifier. Correction of the difficulty can often be accomplished by means of bypassing, shielding, filtering, or choking means, as exemplified in Fig. 8-1. A 250-pF bypass capacitor is generally suitable. An RF choke may have a value from 5 to 7 $\mu$H for frequencies in the range from 30 to 110 MHz, or 1.5 $\mu$H for frequencies in the range from 80 to 200 MHz.

In most cases, "audio rectification" occurs in a preamp, because the audio signal has a low level and the preamp is followed by a high-gain sequence of amplifiers. A useful preliminary check is to vary the setting of the volume control. If the interference is reduced in intensity when the volume control is turned down, it is indicated that the trouble is located ahead of the volume control. However, if the volume control has no effect on the interference level, the technician should look for

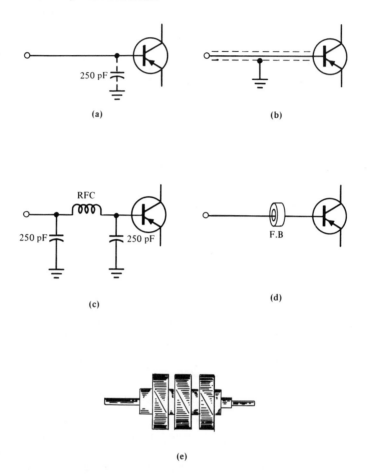

**Figure 8-1** Representative interference filter arrangements: **(a)** bypass capacitor; **(b)** shielding; **(c)** pi-filter section; **(d)** ferrite bead; **(e)** choke coil.

the trouble in the circuitry following the volume control. Sometimes it will be found that part or all of the interference is gaining entry via the power cord. In such a case, a power-line filter such as that shown in Fig. 8-2 may be effective. If some interference is still present, RF filtering will be required in the audio amplifier. A good arrangement is depicted in Fig. 8-3. Values for capacitors C1, C2, and C3 must be determined experimentally for a particular amplifier. In other words, the capacitance values must be sufficiently great to bypass the RF interference; on the other hand, excessive capacitance will impair the high-frequency response of the amplifier.

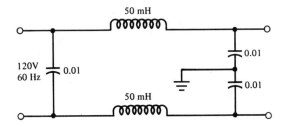

**Figure 8-2**   Basic power-line filter arrangement.

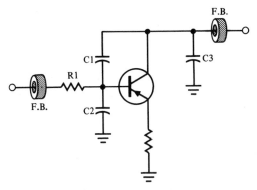

**Figure 8-3**   Ferrite beads supplement bypass capacitors for suppression of RFI.

Radio-frequency interference occasionally enters an audio amplifier at its output end. For example, speaker leads may happen to be resonant at the interfering frequency, and function as an antenna. Thus, an 8-ft length of speaker lead is resonant at about 30 MHz. Therefore, it may be found helpful to bypass the audio-output circuit to ground through small capacitors. If an audio amplifier is properly stabilized, it will tolerate comparatively large values of capacitance across the speaker terminals without serious deterioration of performance. In the case of a microphone or tape preamp, "audio rectification" is most likely to occur in the first stage. With reference to Fig. 8-4, either a single transistor may be employed, or a Darlington pair may be utilized. RF interference suppression is provided by a 1-kΩ resistor and a 200-pF capacitor, in the case of a single transistor. However, if a Darlington pair is used, a capacitance value to 20 pF is utilized. These

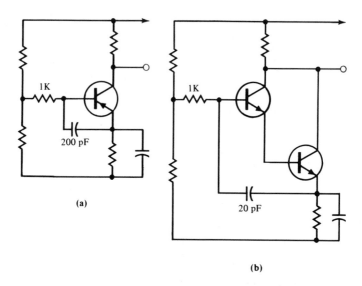

(a)

(b)

**Figure 8-4**   RFI filter arrangements for input preamp stage: **(a)** single transistor configuration; **(b)** Darlington-pair configuration.

filter arrangements will attenuate interference over TV channels 4 through 6, and also through the 88–108 MHz FM band. In the event that interference is being caused by AM broadcast fields, the 1-kΩ resistor should be omitted, and a 1-mH RF choke used instead; also, the capacitance value should be doubled. In the case of UHF interference, a ferrite bead is used instead of a 1-kΩ resistor, and a 10-pF capacitor is utilized.

## 8-2   SHIELDING AND FILTERING METHODS

Sometimes RFI becomes noticeable only when the pickup arm or the turntable of a phono player is touched. In such a case, a ground wire should be connected between the pickup arm and the preamp chassis ground. In the event that the pickup headshell is fabricated from Bakelite or plastic, a small metallic shield may be inserted between the cartridge and the pickup arm, as depicted in Fig. 8-5. The shield plate should be grounded to the pickup arm. Again, RFI may become noticeable only when a microphone is grasped. This difficulty can often be corrected by connecting a ground wire between the microphone housing and the preamp chassis ground. "Audio rectification" can occur as a

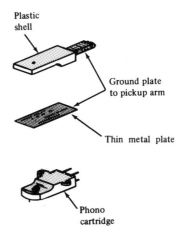

Plastic
shell

Ground plate
to pickup arm

Thin metal plate

**Figure 8-5** A grounded shield plate may be inserted between a cartridge and the pickup arm.

Phono
cartridge

result of poor ground connections or poor solder bonds (see Fig. 8-6). If a low-ohms meter is applied across a poor connection of this type, a different resistance reading will be observed when the test leads are reversed.

Even if a ground connection is good, and has a linear resistance characteristic, it is sometimes helpful to increase the inductance of the lead, and thereby provide some RF filter action. For example, suppose that the emitter of a preamp transistor is connected through a resistor to ground, as depicted in Fig. 8-3. To reduce the amplitude of RFI voltage at the emitter terminal, it is helpful in some situations to connect an RF choke between the emitter terminal and the ground lead. This RF choke should have an inductance value in the range from 1 to 10 mH; its optimum value may be determined experimentally. The effect of this RF choke is to impede the flow of high-frequency current in the emitter lead. If the RFI is in the UHF range, a ferrite bead may prove more effective than a conventional inductor.

When a difficult RFI problem is encountered in a hi-fi system, it may become necessary to enclose some or all of the equipment in a screened structure. In other words, the equipment can be placed within a decorative cabinet that has been lined with copper screen, for example. Radio-frequency interference cannot penetrate the screening. Note that it is necessary that the screening be connected to a good earth ground, such as a cold-water pipe. If "audio rectification" persists after the equipment has been shielded in this manner, it is indicated that the interference is gaining entry via the power cord or the speaker leads. Therefore, a power-line filter will probably be required, or the speaker leads will need to be bypassed to ground. The power-line filter, if used,

## A GOOD SOLDER CONNECTION

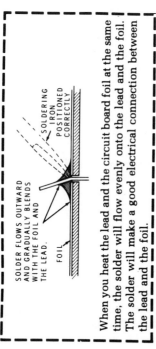

SOLDER FLOWS OUTWARD
AND GRADUALLY BLENDS
WITH THE FOIL AND
THE LEAD.

FOIL

SOLDERING
IRON
POSITIONED
CORRECTLY

When you heat the lead and the circuit board foil at the same time, the solder will flow evenly onto the lead and the foil. The solder will make a good electrical connection between the lead and the foil.

## POOR SOLDER CONNECTIONS

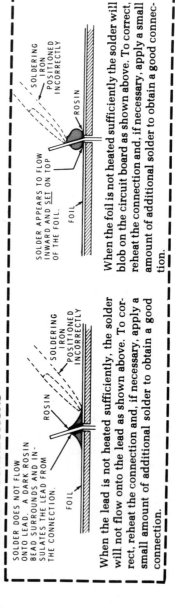

SOLDER DOES NOT FLOW
ONTO LEAD. A DARK ROSIN
BEAD SURROUNDS AND IN-
SULATES THE LEAD FROM
THE CONNECTION.

ROSIN

SOLDERING
IRON
POSITIONED
INCORRECTLY

FOIL

When the lead is not heated sufficiently, the solder will not flow onto the lead as shown above. To correct, reheat the connection and, if necessary, apply a small amount of additional solder to obtain a good connection.

SOLDER APPEARS TO FLOW
INWARD AND SET ON TOP
OF THE FOIL.

ROSIN

SOLDERING
IRON
POSITIONED
INCORRECTLY

FOIL

When the foil is not heated sufficiently the solder will blob on the circuit board as shown above. To correct, reheat the connection and, if necessary, apply a small amount of additional solder to obtain a good connection.

**Figure 8-6**   Bad solder connections can cause "audio rectification."

(Courtesy of Heath Co.)

should be mounted on the inner wall of the screened structure, at the point of entry for the power cable. Similarly, bypass capacitors should be mounted on the inner wall at the point of exit for the speaker leads.

## 8-3    AUTOMOBILE NOISE TROUBLESHOOTING

Apart from "audio rectification," excessive motor noise is very likely to be encountered in automobile installations, unless the sources of motor noise have been suppressed. These noise sources include the ignition system, the alternator or DC generator, relay-type voltage regulators, electric motors, gas-gauge installations, and various electrical and electromechanical accessories. A circuit arrangement for a basic ignition system is depicted in Fig. 8-7. This is the conventional electromechanical system. When a motor noise trouble symptom occurs, its source must be localized. The technician should tune the radio off-station (if the audio amplifier is driven by a tuner) and analyze the noise output with the engine running. If the noise level decreases when the headlights are turned on, he concludes that the voltage regulator is producing at least a part of the interference. Next, he removes the antenna lead from the radio; this test may result in reduction or elimination of the noise.

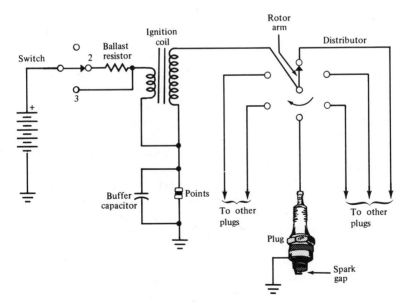

**Figure 8-7**    Circuit arrangement for a basic ignition system.

In such a case, the technician looks first for an open shield braid on the coaxial antenna lead, an ungrounded hood, ungrounded fender, or other metallic structure. Another test is made by turning the volume control to its minimum position. If the noise level is unaffected, the noise voltages are probably gaining entry via the DC power lead. The case of the radio must also be well grounded; the technician routinely checks for a loose or broken ground wire.

A suppressor resistor and a bypass capacitor for an ignition coil may be installed as exemplified in Fig. 8-8. Note that carbon spark-plug wire can be utilized instead of a suppressor resistor. A typical length of carbon spark-plug wire has a resistance in the range from 10 kΩ to 100 kΩ. Sometimes, an aged section of carbon spark-plug wire develops an abnormally high resistance, and must then be replaced. Bypass capacitors housed in metal cans are widely used, and are usually satisfactory; in difficult situations, however, the technician may find it helpful to use coaxial bypass capacitors. The appearance of a typical feedthrough capacitor is seen in Fig. 8-9. Note that emergency-brake cables, and any power wires that pass through the firewall occasionally pick up noise voltages and reradiate this interference to the radio power leads. This difficulty can often be overcome by installing an L-section filter such as that shown in Fig. 8-10, particularly when the radiating wire or cable cannot be grounded and cannot be bypassed.

Note that the filter inductor in Fig. 8-10 must carry appreciable current, and that wire with approximately the same diameter conductor as the power lead should be used. It is good practice to install the interference filter on the radio chassis, so that a short connecting lead can be used to the load circuitry. As shown by the dotted lines in the diagram, it may be found helpful to connect the bypass capacitor at the input end of the filter coil. In severe situations, bypass capacitors can be connected at each end of the inductor, thereby forming a pi filter configuration. As noted previously, the voltage regulator may also be a noise source. With reference to Fig. 8-11, the filtering arrangement shown will be found effective. In many cases, C1 alone will suffice. However, if the noise remains noticeable, C2, C3, and R may be included also.

Sometimes the gasoline-gauge mechanism becomes noisy. This source of noise becomes apparent when the automobile is being driven along a rough road. The customary method of controlling the noise is to bypass one or both terminals of the meter to ground. A capacitance value of 0.5 μF is suitable. Occasionally, the horn circuit will develop a popping type of noise interference when one is traveling along rough roads. In such a case, the wire to the horn should be bypassed to ground with a 0.5-μF capacitor. Difficult noise and RFI problems are often

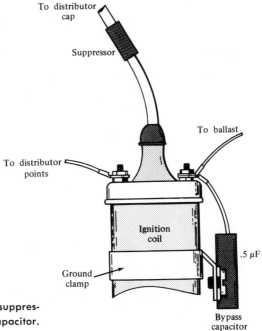

To distributor
cap

Suppressor

To ballast

To distributor
points

Ignition
coil

.5 μF

Ground
clamp

Bypass
capacitor

**Figure 8-8**   Example of suppressor resistor and bypass capacitor.

**Figure 8-9**   Appearance of a typical feedthrough capacitor.

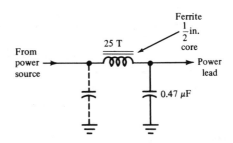

Ferrite
$\frac{1}{2}$ in.
core

25 T

From
power
source

Power
lead

0.47 μF

**Figure 8-10**   Typical L-section interference filter for a power lead.

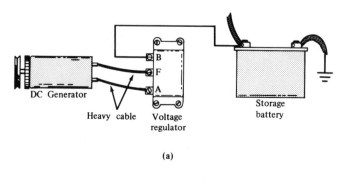

(a)

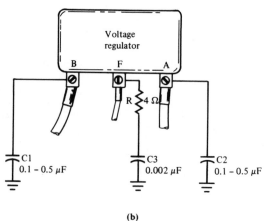

(b)

**Figure 8-11** A generator type of battery charging arrangement: **(a)** regulator circuitry; **(b)** connection of bypass capacitors.

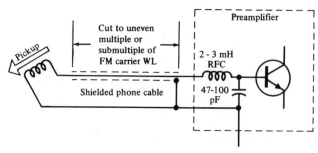

**Figure 8-12** RFI trap and filter arrangement for an FM transmitter phono installation.

tracked down to some structural part of an automobile that is imperfectly grounded to the frame. Flexible copper braid can be used to bond such structural parts to the main metallic portion of the vehicle.

**Trap Action of Shielded Cable**   Radio-frequency interference in FM broadcast stations is likely to be encountered with conventional phono pickups. The input circuit can develop interference owing to "audio-rectification" if the turntable is installed in proximity to the transmitter. In this situation, the RF filter network used in the preamp input circuit should be supplemented by a shielded pickup cable that is cut to a suitable length that provides trap action. With reference to Fig. 8-12, the cable should be cut to an odd multiple or to an odd submultiple of a quarter wavelength at the operating frequency of the transmitter. As an illustration, one-quarter wavelength at 100 MHz is equal to a length of 0.75 meter (29.5 in.). In this application, the shielded cable is grounded only at the amplifier end; the pickup end of the cable is left ungrounded so that RF energy will "see" a very high impedance at the input end of the cable. The ground connection to the cable should be both to the preamplifier and to a good earth ground, such as a cold-water pipe. Characteristics of tuned stubs are summarized in Fig. 8-13 on page 246.

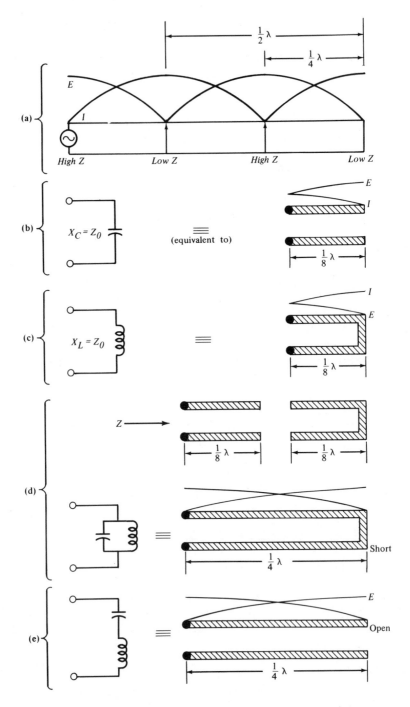

**Figure 8-13** Short-circuited and open-circuited line sections (stubs) are equivalent to resonant circuits.

# Resistor Color Codes

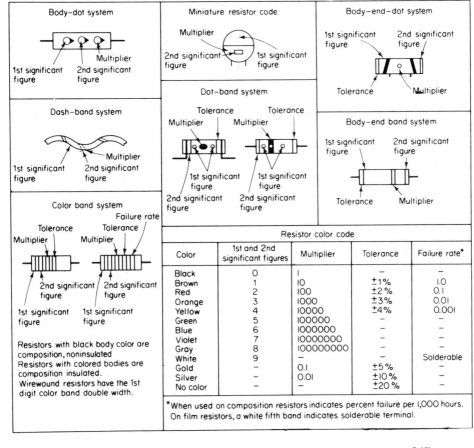

**Body-dot system**

1st significant figure  2nd significant figure  Multiplier

**Dash-band system**

1st significant figure  2nd significant figure  Multiplier

**Color band system**

Tolerance  Multiplier  Tolerance  Multiplier  Failure rate

2nd significant figure  2nd significant figure

1st significant figure  1st significant figure

Resistors with black body color are composition, noninsulated
Resistors with colored bodies are composition insulated.
Wirewound resistors have the 1st digit color band double width.

**Miniature resistor code**

Multiplier
2nd significant figure  1st significant figure

**Dot-band system**

Tolerance  Tolerance
Multiplier  Multiplier

1st significant figure  1st significant figure
2nd significant figure  2nd significant figure

**Body-end-dot system**

1st significant figure  2nd significant figure

Tolerance  Multiplier

**Body-end band system**

1st significant figure  2nd significant figure

Tolerance  Multiplier

**Resistor color code**

| Color | 1st and 2nd significant figures | Multiplier | Tolerance | Failure rate* |
|-------|-------------------------------|------------|-----------|---------------|
| Black | 0 | 1 | – | – |
| Brown | 1 | 10 | ±1% | 1.0 |
| Red | 2 | 100 | ±2% | 0.1 |
| Orange | 3 | 1000 | ±3% | 0.01 |
| Yellow | 4 | 10000 | ±4% | 0.001 |
| Green | 5 | 100000 | – | – |
| Blue | 6 | 1000000 | – | – |
| Violet | 7 | 10000000 | – | – |
| Gray | 8 | 100000000 | – | – |
| White | 9 | – | – | Solderable |
| Gold | – | 0.1 | ±5% | – |
| Silver | – | 0.01 | ±10% | – |
| No color | – | – | ±20% | – |

*When used on composition resistors indicates percent failure per 1,000 hours.
On film resistors, a white fifth band indicates solderable terminal.

# Capacitor Color Codes

## Molded mica capacitor codes (capacitance given in MMF)

| Color | Digit | Multiplier | Tolerance | Class or characteristic |
|---|---|---|---|---|
| Black | 0 | 1 | 20 % | A |
| Brown | 1 | 10 | 1% | B |
| Red | 2 | 100 | 2% | C |
| Orange | 3 | 1000 | 3% | D |
| Yellow | 4 | 10000 | – | E |
| Green | 5 | | 5% (ELA) | F (JAN) |
| Blue | 6 | | | G (JAN) |
| Violet | 7 | | | |
| Gray | 8 | | | I (ELA) |
| White | 9 | | | J (ELA) |
| Gold | | 0.1 | 5% (JAN) | |
| Silver | | 0.01 | 10% | |

Class or characteristic denotes specifications of design involving Q factors, temperature coefficients, and production test requirements.
All axial lead mica capacitors have a voltage rating of 300, 500, or 1000 volts, for 4.0 MMF whichever is greater.

## Molded paper capacitor codes (capacitance given in MMF)

| Color | Digit | Multiplier | Tolerance |
|---|---|---|---|
| Black | 0 | 1 | 20 % |
| Brown | 1 | 10 | |
| Red | 2 | 100 | |
| Orange | 3 | 1000 | |
| Yellow | 4 | 10000 | |
| Green | 5 | 100000 | 5% |
| Blue | 6 | 1000000 | |
| Violet | 7 | | |
| Gray | 8 | | |
| White | 9 | | 10 % |
| Gold | | | 5 % |
| Silver | | | 10 % |
| No color | | | 20 % |

**Molded paper tubular**

1st / 2nd } significant figures
Multiplier
Tolerance

1st / 2nd } significant voltage figures
Add two zeros to significant voltage figures. One band indicates voltage ratings under 1000 volts.

Indicates outer foil. May be on either end. May also be indicated by other methods such as typographical marking or black strip.

## Molded–insulated axial lead ceramics

1st / 2nd } significant figures
Multiplier
Tolerance
Temperature coefficient

## Typographically marked ceramics

Temperature coefficient
Capacity
Tolerance

## JAN letter / Tolerance

| JAN letter | Tolerance 10 MMF or less | Tolerance Over 10 MMF |
|---|---|---|
| C | ±0.25 MMF | |
| D | ±0.6 MMF | |
| F | ±1.0 MMF | ±1% |
| G | ±2.0 MMF | ±2% |
| J | | ±5% |
| K | | ±10% |
| M | | ±20% |

## Extended range T.C. tubular ceramics

1st / 2nd } significant figures
Multiplier
Tolerance
Temp. coeff. multiplier
T.C. significant figure

## Color band system

1st / 2nd } significant figures
Multiplier
Tolerance

Resistors with black body color are composition, non insulated.
Resistors with colored bodies are composition, insulated.
Wire–wound resistors have the 1st digit color band double width.

## Resistor codes (resistance given in ohms)

| Color | Digit | Multiplier | Tolerance |
|---|---|---|---|
| Black | 0 | 1 | ±2% |
| Brown | 1 | 10 | ±1% |
| Red | 2 | 100 | ±2% |
| Orange | 3 | 1000 | ±3%* |
| Yellow | 4 | 10000 | GMV* |
| Green | 5 | 100000 | ±5% |
| Blue | 6 | 1000000 | ±8%* |
| Violet | 7 | 10000000 | ±12 1/2 %* |
| Gray | 8 | 0.01 (ELA alternate) | ±30%* |
| White | 9 | 0.1 (ELA alternate) | ±10% (ELA alternate) |
| Gold | | 0.1 (JAN and ELA preferred) | ±5% (JAN and ELA preferred) |
| Silver | | 0.01 (JAN and ELA preferred) | ±10% (JAN and ELA preferred) |
| No color | | | ±20% |

*GMV = guaranteed minimum value, or −0,100% tolerance.
±3, 6, 12 1/2, and 30% are ASA 40, 20, 10, and 5 step tolerances.

## Extended range T.C. tubular ceramics

Tolerance
1st / 2nd } significant figures
Multiplier

## Body–end band system

1st / 2nd } significant figures
Tolerance   Multiplier

| Disc ceramics (5-dot system) | Ceramic capacitor codes (capacity given in MMF) | | | | | | | High capacitance tubular ceramics insulated or non-insulated |
|---|---|---|---|---|---|---|---|---|
| 1st significant 2nd figures, Multiplier, Tolerance, Temperature coefficient | Color | Digit | Multiplier | Tolerance | | Temperature coefficient PPM/°C | Extended range Temp. Coeff. | | 1st significant 2nd figures, Multiplier, Tolerance |
| | | | | 10 MMF or less | Over 10 MMF | | Signifi-cant figure | Multiplier | |
| | Black | 0 | 1 | ±2.0 MMF | ±20% | 0(NP0) | 0.9 | −1 | |
| | Brown | 1 | 10 | ±0.1 MMF | ±1% | −33(N033) | | −10 | |
| | Red | 2 | 100 | | ±2% | −75(N075) | 1.0 | −100 | Voltage (optional) |
| | Orange | 3 | 1000 | | ±2.5% | −150(N150) | 1.5 | −1000 | |
| | Yellow | 4 | 10000 | | | −220(N220) | 2.2 | −10000 | |
| Disc ceramics (3-dot system) | Green | 5 | | ±0.5 MMF | ±5% | −330(N330) | 3.3 | +1 | Temperature compensating tubular ceramics |
| | Blue | 6 | | | | −470(N470) | 4.7 | +10 | |
| 1st significant 2nd figures, Multiplier | Violet | 7 | | | | −750(N750) | 7.5 | +100 | 1st significant 2nd figures, Multiplier, Tolerance |
| | Gray | 8 | 0.01 | ±0.25 MMF | | −30(P030) | | +1000 | |
| | White | 9 | 0.1 | ±1.0 MMF | ±10% | General purpose bypass and coupling +100(P100) (Jan) | | +10000 | |
| | Silver | | | | | | | | |
| | Gold | | | | | | | | Temperature coefficient |
| | Ceramic capacitor voltage ratings are standard 500 volts, for some manufacturers, 1000 volts for other manufacturers, unless otherwise specified. | | | | | | | | |

| Current standard JAN and ELA code | Button silver mica | Molded flat paper capacitors (commercial code) | Molded flat paper capacitors (JAN code) |
|---|---|---|---|
| White (ELA), Black(JAN), 1st significant 2nd figures, Multiplier, Tolerance, Class or characteristics | 1st (when applicable), 2nd for 1st, 3rd for 2nd — sig fig, Multiplier, Tolerance, Class | 1st significant 2nd figures, Voltage, Multiplier, Black or brown body | Sliver, 1st significant 2nd figures, Multiplier, Tolerance, Characteristic |

| Molded ceramics | Button ceramics | Stand-off ceramics | Feed-thru ceramics |
|---|---|---|---|
| Using standard resistor color-code, 1st significant 2nd figure, Multiplier, White band. Distinguishes capacitor from resistor | 1st significant 2nd figures, Multiplier, Viewed from soldered surface | 1st significant 2nd figures, Multiplier, Tolerance, Temperature coefficient | 1st significant 2nd figures, Multiplier, Tolerance, Temperature coefficient |

# APPENDIX III

# Transistor Identification

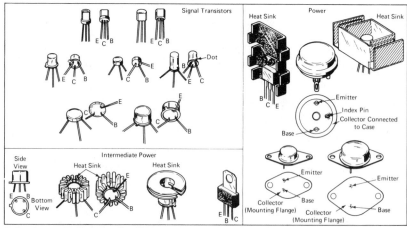

To Test a Transistor You Need to Know Three Things

1. The Basing Configuration (E, B, C, or S, G, D). The Diagram Above Shows Some of the More Common Configurations. If the Transistor Type Number Is Available, the Basing Configuration Can Be Found in the Manufacturer's Handbook. Also, a Schematic May Provide This Information.
2. The Type (NPN or PNP). This Information Can Come From the Circuit, Schematic, or Manufacturer's Handbook.
3. The Power Class. See Diagram Above. (Signal, Intermediate Power, or Power.)

# Diode Identification

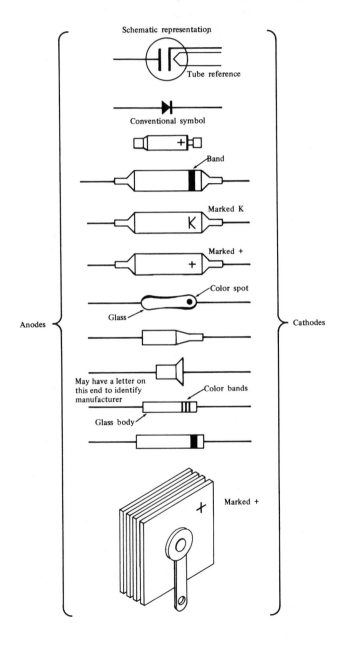

Schematic representation

Tube reference

Conventional symbol

Band

Marked K

Marked +

Color spot

Glass

Anodes

Cathodes

May have a letter on
this end to identify
manufacturer

Color bands

Glass body

Marked +

# Basing Identifications For Typical Transistors

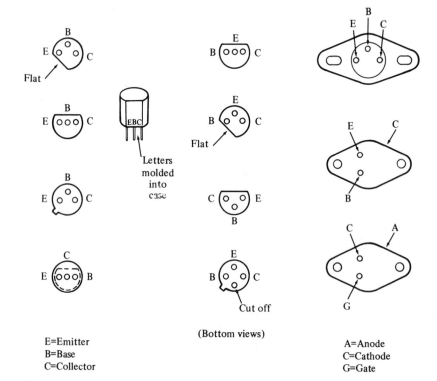

Flat

B
E C

B
E C

B
E C

C
E B

B
E
C

EBC

Letters
molded
into
case

E
B C

E
B C

Flat

C
B E

E
B C

Cut off

B
E C

B
E B

(Bottom views)

B
E C

E
C

B

C
A

G

E=Emitter
B=Base
C=Collector

A=Anode
C=Cathode
G=Gate

# Frequencies in Hertz of the Tempered Scale

| C | C# | D | D# |
|---|---|---|---|
| 16.35 | | | |
| 32.70 | 17.32 | 18.35 | 19.44 |
| 65.41 | 35.65 | 36.71 | 38.89 |
| 130.81 | 69.30 | 73.42 | 77.78 |
| 261.62 | 138.59 | 146.83 | 155.56 |
| 523.25 | 277.18 | 293.66 | 311.13 |
| 1046.50 | 554.36 | 587.33 | 622.25 |
| 2093.00 | 1108.73 | 1174.66 | 1244.51 |
| 4186.01 | 2217.46 | 2349.32 | 2489.01 |
| 8372.02 | 4434.92 | 4698.64 | 4978.03 |
| 16744.03 | 8869.84 | 9397.27 | 9956.06 |

| E | F | F# | G |
|---|---|---|---|
| 20.60 | 21.83 | 23.12 | 24.50 |
| 41.20 | 43.65 | 46.25 | 49.00 |
| 82.41 | 87.31 | 92.50 | 98.00 |
| 164.81 | 174.61 | 185.00 | 196.00 |
| 329.63 | 349.23 | 369.99 | 392.00 |
| 659.26 | 698.46 | 739.99 | 783.99 |
| 1318.51 | 1396.91 | 1479.98 | 1567.98 |
| 2637.02 | 2793.82 | 2959.95 | 3135.96 |
| 5274.04 | 5587.65 | 5919.90 | 6270.93 |
| 10548.08 | 11157.30 | 11839.81 | 12541.86 |

| G# | A | A# | B |
|---|---|---|---|
| 25.96 | 27.50 | 29.14 | 30.87 |
| 51.91 | 55.00 | 58.27 | 61.74 |
| 103.83 | 110.00 | 116.54 | 123.47 |
| 207.65 | 220.00 | 233.08 | 246.94 |
| 415.30 | 440.00 | 466.16 | 493.88 |
| 830.61 | 880.00 | 932.33 | 987.77 |
| 1661.22 | 1760.00 | 1864.65 | 1975.53 |
| 3322.44 | 3520.00 | 3729.31 | 3951.06 |
| 6644.87 | 7040.00 | 7458.62 | 7902.13 |
| 13289.74 | 14080.00 | 14917.23 | 15804.26 |

CCCC = 16.35 Hz is the lowest note of 32 ft pitch
CCC = 32.70 Hz is the lowest note of 16 ft pitch
CC = 65.41 Hz is the lowest note of 8 ft pitch
C = 261.62 Hz is the popularly termed middle C of the key-
board

# Audio-Frequency Spectrum

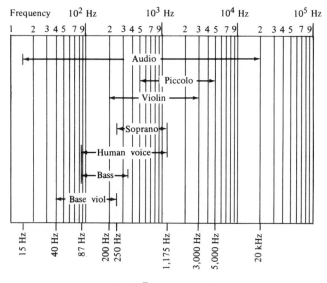

# Basic 70.7 and 25 Volt Speaker Systems

The 70.7- and 25-V speaker-matching systems permit higher operating efficiency in audio power systems. The 70.7-V system is preferred for high-power PA networks. Fig. A8-1 depicts a 70.7-V matching network for three speakers. A matching transformer is installed to match a speaker, or a group of speakers, to the 70.7-V line. This is called a *constant-voltage system,* because the line voltage is comparatively unaffected by switching speakers on or off. Network calculations are as follows:

1. Determine the power rating of each speaker.
2. Add the power values to find the total power demand and use a 70.7-V amplifier with a rated power output at least equal to this demand.
3. Select a 70.7-V matching transformer for each speaker (or for each group of speakers) with appropriate primary wattage ratings.
4. Connect the primary terminals of each transformer across the 70.7-V line from the amplifier output. Note that a primary mismatch up to 25 percent is tolerable.
5. Connect the secondary terminals of each transformer to its speaker (or group of speakers), observing the matching ohms tap.
6. If the matching transformers are rated in impedance values, the primary wattage of a transformer may be calculated as follows:

$$Z_p = \frac{70.7^2}{P}$$

where $Z_p$ is the rated primary impedance and $P$ is the wattage rating of the speaker.

It follows that the following power and impedance relations result:

1 W corresponds to 5000 ohms $Z_p$
2 W corresponds to 2500 ohms $Z_p$
5 W corresponds to 1000 ohms $Z_p$
10 W corresponds to 500 ohms $Z_p$

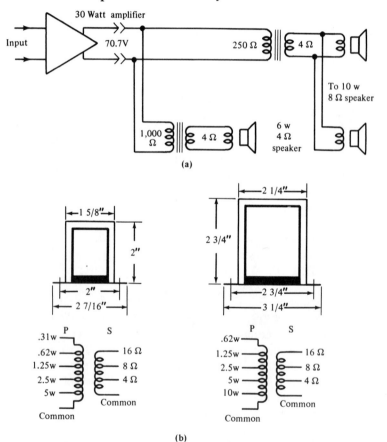

**A-8-1** Example of a 70.7-volt speaker-matching network: **(a)** configuration; **(b)** Typical 70.7-V transformer taps and dimensions.

Refer to Fig. A8-1. The 6-W speaker has a 4-Ω voice coil, and the paralleled 10-W speakers have 8-Ω voice coils. In turn, the total power demand is 26 W and the amplifier would be rated for approximately 30 W output. If the above equation is used, the primary impedance for the 6-W transformer would be 833 Ω; a 1000-Ω impedance could be utilized. For the 20-W speaker combination, the primary impedance would be 250 Ω.

# Glossary

A-B TEST    Comparison of sound from two sources, such as comparing original program to tape as it is being recorded by switching rapidly back and forth between them.

ACCOMPANIMENT    Also called *lower* or *great*. The lower manual of an organ, which provides the musical harmony to the solo or melody.

ACETATE BACKING    A standard plastic base for magnetic recording tape.

ACTION    An organ action that denotes the assembly of key contacts and couplers.

AEOLIAN    A very soft organ stop of mild string quality.

AES    Abbreviation for Audio Engineering Society.

AF    Abbreviation for audio frequency, a range that extends from 20 Hz to 20 kHz.

AFC    Abbreviation for automatic frequency control, a circuit commonly used in FM receivers to compensate for frequency drift, to keep the tuner "locked" to a selected station.

AM    Amplitude modulation; a method of superimposing intelligence on an RF carrier by amplitude variation of the carrier.

AMPLIFICATION    Magnification or enlargement.

AMPLIFIER    An electronic device that magnifies or enlarges audio voltage or power signals.

AMPLITUDE    Also called *peak value;* the maximum value of a waveform (with respect to one polarity).

ANODE    The electrode at which electrons leave a device to enter the external circuit.

ARPEGGIO    Technique of playing the notes of a chord in rapid sequence, instead of simultaneously; sometimes accomplished by automatic circuit action.

ATTACK (Related to *rise time.*) The period of time during which a tone increases to full amplitude after a musical instrument starts to emit a tone.

ATTENUATION Opposite of amplification; a reduction of audio voltage or power.

AUDIO A term relating to sound.

AUDIOPHILE One who enjoys experimenting with high-fidelity equipment and who is likely to seek the best possible reproduction.

AUTOTRANSFORMER A transformer designed with a single, tapped winding, that serves as both primary and secondary.

BACKGROUND NOISE Noise inherent in any electronic system.

BAFFLE A partition or enclosure in a speaker cabinet that increases the length of the air path from the front to the rear radiating surfaces of the speaker.

BAROQUE Baroque music is a basic form of composition characterized by ornamentation and powerful climaxes.

BASS The lower or pedal tones provided by an organ.

BASS-REFLEX ENCLOSURE A speaker cabinet enclosure in which a portion of the radiation from the rear of the cone is channeled to reinforce the bass tones.

BEAT A successive rising and falling of a wave envelope owing to alternate reinforcements and cancellations of two or more component frequencies.

BINAURAL A type of sound recording and reproduction. Two microphones, each representing one ear and spaced about 6 in. apart, are used to pick up the sound energy to be recorded on separate tape channels. Playback is accomplished either through separate amplifiers (or a two-channel amplifier) or special headphones wired for binaural listening.

BOURDON A low-pitched wood-flute organ pipe.

BRASS A generalized term that denotes tones resembling those from brass instruments such as the tuba, trumpet, or cornet.

BRIDGE A precision electrical instrument for the measurement of resistance, capacitance, and inductance values.

BUFFER A device, such as an electron tube or transistor, employed between an AC source and its load, principally for the purpose of isolation.

BUS BAR A bare electrical conductor that connects to various tone sources, or that distributes voltages to various points in an organ system.

CAPACITOR (Obs: *condenser.*) Any device designed for storage of electrostatic field energy.

CAPSTAN The spindle or shaft of a tape transport mechanism that pulls the tape past the heads.

CAPTURE RATIO An FM tuner's ability to reject unwanted co-channel signals. If an undesired signal is more than 2.2 dB lower than a desired signal, the undesired signal will be completely rejected.

CARDIOID PATTERN   A heart-shaped directional pickup pattern for a microphone that assists in reducing background noise.

CARILLON   A bell-tower voice actuated from an organ keyboard; the bell tones are electronically generated.

CARTRIDGE   A transducer device used with a turntable to convert mechanical channels in a disc into electrical impulses.

CELESTE   An organ stop characterized by a slow beat of 3 or 4 Hz; it is used in the upper register, usually in the diapason family.

CENT   An interval between two tones, with a value of approximately 1/100 semitone.

CERAMIC   A piezoelectric element that is used as the basis of some phonograph pickups; it generates a potential difference when stressed or strained.

CHANGER   A record-playing device that automatically accepts and plays up to 10 or 12 discs sequentially.

CHANNEL   A complete sound path. A monophonic system has one channel; a stereophonic system has two channels; a quadraphonic system has four channels. Monophonic material may be played through a stereophonic system, and quadriphonic material may be played through a stereophonic system. An amplifier may have several inputs, such as microphone(s), tuner; mono, stereo, and quad tape; and phono.

CHANNEL BALANCE   Equal response from left and right channels of a stereo amplifier. A balance control in a stereo amplifier permits adjustment for uniform sound volume from both speakers or a hi-fi system.

CHASSIS   Metal frame, or box, that houses the circuitry of an electronic unit or system.

CHIMES   A bell-like tone produced by striking metal tubes or rods with a hammer, or by an equivalent electronic synthesis.

CHOIR   An organ voice produced by blending several tones (of the same family) that have practically the same pitch, but differing phases. Sometimes, a choir effect is simulated by blending several tones with a phase difference produced by frequency-modulating one or more of the tones.

CHORD   A combination of harmonious tones that are sounded simultaneously.

CHORD COUPLING   An organ coupling made wherein all tones for a specific chord can be played by depressing a single button or key.

CHORD ORGAN   An organ arranged for playing a variety of chords in harmony with solo tones. Each chord is played by depressing a single button or key.

CHORUS EFFECT   Same as CHOIR.

CHROMATIC KEYBOARD   A keyboard with the black notes placed at the same height as the white notes, and with the same widths, to facilitate playing of chromatic scales.

CHROMATIC PERCUSSION   Percussive effects that are applied to notes of an organ, to simulate struck strings, plucked strings, marimba, or xylophone voices.

CHROMATIC SCALE   A scale composed entirely of half-steps.

CIPHER   A tone that sounds when no key is depressed, owing to malfunction.

CLARINET   An organ stop for a voice that simulates clarinet tones.

CLAVIER   Any keyboard or pedal board operated with either the hands or feet. A hand-operated clavier is more often termed a MANUAL.

COMPENSATOR   A fixed or variable circuit built into a preamplifier that compensates for bass and treble alterations that were made during the recording process.

COMPLEX TONE   An audio waveform composed of a fundamental frequency and a number of integrally related harmonic frequencies (a pitch and a number of related overtones).

COMPLIANCE   Physical freedom from rigidity that permits a stylus to track a record groove precisely, or a speaker to respond to an audio signal precisely.

CONCORDANT   A series of musically meaningful tones.

CONSOLE   A cabinet that houses an electronic organ.

CONTRA   When prefixed to the name of a musical instrument, this term signifies that the tones have been lowered one octave.

CORNOPEAN   An organ voice with a rich and hornlike tone color.

COUNTERBASS   Also termed *contrabass;* this term denotes a second bass note that will harmonize with a particular chord.

COUPLER   A stop or tab that permits the tones on one manual of an organ to be played with the tones of another manual, or that permits the sounding of octavely related tones on the same manual.

CPS   Abbreviation for cycles per second; *see* HERTZ, CYCLE, and CYCLES PER SECOND.

CRESCENDO   A pedal or equivalent control for an electronic organ that rapidly brings all stops into play; an increase in voice output to maximum power capability.

CROSSOVER NETWORK   Filtering circuit that selects and passes certain ranges of audio frequencies to the speakers that are designed for the particular ranges.

CROSSTALK   In stereo high-fidelity equipment, crosstalk signifies the amount of left-channel signal that leaks into the right channel, and vice versa.

CRYSTAL   A natural piezoelectric element that is used in some phono pickup cartridges and microphones.

CYCLE   One complete reversal of an alternating current, including a rise to maximum in one direction, a return to zero, a rise to maximum in the other direction, and another return to zero. The number of cycles occurring in one second is defined as the frequency of an alternating current. The word *cycle* is commonly interpreted to mean cycles per second, in which case it is a measure of frequency. The preferred term is hertz.

CYCLES PER SECOND   An absolute unit for measuring the frequency or "pitch" of a sound, various forms of electromagnetic radiation, and alternating electric current. *See* HERTZ.

CYMBAL   A high-pitched metallic organ stop that simulates the metallic clashing sound of orchestra cymbals.

DAMPING   Prevention of vibrations, response, or resonances that would cause distortion if unchecked. Mechanical control is by friction; electrical control is by resistance.

DECAY   A period of time over which a tone decreases from peak volume to inaudibility. It is characterized as an exponential function that defines the natural law of decay (and growth).

DECIBEL (dB)   A unit for measuring relative power levels. One dB is equal to one-tenth of a bel, and is about the smallest change that can be detected by a critical listener.

DEEMPHASIS   An attenuation of certain frequencies; in playback equalization deemphasis offsets the preemphasis given to the higher frequencies during the recording process.

DELAY LINE   An electromechanical transmission line (or equivalent) for delaying a signal or impulse in passage between the input and output terminals; often terminated in comparatively high or low impedances, to obtain energy reflections (reverberation).

DIAPASON   The basic tone color of traditional organ voices, as produced by open or stopped pipes.

DIAPHRAGM   Thin, flexible sheet that vibrates when struck by sound waves, as in a microphone, or which produces sound waves when moved back and forth at an audio-frequency rate, as in a headphone or a speaker.

DIODE   A unilateral electronic device that is used in rectification, wave-shaping, switching, and other circuit applications.

DISCORDANT   A description of tones that are unrelated by established principles of harmony.

DISTORTION   Deviations from an original sound that occur in the reproduction process. Harmonic distortion disturbs the original relationship between a tone and other tones naturally related to it. Intermodulation distortion introduces new tones that result from the beating of two or more original tones.

DIVIDER   A circuit, device, or arrangement that reduces a signal voltage to a certain fraction of its input value, or that generates a subharmonic of an input signal frequency.

DIVIDING NETWORK   Same as CROSSOVER NETWORK.

DOPPLER TONE CABINET   A tone-cabinet design in which one or more speakers are rotated or in which a baffle is rotated to produce a mechanical tremolo / vibrato effect.

DOUBLE TOUCH   A key-contact design for an electronic organ that provides actuation of an additional circuit when somewhat more than normal finger pressure is applied.

DRAWBAR    An arrangement for combining tones in voicing systems; a drawbar is pushed in and pulled out, instead of being pressed as a stop tab.

DUCTED PORT    A form of bass-reflex speaker enclosure in which a tube is mounted behind the reflex port.

DULCIANA    A flute voice with a small and slightly stringy tone.

DYNAMIC CARTRIDGE (electrodynamic)    A magnetic phono pickup in which a moving coil in a magnetic field generates voltages to form an audio signal.

DYNAMIC MICROPHONE    A microphone that operates on the same basic principle as a dynamic cartridge.

DYNAMIC RANGE    The range of loudness, or sound intensity, that an audio instrument can reproduce without distortion.

ECCLES-JORDAN OSCILLATOR    Also termed a flip-flop, or bistable multivibrator; used for frequency division in electronic organ networks.

EFFECTIVE CURRENT    The value of alternating or varying current that will produce the same amount of heat as the same value of direct current. Also called rms current.

EFFICIENCY    In a speaker, the ratio of power output to the power input, expressed as a percentage; the higher the percentage, the better is the efficiency.

ELECTROMAGNETIC    Pertaining to a phenomenon that involves the interaction of electric and magnetic field energy.

ELECTROSTATIC SPEAKER    A type of speaker in which sound is produced by charged plates that are caused to move while one is changed from positive to negative polarity, resulting in forces of attraction or repulsion.

ENCLOSURE    A housing that is acoustically designed for a speaker or speakers.

ERASE HEAD    The leadoff head in a tape recorder that erases previous recordings from the passing tape by generating a strong and random magnetic field.

EXPRESSION CONTROL    An organ volume control, usually operated with the right foot.

EXTENDED OCTAVE    A tone above or below a note on a standard keyboard that sounds when a specific coupler is actuated.

FAST DECAY    A rapid attenuation of a tone after its keyswitch has been released.

FEED REEL    The reel in a tape recorder that supplies the tape.

FET (field-effect transistor)    A transistor of the voltage-operated device classification, instead of the current-operated type as, for example, a bipolar transistor.

FIDELITY    The faithfulness of sound reproduction.

FILTER NETWORK    A reactive network that is designed to provide specified attenuation to signals within certain frequency limits; basic filters are termed low-pass, high-pass, bandpass, and band-reject designs.

FLAT    A note that is a half-step or semitone lower than its related natural pitch.

FLAT RESPONSE    A characteristic of an audio system whereby any tone is reproduced without deviation in intensity for any part of the frequency range that it covers.

FLUTE    A basic electronic organ tone color that simulates the orchestral flute.

FLUTTER    A form of distortion caused when a tape transport or a turntable is subject to rapid speed variation.

FM    Frequency modulation.

FM STEREO    Broadcasting over FM frequencies of two sound signals within a single channel. A *multiplexing* technique is utilized.

FOLDED HORN    A type of speaker enclosure that employs a horn-shaped passageway that improves bass response.

FORMANT FILTER    A waveshaping network or device that changes the waveform of a tone-generator signal into a desired musical tone waveform.

FORTE    A forte tab (solo tab) increases the volume of other tabs that are depressed at the time; a forte tab has no voice of its own.

FOUNDATION VOICE    A definitive organ voice, such as the diapason and dulciana voices.

FREE-RUNNING OSCILLATOR    An oscillator that generates an output in the absence of a synchronizing signal or a trigger signal, as opposed to a monostable or a bistable flip-flop.

FREQUENCY    The number of complete vibrations or cycles completed in one second by a waveform, and measured in hertz.

FREQUENCY MODULATION    A method of broadcasting that varies the frequency of the carrier instead of its amplitude. FM is the selected high-fidelity medium for broadcasting high-quality program material.

FREQUENCY RANGE    The limiting values of a frequency spectrum, such as 20 Hz to 20 kHz.

FREQUENCY RESPONSE    The frequency range over which an audio device or system will produce or reproduce a signal within a certain tolerance, such as ±1 dB.

FUNDAMENTAL    The normal pitch of a musical tone; usually, the lowest frequency component of a tonal waveform.

GAIN    The value of amplification that a signal obtains in passage through an amplifying stage or system.

GATE CIRCUIT    A circuit that operates as a selective switch and permits conduction over a specified interval.

GEMSHORN    A flute organ voice with a bright tone color.

GENERATOR    A tone or signal source, such as an oscillator, frequency divider, magnetic tone wheel, etc.

GLIDE    Also termed *glissando*. A rapid series of tones, produced by a slight shift in pitch of successive tones.

GLOCKENSPIEL    Also called *orchestra bells*. An electromechanical arrangement that simulates the bells used in orchestras.

GREAT MANUAL    Also called *accompaniment manual* or *lower manual*. A keyboard used for playing the accompaniment to a melody.

HALF-TONE    Also called SEMITONE. The relation between adjacent pitches on the tempered scale.

HARMONIC    A frequency component of a complex waveform that bears an integral relation to the fundamental frequency. Also called OVERTONE.

HARMONIC DISTORTION    *See* DISTORTION.

HARMONY    Musical support for a melody, consisting of two or more notes played simultaneously.

HEAD    Electromagnetic device used in magnetic tape recording to convert an audio signal to a magnetic pattern, and vice versa.

HEADPHONES    Small sound reproducers resembling miniature speakers used either singly or in pairs, usually attached to a headband to hold the phones snugly against the ears. Available in monophonic or stereophonic design.

HERTZ    Unit of frequency equal to one cycle per second. Abbreviation is Hz.

HILL-AND-DALE    A phonograph reproduction system in which the stylus moves up and down instead of sideways, or laterally.

HORN    Component part of a speaker design in which mechanical vibrations are coupled to the air by a flaring hornlike passageway, instead of a cone.

HUM    Noise generated in an audio or other electronic device by a source or sources of electrical disturbance.

IC    Abbreviation for *integrated circuit*. Integral solid-state units that include transistors, resistors, semiconductor diodes, and often capacitors, all of which are formed simultaneously during fabrication.

IHFM (IHF)    Refers to the Institute of High Fidelity Manufacturers, now called the Institute of High Fidelity, Inc. This group devises and publishes standards and ratings for high-fidelity equipment.

IMAGE REJECTION    The ability of a receiver to reject interference that is produced by an undesired input frequency that beats with the local-oscillator frequency, to produce an abnormal IF frequency.

IMPEDANCE    An electrical unit, expressed in ohms, that denotes the amount of opposition to alternating-current flow by a device or a circuit.

INFINITE BAFFLE    A speaker mounting arrangement in which the front and back waves from a cone are totally isolated from each other.

INPUT    Connection through which an electric current is fed into a device, circuit, or system.

INTERMODULATION DISTORTION (IM)    Two distinct and separate test frequencies are mixed in an amplifier, and their difference-frequency output is measured in IM percentage. *Also see* DISTORTION.

INTERVAL    The difference in pitch between two musical tones.

JACK    A female receptacle for a plug-type connector.

KEYBED    A shelf or horizontal surface on which a keyboard is mounted.

KEYBOARD    A bank of keys, comprising black and white sets, arranged in ascending tones.

KEYNOTE    The tonic, or first note of a particular scale.

KEYSWITCH    A switch that closes when a key is depressed, thereby actuating a tone generator.

KINURA    A reed stop that has dominant harmonics and a subordinate fundamental.

LATERAL SYSTEM    A system of disc recording in which a stylus moves from side to side (laterally).

LESLIE SPEAKER    A generic term, originally a trade name, denoting a tone cabinet with a mechanical tremolo / vibrato assembly.

LEVEL INDICATOR    A neon bulb, meter, or "eye" tube, used to indicate recording levels.

LISSAJOUS FIGURES    An $XY$ plot of voltage or current phase relations, usually produced automatically on the screen of a cathode-ray tube.

LOAD    A device, circuit, or system that absorbs or converts power from an electrical source, as a speaker converts power from an amplifier.

LOUDNESS CONTROL    An audio-frequency filtering arrangement that boosts the treble and particularly the bass tones in an amplifier as the volume level is reduced; it compensates for the listener's reduced sensitivity to tones at the extreme ends of the audio range at low volume levels.

MAGNETIC TAPE    Plastic tape with an iron-oxide coating for magnetic recording.

MANUAL    Also termed a CLAVIER.

MANUAL PLAYER    Manual record-playing device used with a changer-type machine.

MASTER OSCILLATOR    A source of a tone signal; it may be utilized directly, or it may be processed through one or more frequency dividers; these are also oscillators, but are of the driven type.

MECHANICALS    Organ effects that are not voices in the strict sense of the term; thus, forte (solo), percussion effects, and couplers.

MECHANICAL TONE GENERATOR    A mechanical unit for generation of electrical impulses that are subsequently converted into audible tones.

MEGOHM    A multiple unit that denotes one million ohms.

MELODIA    An organ solo stop of the flute family.

MELODY    Also called a TUNE; usually played sequentially note by note on the swell or solo manual.

MICRO    A prefix that denotes one-millionth.

MILLI    A prefix that denotes one-thousandth.

MIXING    A blend of two or more electrical signals or acoustic waves.

MONOPHONIC    A recording and reproduction system in which all program material is processed in one channel.

MODULATION    A process wherein low-frequency information is encoded into a higher-frequency carrier or subcarrier; subdivisions include amplitude, frequency, and phase modulation, with various combinations and derivatives thereof.

MULTIPLEXING    A system of broadcasting in which two or more separate channels are transmitted on one FM carrier, as in stereophonic broadcasting.

MULTIVIBRATOR    A relaxation oscillator, usually developing a semi-square waveform. Subclassifications include the astable, monostable, and bistable types.

MUTING    A silencing process or action.

NAB CURVE    Tape-recording equalization curve established by the National Association of Broadcasters.

NAZARD    An organ voice that simulates a piccolo-type organ pipe voice.

NEON LAMP    A gas diode that emits an orange glow, and operates as an indicator, protective switch, regulator, relaxation oscillator, or divider.

NETWORK    A comparatively elaborate electrical or electronic circuit arrangement.

NONCHROMATIC PERCUSSION    A percussion effect that has no dominant pitch, such as wood-block, drum, castanet, or cymbal effects.

NOTE    A single musical tone, identified by the letters A through G, plus sharp or flat superscripts.

OCTAVE    A pair of tones are separated by an octave if .the limiting tones have a frequency relation of 2-to-1.

OCTAVE COUPLING    An organ coupling arrangement wherein the depression of a key causes another note an octave higher or lower in pitch to sound simultaneously.

OHM    The unit of electrical resistance, defined as a unitary voltage/current ratio.

OSCILLATOR    An electronic, electrical, or mechanical generator of an electrical signal.

OUTPHASING    An organ voicing method wherein specified harmonics or subharmonics are added to or subtracted from a tone signal prior to its application to a formant filter. In a *chiff* outphasing circuit, certain harmonics are added to the tone signal during its attack period.

OUTPUT    A connection or conductor through which an electrical signal emerges from an electrical or electronic device, circuit, or system.

OVERTONE    Same as HARMONIC.

PARTIAL    Any one of the various frequencies contained in a complex waveform that corresponds to a musical tone.

PATCH CORD    A shielded cable utilized to connect one audio device to another.

PEDAL   The pedal keyboard of an electronic organ; also termed CLAVIER.

PEDAL CLAVIER   A pedal keyboard.

PEDAL DIVIDER   A frequency-divider section associated with the tone generators actuated by the foot pedals.

PEDAL GENERATOR   A tone generator utilized to produce the bass notes of an organ.

PEDAL KEYBOARD   Same as PEDAL CLAVIER.

PERCUSSION   Characteristic tones, as produced by plucking or striking strings.

pF   Abbreviation for *picofarad*.

PHASE   Position occupied at any instant in its cycle by a periodic wave; a part of a sound wave or signal with respect to its passage in time. One signal is said to be in phase, or to lead, or to lag, another reference signal.

PHASE INVERTER   An amplifier that provides an output that is 180 deg out of phase with its input, or an amplifier that provides a pair of output voltages that are 180 deg out of phase with each other.

PHASE-SHIFT OSCILLATOR   An oscillator that obtains its own input from a 180-deg phase-shifting network connected between its input and output terminals.

PICKUP CARTRIDGE   A device used with a turntable to convert mechanical variations into electrical impulses.

PICOFARAD   A unit equal to one micro-microfarad.

PISTON   An organ stop that is operated by pulling or pushing a knob. A piston generally operates groups of conventional stops.

PITCH   That characteristic of a sound which places it on a musical scale.

PIZZICATO   An organ sound effect that simulates the rapid plucking of strings.

PLAYBACK HEAD   The last head of a tape recorder, or the only head on a tape player, which converts the magnetic pattern impressed on a passing tape into an audio signal.

PLUG-TYPE CONNECTOR   A mating connector for a jack.

PM   Permanent magnet.

POLYESTER BACKING   A plastic material used as a base for magnetic recording tape.

POWER   A unit of the rate at which work is done, or energy is consumed, or energy is generated; electrical power is measured basically in rms watts.

POWER AMPLIFIER   An amplifier that drives a speaker in an audio system.

POWER OUTPUT   The signal power delivered by an audio amplifier, measured in watt units.

POWER SUPPLY   A source of electrical energy; usually, an arrangement that converts alternating current into virtually pure direct current.

PREAMPLIFIER   Amplifying arrangement that steps up a very weak input signal to a suitable level for driving an intermediate amplifier or a power amplifier.

PRE-EMPHASIS   A deliberate exaggeration of the high-frequency components in an audio signal.

PRESET   A control that turns on a group of voices or that turns them off without actuating any tabs.

PRINT-THROUGH   Magnetization of a layer of tape by an adjacent layer.

PULSE   An electrical transient, or a series of repetitive surges.

QUADRAPHONIC   A system whereby sound that is picked up by four separate microphones is recorded on separate channels and played back through separate channels that drive individual speakers.

QUALITY   Relates to the harmonic content of a complex tonal waveform; also termed TIMBRE.

QUARTER-TRACK RECORDER   A tape recorder that utilizes one-quarter the width of the tape for each recording; in stereo operation, two of the four tracks are used simultaneously.

QUIETING   Standard of separation between background noise and the program material from a tuner.

RECORD HEAD   The second head of a tape recorder; used to convert an audio signal to a magnetic pattern on the passing tape.

RECORD-PLAYBACK HEAD   A head on a tape recorder that performs both recording and playback functions.

RECORDING AMPLIFIER   An amplifying section in a tape recorder that prepares an audio signal for application to the record head, and bias current to the erase head.

REED   One of the basic tone-color groups of organ voices, which simulates orchestral reeds.

REGISTER   A range of notes included by a clavier or manual; range of notes employed in playing a particular musical composition.

RELAY   An electromagnetically operated switching device.

RESULTANT   Denotes a tone that is produced when two notes a fifth apart and an octave higher than the desired note are sounded to produce the desired pitch; a mode of generating SYNTHETIC BASS.

REVERBERATION   A persistence of sound waves, caused by natural or by artificial echoes.

RHYTHM SECTION   An organ section that generates nonchromatic percussion effects in a periodic manner, either automatically or manually.

RIAA CURVE   Standard disc-recording curve specified by the Record Industry Association of America.

ROLLOFF   The rate at which a frequency-response curve decreases in amplitude; it is usually stated in dB per octave, or dB per decade.

RUMBLE   A low-frequency vibration originating from a vibrating electric motor in a turntable.

RUMBLE FILTER   A low-frequency filter circuit designed to minimize or to eliminate rumble interference.

SCALE   A series of eight consecutive whole notes.

SCRATCH FILTER   A high-frequency filter circuit that minimizes scratchy sounds in playback of deteriorated discs.

SELECTIVITY    A measure of the ability of an electronic device to select a desired signal and to reject adjacent interfering signals; also termed *bandwidth*.

SEMITONE    The relation between adjacent pitches on the tempered scale.

SENSITIVITY    The minimum value of input signal that is required by an electronic unit, such as a tuner, to deliver a specified output signal level.

SEPARATION    The degree to which one channel's information is excluded from another channel; customarily expressed in dB units.

SFORZANDO    A form of CRESCENDO, but also employing discordant tones.

SHARP    Removed by a semitone from a reference pitch.

SIGNAL-TO-NOISE RATIO    The extent to which program material exceeds the background noise level; customarily expressed in dB units.

SINE WAVE    Graphical representation of simple harmonic motion.

SOFT-SUSPENSION SPEAKER    A speaker design without inherent springiness; it utilizes the reaction of a trapped backwave for restorative force.

SOLO MANUAL    The upper manual of a two-manual organ; also called a SWELL MANUAL.

SPEAKER    An electrical transducer that changes electrical energy into sound energy.

SQUAWKER    A midrange speaker.

STANDING WAVES    Reflected waves that alternately cancel and reinforce at various distances.

STEREOPHONIC SOUND    A system wherein sound energy that is picked up by two separated microphones is recorded on separate channels and is then played back through separate channels that drive individual speakers.

STOP    A tab or other switch form that selects and/or mixes various voices and footages in an electronic organ system.

STRING    One of the four basic tone-color groups that simulates orchestral strings.

STROBOSCOPIC DISC    A cardboard or plastic disc with a specialized printed design suitable for checking turntable speed.

STYLUS    A phonograph needle.

SUBHARMONIC    An integral submultiple of the fundamental frequency in a tonal waveform.

SUPER-TWEETER    A speaker designed to reproduce the highest frequencies in the audio range.

SUSTAIN    An effect produced by a note that diminishes in intensity gradually after the key has been released.

SWELL MANUAL    The upper manual of an organ; also termed the SOLO MANUAL.

SYNTHETIC BASS    A method of bass-tone generation that depends on the nonlinear response of the ear; pertinent harmonics are intensified, and although the fundamental is not present, the listener obtains the impression that the tone is complete.

T PAD    A three-element fixed attenuator.

TABLET (TAB)    A rocker-type switch control that selects an organ voice or footage.

TAKE-UP REEL    A reel on a tape recorder that winds the tape after it passes the heads.

TAPE DECK    A tape unit without a power supply or speaker.

TEMPERAMENT    A mode of tuning an instrument scale so that successive tones correspond to specified intervals.

TEMPERED SCALE    An arrangement of musical pitches such that successive notes have equal frequency ratios.

TERMINAL    Electrical connection point.

TIBIA    An organ voice that simulates flute tones.

TIMBRE    Also termed TONE COLOR. The distinguishing quality of a sound that depends primarily upon harmonic content, and secondarily upon volume.

TONE    The fundamental frequency or pitch of a musical note.

TONE ARM    A pivoted arm on a turntable that houses the pickup cartridge.

TONE BURST    A test signal comprising short sequences of sine-wave energy.

TONE COLOR    Also termed TIMBRE. Classified as DIAPASON, FLUTE, STRING, or REED.

TONE CONTROL    A control that provides variation of an amplifier's frequency response.

TONE GENERATOR    An organ section that generates the basic voice waveforms.

TRACKING    The path of a phono stylus within the grooves of a disc.

TRANSDUCER    A device that converts one form of energy into another form.

TRANSIENT    An electrical surge.

TRANSIENT RESPONSE    The ability of a speaker to follow sudden changes in signal level.

TREMOLO    An amplitude modulation of a tone at a rate of approximately seven hertz.

TUNING FORK    A precision source of pitch, usually designed as a U structure, and supported at its nodal point.

TURNTABLE    A *record player*.

VARISTOR    A voltage-dependent resistor.

VIBRATO    A frequency modulation of a tone at a rate of approximately seven hertz.

VOICE    An organ tone of specified timbre.

VOLUME    Same as EXPRESSION. A relative sound level.

WATT    A power unit, equal to the product of one volt and one ampere.

WOOFER    A speaker designed to reproduce bass tones.

WOW    A form of distortion that occurs when a magnetic tape varies back and forth in speed, or a turntable varies similarly in rpm.

Wow-wow    A very slow vibrato effect.

# Index

White noise, 157
Whizzer cone, 197
Wire
    bus, 208
    contact, 208
    harness, 208
    wound rheostat, 191
Woofer, 3
Worst case, 64, 85
Wow, 44

Wow-wow, 222

Y mixer, 206

Zener breakdown, 211
Zero
    bias, 84
    degrees, 227